The Ultimate Business Guru Book

D0626323

THE
ULTIMATE
BUSINESS
GURU

BOOK

50 thinkers
who made management

Stuart Crainer

CAPSTONE

First Published 1998
Reprinted 1998
Capstone Publishing Limited
Oxford Centre for Innovation
Mill Street
Oxford OX2 0JX
United Kingdom
http://www.capstone.co.uk

British Library Cataloguing in Publication Data
A CIP catalogue record for this book is available from the British Library

ISBN 1-900961-59-8

Typeset in 11/14 Plantin by
Sparks Computer Solutions, Oxford
http://www.sparks.co.uk
Printed and bound by
T.J. International Ltd, Padstow, Cornwall

This book is printed on acid-free paper

Contents

F

G

H

J

K

L

M

N

O

P

S

T

W

Acknowledgments

Mark Allin and Richard Burton of Capstone continue to pick up the tab for lunch. Someone has to. Also, I would like to thank all at AMACOM in New York who have enthusiastically published and promoted my books in the United States.

The usual suspects also provided assistance and occasional inspiration. Along the way, I have met and interviewed many of the contemporary thinkers featured in this book. I would therefore like to thank them all for their time and generosity.

'The only thing worse than slavishly following management theory is ignoring it completely.'

The Economist[1]

Introduction

According to the British poet Philip Larkin, sexual intercourse began in 1963. Modern management thinking announced itself a little earlier when, in his masterly 1954 book, *The Practice of Management,* Peter Drucker confidently asserted that management had arrived as 'a distinct and a leading group in industrial society. Rarely, if ever, has a new basic institution, a new leading group, emerged as fast as has management since the turn of the century. Rarely in human history has a new institution proved indispensable so quickly.'[2]

Over 40 years later, Drucker's bold pronouncement holds true. We are all managers now, whether we manage hospitals, schools, funeral parlours, farms or football teams. Politicians embrace management with their focus groups and managerial jargon.[3] Management is the art and science of our times and management thinkers have become its high priests, the gurus.

Their ideas – in the age of knowledge and intellectual capital – are the new corporate currency.

'Business people need to understand that it is ideas that move history,' says marketing guru, Philip Kotler.[4] What business thinkers say and write matters. History is moving and it is moving in their direction. Harvard Business School's Michael Porter is no longer simply a distinguished academic, but a consultant to entire countries who writes books about the competitive advantage of nations. Kenichi Ohmae is no longer a McKinsey consultant revealing the secrets of the Japanese approach to strategy, but an aspiring politician drafting manifestos for the governments of the world. Charles Handy has become a bestselling social philosopher rather than a business school academic. And Tom Peters, the archetypal popular management theorist, has expanded his repertoire to encompass everything from the managerial lessons of cooking to the powers of Zen Buddhism.

New horizons have produced broader ambitions. No longer does a new management idea aim to change one aspect of a particular job. Most are intent on changing the world. The word 'revolution' can increasingly be found on dustjackets (even though between the covers there is often little that is original let alone revolutionary). In the early 1990s, reengineering gurus Michael Hammer and James Champy proclaimed their own revolution. With typical gusto, they said that their big idea, reengineering, was concerned with 'rejecting conventional wisdom and received assumptions of the past ... it is about reversing the industrial revolution ... tradition counts for nothing. Reengineering is a new beginning.' RIP Adam Smith. A few years on, we are still awaiting the new beginning and reengineering is fading into history.

There are brave new worlds – and words – aplenty. The sheer mass of new material suggests that quantity comes before quality. There is a steady supply of new insights into old ideas. Management theorizing has become adept at finding new angles on old topics. There is nothing wrong with this. Indeed, management is fundamentally concerned with seeking out modern approaches to age-old dilemmas. The final word on a subject such as leadership is unlikely ever to be uttered.

As Champy and Hammer's capacity for soundbites suggests, managerial theorizing is no longer a world of timid academics and obscure journals. 'Gurus aren't teams – they are stars; and like other stars their reputation and success is built upon their personal performance', say academics Timothy Clark and Graeme Salaman, students of the guru business. 'Gurus perform, and the power of their performance justifies their appearance fees, reverential treatment and influence.'[5] Management, the universal science, has become populist. It is theory with attitude. The skyline is crowded with an array of thinkers and gurus, each armed with a magic potion to cure all known corporate ills.

And, inevitably, there are critics aplenty. 'I think it is a packaged goods business. There is an unquenchable thirst. If you take the premise, as I do, that corporations are the dominant social institutions of our age you have to reckon with the fact that corporations are very influential. Certain trappings go with the party – a whole group of jesters like me,' says Richard Pascale, author of *Managing on the Edge* and as thoughtful a jester as you are likely to find. 'It is part of the fanfare surrounding these institutions. With that comes a constant churn of material for corporate chieftains to feed on. Because of their prominence in society this is always going to be with us though, among the CEOs I speak to, there is a certain cynicism about the material.'[6]

Richard Pascale is undoubtedly right. There is a great deal of skepticism about many of today's managerial ideas. Managerial thinking is adorned – and too often tainted – with ever greater hype and hyperbole. The emerging agenda can be seen as driven by the media as much as by the research interests of academics or the needs of business.

Depending on your perspective, this can be attributed to the substantial financial rewards available for those with the next bright idea to sweep the globe, or as a sign of ever-increasing desperation among managers to find ways in which they can make sense of the business world. Alternatively, and more positively, you can regard the merry go-round of ideas as an indication of just how vital effective management is to the economies and people of the world.

Inventing the guru

It was not always like this. There was a time when management thinkers worked quietly and diligently away in the hallowed halls of academia, carefully penning dense articles and books to be published in obscure journals. (Of course, some still do so.) In the 1950s there were people like Douglas McGregor, Frederick Herzberg and Abraham Maslow. In the 1960s there was Alfred Chandler, Ted Levitt and Igor Ansoff, leading into the 1970s when Henry Mintzberg first came to prominence. At the time they were recognized as significant thinkers in the field of management. They wrote books that didn't sell in huge numbers, but were significant enough to prove influential. They wrote articles in academic journals, gave the occasional seminars and worked as consultants for a few large corporations. As virtually all worked for major business schools with generous salaries, they did just fine. It was a good business to be in, but nothing special. In the 1960s and 1970s you did actually get paid more if you ran an organization.

The world of management thinking has been transformed. It touches everyone, everywhere. Today, there can hardly be a manager in the Western world who has not been to an event promoting a particular individual's view of how they should be managing their business. And then there are the consultants with their theories and formulae; the business schools with their resident experts advocating particular tools and techniques. There is no escape from the maelstrom of bright ideas.

The onslaught of ideas is not always welcomed or celebrated. Indeed, barely a week goes by without another article, report or book lambasting management theorists as a group of publicity-seeking megalomaniacs who make far too much money and whose ideas are usually little more than common sense. There is some truth in all these accusations.

The gurus tend to come from much the same backgrounds and often say much the same things. The passage to guru status usually involves a progression from an American business school (preferably Harvard); to articles in a leading American business journal (the *Harvard Business Review* or *Strategy & Business*); and from there to work with a big name consulting company (McKinsey, BCG, Bain or Booz.Allen & Hamilton). From there it is a long trek – via PR companies, publishers, publicists, marketing advisers – and it involves a lot of handshaking, travel and some measure of sycophancy.

The management guru industry is largely an American one. Indeed, the American management model has dominated the twentieth century. Only at the very end of the century is a convincing case being made for more global interpretations of American truisms. (Thanks to the slow rise of a group of thinkers not based in the United States – including Europeans such as Geert Hofstede, Gunnar Hedlund, Charles Handy, Andrew Campbell, Charles Hampden-Turner and Fons Trompenaars.) Historically, in management thinking at least, it has certainly helped to be American. Some gurus have taken this requirement very seriously – Igor Ansoff, the father of strategic management, was born in Vladivostock to a Russian mother and an American father; Peter Drucker was born in Austria and Ted Levitt, the marketing guru, was born in Germany. All moved to America.

While management thinking is clearly open to criticism on a number of fronts – too shallow, too American, too general, too populist – its comparative youth should not be overlooked. It is easy to forget that, as sciences go, management is in its infancy. As the thinkers in this book prove, management thinking is largely a creature of the twentieth century (48 of the 50 thinkers included here were alive during the twentieth century).

Management literature – aside from the unread and esoteric – has an even shorter history. The first 50 years of the century saw a handful of influential and useful management texts – works by the like of Chester Barnard, Mary Parker Follett, Frederick W. Taylor and Henri Fayol. Between 1950 and 1982, from McGregor to Mintzberg, there was a steady but unspectacular increase in numbers. Peter Drucker's seminal texts of this period were intellectual spectaculars rather than bestsellers. Then it took off. After the publication of Peters and Waterman's *In Search of Excellence* in 1982, the business book market exploded and has continued to mushroom in size ever since. Tens of thousands of business titles are now published every year.

Look also at academia. Compared to most other disciplines, management has only just arrived on the scene. While management has been a fundamental activity throughout history, the recognition and study of management as a discipline and profession is a thoroughly modern phenomenon. Only in the twentieth century has management come of age, gaining respectability and credence. Even now, the study of management is still in a fledgling state. Business schools like to give the impression of age-old permanence and wisdom but, in fact, their lineage is relatively short.

In the US, Chicago University's business school was founded in 1898; Amos Tuck at Dartmouth College, New Hampshire – founded in 1900 – was the first graduate school of management in the world; and Harvard offered its first MBA in 1908 and established its graduate business school in 1919. In Europe structured study of management is even younger. France's INSEAD offered an MBA for the first time in 1959. (The dearth of European business education was such that in 1970 only one member of INSEAD's faculty had a business doctorate – all now do.) It was not until 1965 that the UK's first two public business schools (in Manchester and London) were opened. The august academic institutions, Cambridge and Oxford Universities, have only embraced management in the last decade. Such statistics pale into insignificance when set against the centuries spent educating lawyers, clerics, soldiers, teachers and doctors in formal, recognized institutions.

Fashion slaves

Young disciplines (and their disciples) are apt to be hijacked, taken off in new, unexpected directions. They are pliable, sometimes uncontrollable. Management has proved this point with admirable gusto. New fashions come along and are grabbed. Managers are as fashion conscious as narcissistic thirteen-year-olds. Give them a distant glimpse of a bandwagon and they will leap aboard with abandon.

Research into the popularity of quality circles, carried out by two Columbia University academics, found that at the height of their popularity, between 1981 and 1982, coverage of quality circles was 'unreasoned, emotional and unqualifiedly positive'. After 1982, the bandwagon ground to an abrupt halt. Suddenly the coverage dried up and what there was became more questioning and increasingly negative. 'What makes this finding especially sobering is that a similar process might very well occur with fashions that have a much more profound effect than quality circles did – for example downsizing', said Eric Abrahamson, one of the researchers.[7]

Celebrants of the latest fashion can easily become fashion victims. One trenchant critic of this sad managerial propensity is the Canadian strategy guru, Henry Mintzberg. He was among the most critical of the reengineering fad – 'There is no reengineering in the idea of reengineering', he said. 'Just reification, just the same old notion that the new system will do the job. But because of the hype that goes with any new management fad, everyone has to run around reengineering everything. We are supposed to get superinnovation on demand just because it is deemed necessary by a manager in some distant office who has read a book. Why don't we just stop reengineering and delayering and restructuring and decentralizing and instead start thinking?'[8]

The answer is simple: thinking is hard; action, even if it is foolish, is easy. Managers retain an unquenchable desire for instant solutions that tackle all their problems in one fell swoop. Managers believe in the big idea. This is akin to an adolescent believing that a fashionable set of clothes will change their personality and lead them into a new world of happiness and romantic fulfillment. The result can be that executives are in touch with the gurus, but woefully out of touch with reality. Fashion conscious organizations end up attempting to implement every bright idea their senior executives have recently come across – research by George Binney and Colin Williams of the UK's Ashridge Management College found one company with 19 initiatives simultaneously underway. Inflicting ill-advised ideas on their organization occupies the time of many thousands of managers. For some it is a full-time job.

It seems that managers are in need of security and reassurance. They want a formula or a case study before making a move. They want a neat and tidy rationale, a decision-making system. At the same time, they continue to base the majority of their decisions on instinct. Managers may have absorbed the latest thinking on core competencies, but are more likely to make a decision on prejudice or personal opinion rather than a smart theory. Forget the science, managers are human after all.

Another paradox is that the global managerial search for security and reassurance leads managers to read books and listen to gurus whose message is anything but reassuring. The currency of Tom Peters, Richard Pascale or Charles Handy is insecurity and uncertainty. There is, perhaps, the reassurance that the gurus are identifying trends, feelings and fears which managers are already experiencing, but it is usually scant recompense for a sweat-drenched shirt and an uncomfortable feeling at the pit of your stomach that you are as dispensable as a piece of office furniture. The gurus aren't automatic dispensers of saccharined placebos. (Though, if that is what you want, there are plenty of alternatives to choose from.)

Inevitably, there is a degree of one-upmanship among the managerial audience. CEOs may view the latest idea with disdain, but aspiring managers cast around for recipes for success and ideas that can distinguish them from the crowd. Up and coming managers feel pressure to keep up-to-date with the latest thinking and fashions. They want to be in touch. If your son or daughter discovers that you have never heard of the latest pop sensation they are incredulous and days of inevitable baiting follow as they bemoan your advanced age. Managers behave very similarly when they discover a colleague who knows nothing of the latest addition to the managerial vocabulary. Of course, jargon is an essential tool in the guru's armory. Managers are addicted to jargon and gurus exploit their craving. Managers like to know what 'reengineering' means before their colleagues. As the inventor of the latest buzzword the guru can travel the world unraveling its true meaning to enraptured audiences.

More broadly, the guru industry is helped by the fact that, though they may be professionals, managers remain slightly reticent and ill-at-ease with the worth of their profession. Managers feel a need to explain themselves in a way in which lawyers or doctors do not. They are professionals, but where is the kudos? After all, young children do not express strong urges to become chief executives – and those that do are more likely to be taken to child psychologists than to witness their first production line in operation. Managers frequently explain themselves with their business cards and their job titles. They explain themselves through their company cars and the stunning variety of executive perks. And they seek legitimacy through the acquisition of knowledge.

The books gathering dust on their shelves are not merely decorative. They are statements. The executives with *The Age of Unreason* hovering unread above their desks are acknowledging their *willingness* to think, to acquire new skills, to make a difference. (This does not mean that they think, acquire new skills or make a difference.) For their intent alone, managers the world over should be congratulated. Their desire for self-improvement is open to ridicule, folly and fashion, but it is also a fundamental part of management, of business and of humanity.

The source of ideas

This book identifies 50 of the most important management thinkers. It comes with the simple caveat that no selection can be definitive. In such a global and crowded field it is often difficult to identify original instigators from followers. Even so, all 50 have had a significant impact on management thinking as well as on how managers manage their businesses.

The 50 include consultants, academics and even some executives.

Consultants (10)

- Marvin Bower
- Dale Carnegie
- James Champy
- W. Edwards Deming
- Peter Drucker
- Bruce Henderson
- Joseph Juran
- Kenichi Ohmae
- Tom Peters
- Frederick Taylor

Executives (10)

- Chester Barnard
- Henri Fayol
- Henry Ford
- Harold Geneen
- Konosuke Matsushita
- Akito Morita
- David Packard
- Alfred P. Sloan
- Robert Townsend
- Thomas Watson Jr

Academics (28)

- Igor Ansoff
- Chris Argyris
- Warren Bennis
- Alfred Chandler
- Mary Parker Follett
- Sumantra Ghoshal
- Gary Hamel
- Charles Handy
- Frederick Herzberg
- Geert Hofstede
- Elliott Jaques

- Rosabeth Moss Kanter
- Philip Kotler
- Ted Levitt
- Kurt Lewin
- Douglas McGregor
- Abraham Maslow
- Elton Mayo
- Michael Porter
- Richard Pascale
- Laurence Peter
- John Naisbitt
- Henry Mintzberg
- Edgar Schein
- Peter Senge
- Alvin Toffler
- Fons Trompenaars
- Max Weber

Historical influences (2)

- Nicolo Machiavelli
- Sun-Tzu

There are a number of interesting things about this list. The most obvious feature is that there are only two women (Mary Parker Follett and Rosabeth Moss Kanter). In truth, there are few other credible candidates. Jane Mouton, Lilian Gilbreth and Britain's Rosemary Stewart are the only three others who come to mind and the input of all three was significant but limited.

The second feature is the American dominance. Of the modern day thinkers, there are only small groups of Europeans (Fayol, Hofstede, Handy, Parkinson and Trompenaars); Japanese (Matsushita, Morita and Ohmae) and a small number of others (the Australians Mayo and Henderson, and the Indian Ghoshal).

If you make such a selection in 20 years' time I suspect it would be radically different with more women and more non-Americans. Blind faith in the American management model appears to have slipped. 'American managerial history is largely inward-focused and self-congratulatory', noted Richard Pascale in *Managing on the Edge*.

Tomorrow's gurus are scattered around the world and Europe is growing in intellectual influence. London Business School, for example, is home to Sumantra Ghoshal and Arie de Geus, as well as hosting forays from visiting professor Gary Hamel. France's INSEAD is home to rising stars, such as Chan Kim, in addition to long-established luminaries like Yves Doz and Henry Mintzberg. 'There is a European school of theory which is much less deterministic than American models. It is concerned with creating things dynamically and there is a critical mass of people who think along similar lines,' says one of the new generation of thinkers, London Business School's Don Sull, an American.

I also anticipate that the growing influence of consultants will lead to their increasing domination of the market in ideas. Recent years have seen a radical change in the ideas industry. Not only is the business more aggressively marketed and unashamedly populist, but the source of the best ideas has shifted from business schools to consultancies. Clearly, the businesses of both consultants and business schools are ideas driven. For management consultants, a fresh insight is highly marketable. It can speedily be integrated into a package sold *en masse* to companies. It is an obvious commercial fact that consultants who appear to be a step ahead of the game will attract more clients.

The same commonsensical rule applies to business schools. A school that has a reputation for being genuinely innovative and fresh in its thinking and its insights has a headstart on one that simply follows in the wake of others. Little wonder then that business schools fall over themselves to attract the intellectual thought leaders. The result is a merry-go-round of business school academics. Big names are traded and hawked. The annual meeting of the American Academy of Management was compared by one senior academic to an 'intellectual meat market'. Some are poached – Sumantra Ghoshal's move from INSEAD to London Business School was one instance of a big name taking the bait. (Other leading thinkers prefer to acquire visiting professorships depending on their vacation preferences.)

Amid the brain drains and brain gains, business schools can point to a lengthy pedigree of innovative research that has unquestionably changed management. Early management theorists such as Chester Barnard and Mary Parker Follett had strong academic connections.

The human relations school of the late 1950s was inspired by MIT-based Douglas McGregor who attracted the likes of Warren Bennis, Ed Schein and Chris Argyris to his team. Harvard Business School alone has a lengthy lineage of original thinkers. These include Alfred Chandler in the 1960s; marketing guru Ted Levitt; Chris Argyris; Rosabeth Moss Kanter; Michael Porter; and John Kotter.

Undoubtedly there remains a nucleus of highly original thinkers at the world's business schools. The present Harvard group – Kotter, Kanter, Porter *et al.* – have repeatedly broken new ground and are genuinely influential. Harvard's near neighbour MIT can point to the influence of Peter Senge, Ed Schein and Lester Thurow. Elsewhere, London Business School can boast the formidable Ghoshal, as well as having Gary Hamel as a visiting professor. Other notables, such as Henry Mintzberg and Philip Kotler, are business school based. Charles Handy came to theorizing at MIT and was then at London Business School. In fact, of the great management theorists, Peter Drucker is the only – but a significant – exception: Drucker has resolutely eschewed the temptation of a big name business school.

And yet, despite the names and brains, recent history has seen business schools gradually lagging behind in the war of ideas. A review of the significant management ideas of the 1980s and 1990s quickly reveals that most had their origins in management consultancies rather than in business schools.

First came what could loosely be termed 'excellence', spawned by Peters and Waterman's bestselling *In Search of Excellence*. At the time of researching and writing the book, the duo were McKinsey consultants.

Excellence led to the quality movement of the 1980s. Once again its inspirations came from outside business schools. The likes of W. Edwards Deming, Joseph Juran and Philip Crosby were more likely to be sneered at by business schools than welcomed into the fold. Despite the fact that many business schools now run programs and courses on quality, TQM, Just-in-Time and other techniques, there are comparatively few influential books on the subjects written by business school academics.

Then came the concept of the learning organization. Here, at least, the business schools can claim to have played the leading role. The bestselling *The Fifth Discipline*, which effectively launched the subject into public consciousness, was written by MIT's Peter Senge. The entire concept could also be seen as building on the work of Chris Argyris at Harvard.

The 1990s, however, have seen a steady procession of big ideas generated by consultants rather than business schools. Reengineering was a classic consulting big idea, one that could be easily converted into a package and given the hard sell. The current fascination with knowledge management and intellectual capital is also manna for consultants. It is notable that of the three books currently boasting the title *Intellectual Capital* none came from business schools. The business bestseller lists are bereft of big business school names. In the last five years only Hamel and Prahalad's *Competing for the Future* was pioneering, successful and business school generated.

The business school defense to accusations that their ideas have dried up is that consultants are highly adept at taking academic work and popularizing it. This is undoubtedly true. The reverse is also equally true: business schools are very good at coming up with ideas and then burying them in the same way as dogs bury particularly tasty bones. Business school research – often written in tortuous prose – is published via academic journals and expensive research reports with limited circulations. (Tom Peters has pointed out that a lot of the material in *In Search of Excellence* was actually dug up from research that lay buried in business schools.)

In the past consultants and educators tended to view each other with skepticism and not a little snobbery. Consultants sought to distance themselves from the ivory towers of academia. While academics dealt in theories, consultants proclaimed themselves to be masters of implementation. (This conveniently overlooked the fact that management consultants for top firms are recruited from business schools.)

Thanks to the fact that the consultants are generating new ideas, theory and practice appear more closely intertwined. (This has not made it any easier for bright ideas to become best practice – look at reengineering.) Conversion to the need to combine implementation with theory has not come cheaply. It is estimated that McKinsey now spends between $50 and $100 million a year on 'knowledge building'. It claims, somewhat dauntingly, to spend more on research than Harvard, Wharton and Stanford combined. To put this in perspective, London Business School's annual revenue from its research activities is a relatively meager £4.5 million – and LBS is unquestionably one of the leading sources of business school research.

'Bestselling books by consultants get attention and appear to be unearthing new ideas, but usually the consultants are midwives. You shouldn't confuse midwifery with conception,' counters London Business School's Research Dean, Professor Nicholson. 'There is a lot of brilliant translation. Consultants learn from experience and then generalize, but it is not systematic and their work is limited. Ideas such as organizational culture or empowerment weren't invented by consultants. When you trace ideas back you usually find yourself with academic research.'[9]

Even so, the borders between consulting and business schools are likely to become even more blurred in the near future. Ashridge Management College, for example, has its own consulting company. After all, it is well established for many business school academics to top up their academic salaries with consulting work. Some of the big names run their own consulting companies. Rosabeth Moss Kanter of Harvard Business School is also co-founder and chairman of Goodmeasure, which specializes in organizational change, innovation and the effective implementation of strategy. Kanter's Harvard colleague, Michael Porter, has his own consulting company, Monitor; and Gary Hamel has Strategos, as well as spending time at London Business School.

Clearly, the fact that consultants and business schools are moving closer together in a variety of ways has implications for the generation of ideas. Looking to the future, it is possible to envisage an elite of business schools continuing with high-quality research while the remainder follow behind as interpreters and translators. It is also possible to foresee far greater movement between the worlds of consulting and business schools than ever before. This could be mutually beneficial. Under continual pressure, as they shuttle from project to project, consultants would benefit more from being given the space, time and opportunity to study the implications of their work more thoroughly and systematically. Similarly, academics could benefit from closer contact with the immediacy of consulting work. The result could be a more balanced output of ideas with business schools re-

claiming their place as factories of ideas rather than becoming producers of executive programs. Whatever their source, it is unlikely
that the flood of ideas will come to a halt. And, whatever your views
on their originality or capacity for self-marketing, the business gurus
will continue to be the richest vein of bright ideas.

The selection

For ease of reference, *The Ultimate Book of Business Gurus* is organized alphabetically by thinker. The section on each thinker seeks to
cover their career and central ideas. On the title page of each section
there is a brief résumé of their occupation, dates, key ideas and main
publications. A full list of each of their publications is given in the
Bibliography at the end of the book. In some cases, thinkers hunt in
pairs. I have treated writing duos as two individuals and given both
separate entries. To avoid duplication, one partner receives more attention.

The selection of 50 is open to question and discussion. By way
of consolation and additional information (and as a result of plain
indecision), the Appendix features a further selection of thinkers who
also deserve a place in the business hall of fame.

Stuart Crainer
March 1998

Notes

1   'In defence of the guru', *The Economist*, 26 February 1994.
2   Drucker, Peter F., *The Practice of Management*, Harper & Row,
    New York, 1954.
3   'Politicians are asking management theorists how to plan their
    day, organize their offices and master their emotions. They are
    even asking them how to think about the world,' noted *The Econo-
    mist*, 'Managing the public sector', 20 May 1995.
4   Correspondence with the author, November 1997.
5   Clark, Timothy, and Salaman, Graeme, 'The management guru
    as organizational witchdoctor', *Organization*, Vol. 3 (1), 1996.

6   Interview with the author, July 1996.
7   Griffith, Victoria, 'Ammunition for fighting the fad', *Financial Times*, 15 August 1997.
8   Mintzberg, Henry, 'Musings on management', *Harvard Business Review*, July/August 1996
9   Interview with the author, September 1997.

Igor Ansoff

"The end product of strategic decisions is deceptively simple; a combination of products and markets is selected for the firm. This combination is arrived at by addition of new product markets, divestment from some old ones, and expansion of the present position.**"**

Igor Ansoff

American academic and consultant
Born 1918

Breakthrough ideas

Strategic management
Gap analysis
Synergy

Key book

Corporate Strategy

Igor Ansoff (born 1918) was one of the key figures in the formulation of a clear concept of strategic management.

Ansoff trained as an engineer and mathematician. After leaving Brown University, he worked for the RAND Corporation,[1] initially in the mathematics department, and then the Lockheed Corporation where he was a vice-president. 'The timing of my move to industry was fortuitous, because it influenced my ultimate career path', says Ansoff. 'It occurred at a time when American industry was increasingly confronting environmental discontinuities and turbulence. As a result, my experience at Lockheed focused my attention and trained me to deal with the problem of managing organizations in the face of environmental discontinuities which became the central focus of my attention during the following 30 years.'

In 1963 he left industry for academia, joining Carnegie–Mellon's Graduate School of Business Administration. He then taught at Vanderbilt University and at the European Institute for Advanced Studies in Management in Belgium. He joined the San Diego-based, US International University in 1983 where he is now Distinguished Professor of Strategic Management.

Ansoff's experiences at Lockheed provided the impetus for his first foray into the murky waters of corporate strategy. On a vacation Ansoff grew a beard, consumed half a case of Scotch and contemplated strategy. The end product was his first – and most important – book, *Corporate Strategy*, in which he sought to make sense of the broader implications of what he had learned at Lockheed. Ansoff believed that there was 'a practical method for strategic decision making within a business firm' which could be made accessible to all.

Following on from the work of Alfred Chandler (q.v.), Ansoff's work struck a chord. Until then, strategic planning was a barely understood, *ad hoc* concept. It was practiced, while the theory lay largely unexplored.

The result was a rational model by which strategic and planning decisions could be made. A creature of its times, the model concentrated on corporate expansion and diversification rather than strategic planning as a whole. (When interviewed by the Lockheed CEO, Ansoff had asked what was meant by diversification. The CEO did not know even though this was the strategy the company was then pursuing.) From this emerged the Ansoff Model of Strategic Planning, an intricate and somewhat daunting sequence of decisions.

Central to this was the reassuringly simple concept of gap analysis: see where you are; identify where you wish to be; and identify tasks which will take you there. Ansoff can also lay claim to introducing the word 'synergy' into the management vocabulary. He explained it with uncharacteristic brevity as '2 + 2 = 5'. In addition, Ansoff examined 'corporate advantage' long before Michael Porter cornered the field 20 years later.

Ansoff regarded strategic management as 'the part of management which develops a firm's future profit potential by assuring that it does business in markets which have the potential of satisfying its objectives; that it offers products/services which these markets want; and that it offers them in a way which assures it a competitive advantage'. He distinguished this from what he called operating management – 'the part of management which, using the profit potential, optimizes a firm's profitability through efficient production, distribution and marketing its products/services generated by strategic management'.

To the contemporary observer, Ansoff's work can appear excessively analytical and highly prescriptive. Ansoff himself has honestly admitted that his early model was overly analytical. Early converts to strategic planning as outlined by Ansoff found that 'paralysis by analysis' was a very real threat. 'In retrospect, the incidence of strategic planning failure should not have been surprising. After all, it was a practical invention designed by staffs in business firms as a solution to a problem which was poorly understood, and in the absence of a theory which could have guided the design,' Ansoff has reflected.

Over the last 30 years, Ansoff has worked steadfastly on honing his model so that strategic planning could become a universally available management tool. Along the way he has fuelled a continuing debate with the likes of Henry Mintzberg on the role of creativity and intuition, as opposed to analysis, in the formulation of strategy. In an era where corporate change is increasingly recognized as a fact of life, thinkers argue that solutions are ever more elusive – 'Strategic planning, at best, is about posing questions, more than attempting to answer them', Richard Pascale suggests. Ansoff's model was better suited to a world of answers than one beset by turbulence and uncertainty.

Notes

1 RAND, an acronym for Research and Development, was an American military think-tank established after the war.

Bibliography

Corporate Strategy, McGraw Hill, New York, 1965.
Strategic Management, Macmillan, London, 1979.
Implanting Strategic Management, Prentice Hall, London, 1984.

Chris Argyris

"Because many professionals are almost always successful at what they do, they rarely experience failure. And because they have rarely failed, they have never learned how to learn from failure."

Chris Argyris

American academic
Born 1923

Breakthrough ideas

Organizational learning
Single and double loop learning

Key books

Personality and Organization
Organizational Learning

L ean and ascetic of appearance, **Chris Argyris'** work is driven by a fundamental – some would say flawed – faith in human nature. His romantic optimism is bolstered by his considerable intellect. Argyris (born 1923) is a formidable thinker – even by the lofty standards of his employer, Harvard Business School.

Argyris was brought up in the New York suburbs and spent some time in Greece with his grandparents. Prior to joining Harvard he was at Yale where he was a professor of administrative science. His qualifications embrace psychology, economics and organizational behavior. He is now the James Bryant Conant Professor of Education and Organizational Behavior at Harvard Business School, a post he has held since 1971.

Argyris' early work concentrated on the then highly innovative field of behavioral science. Indeed, his 1957 book, *Personality and Organization* has become one of the subject's classic texts. Argyris argued that organizations depend fundamentally on people and that personal development is, and should be, related to work. The problem, Argyris believed, in many organizations is that the organization itself stands in the way of people fulfilling their potential. The task for the organization is to make sure that people's motivation and potential are fulfilled and well-directed.

Argyris was part of the human relations school of the late 1950s and involved in the work of the National Training Laboratories which had a mesmeric attraction for a host of other important thinkers. 'He was bespectacled, dark-complexioned, and slender, with a narrow face that tended, almost despite himself, to break into a delighted grin when arguments grew hot, as if he was overjoyed at the chance to test himself', says Art Kleiner in *The Age of Heretics*. 'His voice was distinctively mild-mannered and reedy with a slight European tinge. His style of debate was analytical – indeed, his approach to life was passionately devoted to inquiry, reasoning, and theory. But he was drawn to the kinds of problems that most analytical people eschew, the riddles of human nature. In particular, why did people fail to live up to their own professed ideals? Why was so much human behavior so self-frustrating, particularly in organizations?'[1]

These are questions which Argyris has continued to ask with dogged persistence. Central to his process of inquiry has been the entire concept of learning. Argyris has examined learning processes, both in individual and corporate terms, in huge depth. 'Most people define learning too narrowly as mere *problem solving,* so they focus on identifying and correcting errors in the external environment. Solving problems is important, but if learning is to persist managers and employees must also look inward. They need to reflect critically on their own behavior,' he says.[2] Problems with learning, as Argyris has revealed, are not restricted to a particular social group. Indeed, it is the very people we expect to be good at learning – teachers, consultants and other 'professionals' – who often prove the most inadequate at actually doing so.

His most influential work was carried out with Donald Schön (most importantly in their 1974 book, *Theory in Practice,* and their 1978 book, *Organizational Learning*). The combination of the psychologist, Argyris, and the more philosophical, Schön, produced some original perspectives on age old problems.[3]

Argyris and Schön originated two basic organizational models. The first was based on the premise that we seek to manipulate and form the world in accordance with our individual aspirations and wishes. In Model 1 managers concentrate on establishing individual goals. They keep to themselves and don't voice concerns or disagreements. The onus is on creating a conspiracy of silence in which everyone dutifully keeps their head down.

Defense is the prime activity in a Model 1 organization though occasionally the best means of defense is attack. Model 1 managers are prepared to inflict change on others, but resist any attempt to change their own thinking and working practices. Model 1 organizations are characterized by what Argyris and Schön labeled 'single-loop learning' ('when the detection and correction of organizational error permits the organization to carry on its present policies and achieve its current objectives').

In contrast, Model 2 organizations emphasized 'double-loop learning' which Argyris and Schön described as 'when organizational error is detected and corrected in ways that involve the modification of underlying norms, policies, and objectives'. In Model 2 organizations, managers act on information. They debate issues and respond to, and are prepared to, change. They learn from others. A virtuous circle emerges of learning and understanding. 'Most organizations do quite well in single-loop learning but have great difficulties in double-loop learning', concluded Argyris and Schön.

In addition, Argyris and Schön proposed a final form of learning which offered even greater challenges. This was 'deutero-learning', 'inquiring into the learning system by which an organization detects and corrects its errors'.

While defensiveness has remained endemic, corporate fashions have moved Argyris' way. With the return of learning to the corporate agenda in the early nineties, his work became slightly more fashionable. This did not temper the rigor of his output or of his arguments. The questions remained. 'Any company that aspires to succeed in the tougher business environment of the 1990s must first resolve a basic dilemma: success in the marketplace increasingly depends on learning, yet most people don't know how to learn. What's more, those members of the organization that many assume to be the best at learning are, in fact, not very good at it,' he noted in a *Harvard Business Review* article.[4]

The challenge – and mystery – of learning remains profound. The riddle of human nature remains as intractable as ever; and Chris Argyris' curiosity appears undiminished. 'Many professionals have extremely brittle personalities. When suddenly faced with a situation they cannot immediately handle, they tend to fall apart,' he says. 'There seems to be a universal human tendency to design one's actions consistently according to four basic values:

1   To remain in unilateral control;
2   To maximize *winning* and minimize *losing*;
3   To suppress negative feelings; and
4   To be as *rational* as possible – by which people mean defining clear objectives and evaluating their behavior in terms of whether or not they have achieved them.'

As Argyris has repeatedly exposed, on such patterns of behavior are organizations built.

Notes

1 Kleiner, Art, *The Age of Heretics*, Nicholas Brealey, London, 1996.
2 Argyris, Chris, 'Teaching smart people how to learn', *Harvard Business Review*, May–June 1991.
3 Schön is featured in the Appendix.
4 Argyris, Chris, 'Teaching smart people how to learn', *Harvard Business Review*, May–June 1991.

Bibliography

Personality and Organization, Harper, New York, 1957.
Understanding Organizational Behavior, Dorsey Press, Homewood, IL, 1960.
Organizational Learning (with Donald Schön), Addison Wesley, Reading, MA, 1978.
On Organizational Learning, Blackwell, Cambridge, MA, 1992.

Chester Barnard

"I rejected the concept of organization as comprising a rather definite group of people whose behavior is co-ordinated with reference to some explicit goal or goals. In a community all acts of individuals and of organizations are directly or indirectly interconnected and interdependent."

Chester Barnard

American executive
1886–1961

Breakthrough ideas

The nature and scope of executive roles
Company/executive relationship

Key book

The Functions of the Executive

C hester Barnard (1886–1961) was a rarity: a management theorist who was also a successful practitioner. Barnard won an economics scholarship to Harvard, but before finishing his degree he joined American Telephone and Telegraph to begin work as a statistician. He spent his entire working life with the company, eventually becoming President of New Jersey Bell in 1927. *Fortune* Magazine hailed Barnard as 'possibly [having] the most capacious intellect of any business executive in the United States'. He retired in 1952.

Though he was the archetypal corporate man, Barnard's interests were varied. During World War II, he worked as special assistant to the Secretary of the Treasury and co-wrote a report which formed the basis of US atomic energy policy. Barnard also found time to lecture on the subject of management.

Chester Barnard's best known book, *The Functions of the Executive,* collected together his lectures. The language is dated, the approach ornate, but comprehensive. The book continues to attract occasional outbursts of appreciation when discovered by modern thinkers. (It was last resurrected by Peters and Waterman in their 1982 bestseller *In Search of Excellence* who noted: 'Its density makes it virtually unreadable; nonetheless it is a monument'.)

Indeed, much of what Barnard argued strikes a chord with contemporary management thinking. For example, he highlighted the need for communication – he believed that everyone needs to know what and where the communications channels are so that every single person can be tied into the organization's objectives. He also advocated lines of communication that were short and direct. 'The essential functions are, first, to provide the system of communications; second, to promote the securing of essential efforts; and, third, to formulate and define purpose', he wrote.

To Barnard the chief executive was not a dictatorial figure geared to simple short-term achievements. Instead, part of his responsibility was to nurture the values and goals of the organization. Barnard argued that values and goals need to be translated into action rather than meaningless motivational phraseology. Barnard took what would today be called a holistic approach, arguing that 'in a community all acts of individuals and of organizations are directly or indirectly interconnected and interdependent'.

Barnard regarded the commercial organization simply as a means of allowing people to achieve what they could not achieve when merely individuals. He defined an organization as a 'system of consciously co-ordinated activities of forces of two or more persons'. Not surprisingly given the era in which Barnard lived, there was a hint of Taylor's Scientific Management in such observations. For all his contemporary sounding ideas, Barnard was a man of his times – advocating corporate domination of the individual and regarding loyalty to the organization as paramount.

Even so, Barnard proposed a moral dimension to the world of work (one which Taylor certainly did not recognize). 'The distinguishing mark of the executive responsibility is that it requires not merely conformance to a complex code of morals but also the creation of moral codes for others', wrote Barnard. In arguing that there was a morality to management, Barnard played an important part in broadening the managerial role from one simply of measurement, control and supervision, to one also concerned with more elusive, abstract notions, such as values.

Bibliography

The Functions of the Executive, Harvard University Press, Cambridge, MA, 1938.
Organization and Management, Harvard University Press, Cambridge, MA, 1948.

Warren Bennis

"The new leader is one who commits people to action, who converts followers into leaders, and who may convert leaders into agents of change."

Warren Bennis

American academic and administrator
Born 1925

Breakthrough ideas

Leadership as an accessible skill
Adhocracy as an antidote to bureaucracy

Key books

Leaders
An Invented Life
Organizing Genius

P erpetually tanned, with a shining white-toothed smile, **Warren Bennis** (born 1925) appears the archetype of the Californian popular academic. To many he is simply the regular Presidential adviser who brought leadership to a new, mass audience. But there is more to Bennis than that. His lengthy career has involved him in education, writing, consulting and administration. Along the way he has made a contribution to an array of subjects and produced a steady stream of books including the best-selling, *Leaders,* and most recently, *Organizing Genius: The Secrets of Creative Collaboration.*

Now in his seventies, Bennis was the youngest infantry officer in the European theatre of operations during World War II. He recalls the war's end – 'On August 6 1945, I was on patrol duty in Heidelburg, Germany. I was talking to an enlisted man who said that we'd unloaded a super bomb in Japan. Now we can have our lives back, he said. We were all set to go to Japan.'

Returning home, he went to Antioch College as an undergraduate and fell under the influence of his mentor, Douglas McGregor, creator of the motivational Theories X and Y. Later, Bennis followed McGregor to MIT. 'My early work was on small group dynamics, more a classical area of social psychology. I moved from there to T-Groups, sensitivity training and then into change in social systems,' recalls Bennis.[1]

From being an early student of group dynamics in the 1950s; Bennis became a futurologist in the 1960s. His work – particularly *The Temporary Society* (1968) – explored new organizational forms. Bennis envisaged organizations as *adhocracies* – roughly the direct opposite of bureaucracies – freed from the shackles of hierarchy and meaningless paperwork. (The term was later used by Alvin Toffler, among others.)

While Bennis was mapping out potential futures for the business world, he was confronting realities as a university administrator at the State University of New York at Buffalo and as President of the University of Cincinnati. He found that his practice disappointed his theory – a rare example of an academic putting his reputation where his ideas are. 'When I was at the University of Cincinnati I realized that I was seeking power through position, by being President of the university. I wanted to *be* a university president but I didn't want to *do* it. I wanted the influence,' says Bennis. 'In the end I wasn't very good at being a president. I looked out of the window and thought that the man cutting the lawn actually seemed to have more control over what he was doing.'

Bennis returned to the other side of the academic fence. He is now based at the University of Southern California where he is founder of the University's Leadership Institute in Los Angeles.

Explaining the pattern of his career, Bennis reflects: 'I am voraciously curious. At the age of 72 I would like to open more doors for people. People who cannot invent and reinvent themselves must be content with borrowed postures, secondhand ideas, fitting in instead of standing out.'[2]

Yet, despite his varied career – and life – Bennis remains inextricably linked with the subject of leadership. 'I have been thinking about leadership almost as long as I have been thinking', he says in the autobiographical collection, *An Invented Life*.[3] 'It is probably a trap of my own making', he admits. 'My first major article came out in 1959 and was on leadership. Since 1985 most of my work has been in that area. You build up some sort of brand equity and there is a degree of collusion between that and the marketplace – people say leadership that's Bennis. It makes life a little simpler.'

With the torrent of publications and executive programmes on the subject, it is easy to forget that leadership had been largely forgotten as a topic worthy of serious academic interest until it was revived by Bennis and others in the 1980s. Since then, Bennis admits, 'leadership has become a heavy industry. Concern and interest about leadership development is no longer an American phenomenon. It is truly global.'

Bennis' work stands as a humane counter to much of the military-based, hero worship which dogs the subject. Bennis argues that leadership is not a rare skill; leaders are made rather than born; leaders are usually ordinary people – or apparently ordinary – rather than charismatic; leadership is not solely the preserve of those at the top of the organization – it is relevant at all levels; and, finally, leadership is not about control, direction and manipulation.

Bennis' best known leadership research involved 90 of America's leaders. These included Neil Armstrong, the coach of the LA Rams, orchestral conductors, and businessmen such as Ray Kroc of

McDonald's. 'They were right brained and left-brained, tall and short, fat and thin, articulate and inarticulate, assertive and retiring, dressed for success and dressed for failure, participative and autocratic', said Bennis.[4] The link between them was that they had all shown 'mastery over present confusion'. Bennis' message was that leadership is all-encompassing and open to all.

From the 90 leaders, four common abilities were identified: management of attention; of meaning; of trust; and of self. Management of attention, said Bennis, is a question of vision. Indeed, he uses a definition of leadership as: 'The capacity to create a compelling vision and translate it into action and sustain it.' Successful leaders have a vision that other people believe in and treat as their own.

Having a vision is one thing, converting it into successful action is another. The second skill shared by Bennis' selection of leaders is management of meaning – communications. A vision is of limited practical use if it is encased in 400 pages of wordy text or mumbled from behind a paper-packed desk.

Bennis believes effective communication relies on use of analogy, metaphor and vivid illustration as well as emotion, trust, optimism and hope.

The third aspect of leadership identified by Bennis is trust which he describes as 'the emotional glue that binds followers and leaders together'. Leaders have to be seen to be consistent.

The final common bond between the 90 leaders studied by Bennis is 'deployment of self'. The leaders do not glibly present charisma or time management as the essence of their success. Instead, the emphasis is on persistence and self-knowledge, taking risks, commitment and challenge but, above all, learning. 'The learning person looks forward to failure or mistakes', says Bennis. 'The worst problem in leadership is basically early success. There's no opportunity to learn from adversity and problems.'

The leaders have a positive self regard, what Bennis labels 'emotional wisdom'. This is characterized by an ability to accept people as they are; a capacity to approach things in terms of only the present; willingness to treat everyone, even close contacts, with courteous attention; an ability to trust others even when this seems risky; and an ability to do without constant approval and recognition.

Most recently, Bennis has switched his attention to the dynamics of group working. He prefers the terminology of groups rather than the more fashionable teams – 'Teams has a Dilbertian smell to it. Everyone is talking about teams and there is a lot of bullshit written. I'm not sure how useful it is to business people. I think you can learn more from extraordinary groups than the run of the mill. None of us is as smart as all of us. These are exceptional groups with great intensity who had belief in their collective aspiration. The groups are a series of vivid utopias whether they are Xerox's Palo Alto Research Center, the group behind the 1992 Clinton campaign, Lockheed's Skunk Works or the Manhattan Project which invented the atomic bomb'.

The relationship between groups and their leaders is clearly of fundamental interest to Bennis. 'Greatness starts with superb people. Great Groups don't exist without great leaders, but they give the lie to the persistent notion that successful institutions are the lengthened shadow of a great woman or man. It's not clear that life was ever so simple that individuals, acting alone, solved most significant problems.'

Indeed, the heroic view of the leader as the indomitable individual is now outdated and inappropriate. 'The Lone Ranger is dead. Instead of the individual problem solver we have a new model for creative achievement. People like Steve Jobs or Walt Disney headed groups and found their own greatness in them,' says Bennis. 'He or she is a pragmatic dreamer, a person with an original but attainable vision. Ironically, the leader is able to realize his or her dream only if the others are free to do exceptional work. Typically, the leader is the one who recruits the others, by making the vision so palpable and seductive that they see it, too, and eagerly sign up. Inevitably, the leader has to invent a leadership style that suits the group. The standard models, especially command and control, simply don't work. The heads of groups have to act decisively, but never arbitrarily. They have to make decisions without limiting the perceived autonomy of the other participants. Devising and maintaining an atmosphere in which others can put a dent in the universe is the leader's creative act.'

There is a rich strand of idealism which runs through Bennis' work. He is a humanist with high hopes for humanity. 'Most organizations are dull and working life is mundane. There is no getting away from that. So, these groups could be an inspiration. A Great Group is more than a collection of first-rate minds. It's a miracle. I have unwarranted optimism. By looking at the possibilities we can all improve. With T-Groups in the fifties, people said it is not real life. But it shows you the possibilities.' To accusations of romanticism, Bennis puts up a resolute and spirited defense: 'If a romantic is someone who believes in possibilities and who is optimistic then that is probably an accurate description. I think that every person has to make a genuine contribution in their lives and the institution of work is one of the main vehicles to achieving this. I'm more and more convinced that individual leaders can create a human community that will, in the long run, lead to the best organizations.'

Notes

1   Interview with author, December 1997 (as are all other quotations unless otherwise attributed).
2   'Profile of Warren Bennis', *Organization Frontier* 93/3.
3   Bennis, Warren, *An Invented Life*, Addison Wesley, Wokingham, 1993.
4   Quoted in Crainer, Stuart, 'Doing the right thing', *The Director*, October 1988.

Bibliography

The Planning of Change (with Benne K.D. & Chin, R., 2nd edn), Holt, Rinehart & Winston, 1970.
Leaders: The Strategies for Taking Charge (with Burt Nanus), Harper & Row, New York, 1985.
On Becoming a Leader, Addison-Wesley, Reading, MA, 1989.
Why Leaders Can't Lead, Jossey-Bass, San Francisco, CA, 1989.
An Invented Life: Reflections on Leadership and Change, Addison-Wesley, Reading, MA, 1993.
Organizing Genius (with Patricia Ward Biederman), Addison Wesley, Reading, MA, 1997.

Marvin Bower

"In all successful professional groups, regard for the individual is based not on title but on competence, stature and leadership."

Marvin Bower

American management consultant
Born 1903

Breakthrough ideas

Corporate culture and values
Teamworking and project management
Professionalization of management consulting

Key books

The Will to Manage
The Will to Lead

Marvin Bower (born 1903) is the man who did more than any other to create the modern management consulting industry – perhaps only Bruce Henderson of the Boston Consulting Group can come close to Bower's long lasting impact at McKinsey & Company. While few claims can be made for Bower as an outstandingly innovative thinker, he was a rigorous setter of standards and an extraordinarily successful practitioner. Under Bower's astute direction McKinsey became the world's premier consulting firm. Interestingly, recent years have also seen the structure and managerial style of the company receiving plaudits.

Marvin Bower joined the fledgling firm of James O McKinsey (1889–1937) in 1933 at a time when management consulting was still called 'management engineering'. Bower was a Harvard-trained lawyer, originally from Cleveland. Soon after Bower's arrival, McKinsey left to run Marshall Field & Company. He died in 1937 and this left Bower in the company's New York office and A.T. Kearney in the Chicago office. In 1939 the two split with Kearney setting up a new company in his own name.

Bower did not change the name of his firm as he shrewdly decided that clients would demand his involvement in projects if his name was up in lights.

'My vision was to provide advice on managing to top executives and to do it with the professional standards of a leading law firm', said Bower.[1] Consequently, McKinsey consultants were 'associates' who had 'engagements', rather than mere jobs, and the firm was a 'practice' rather than a business. 'The entire ethos of McKinsey was to be very respectable, the kind of people CEOs naturally relate to. That's the enduring legacy of Marvin Bower,' says former McKinsey consultant George Binney.[2]

Throughout the 1940s and 1950s, McKinsey expanded in North America. It opened its first overseas office in 1959, followed by Melbourne, Amsterdam, Dusseldorf, Paris, Zurich and Milan. In 1997, McKinsey had 74 offices in 38 countries.

Bower's gospel was that the interests of the client should precede increasing the company's revenues. 'Unless the client could trust McKinsey, we could not work with them', said Bower. If you looked after the client, the profits would look after themselves. (High charges were not a means to greater profits, according to McKinsey, but a simple and effective means of ensuring that clients took McKinsey seriously.)

Bower's other rules were that consultants should keep quiet about the affairs of clients; should tell the truth and be prepared to challenge the client's opinion; and should only agree to do work which is both necessary and which they could do well. To this he added a few idiosyncratic twists such as insisting that all McKinsey consultants wore hats – except, for some reason, in the San Francisco office – and long socks.

Bower's view was that values maketh the man and the business. American Express chief Harvey Golub, an ex-McKinsey consultant, labels Bower as 'one of the finest leaders in American business ever' and says that 'he led that firm according to a set of values, and it was the principle of using values to help shape and guide an organization that was probably the most important thing I took away'.[3]

Bower also changed the company's recruitment policy. Instead of hiring experienced executives with in-depth knowledge of a particular industry, he began recruiting graduates students who could learn how to be good problem solvers and consultants. This was novel at the time but set a precedent and changed the emphasis of consulting – from passing on a narrow range of experience to utilizing a wide range of analytical and problem solving techniques.

Another element of Bower's approach was the use of teams. He thought of McKinsey as a 'network of leaders'. Teams were assembled for specific projects. The best people in the organization were brought to bear on a particular problem no matter where they were based in the world. 'McKinsey had a culture that fostered rigorous debate over the right answer without that debate resulting in personal criticism', recalls IBM's Lou Gerstner, another McKinsey alumnus.[4]

Though the management consulting world developed a high charging, opportunistic reputation, Bower managed to stand apart. True or not, he created an impression of hard working, clean living, decency. Even now, once recruited, McKinsey consultants know where they stand. The firm's policy remains one of the most simple. 'Seniority in McKinsey correlates directly with achievement', it says. The weak are shown the door. 'If a consultant ceases to progress with the Firm or is ultimately unable to demonstrate the skills and qualities required of a principal, he or she is asked to leave McKinsey', says the company's recruitment brochure.

Bower himself set an impressive example – in 1963, on reaching the age of 60, he sold his shares back to the firm at their book value. McKinsey laid its cards on the table. It played it hard, but straight. If Big Blue was the company to trust; McKinsey was the consulting firm to trust. This is something which McKinsey has largely managed to sustain.

Bower's approach was commonsensical and free of fashionable baggage. 'Business has not changed in the past sixty years. The basic way of running it is the same. There have been thousands of changes in methods but not in command and control. Many companies say they want to change but they need to empower people below. More cohesion is needed rather than hierarchy,' he said in 1995.[5]

The culture Bower created, continues. The mystique of McKinsey – The Firm – is untouched. It has become more than a mere consultancy. It is an ethos. Staid suits and professional standards. Clean-cut and conservative. It is obsessively professional and hugely successful; a slick, well-oiled financial machine not given to false modesty – 'We do not learn from clients. Their standards aren't high enough. We learn from other McKinsey partners,' a McKinsey consultant once confided to *Forbes* magazine.

And yet, McKinsey is not the oldest consultancy company. Arthur D Little can trace its lineage back to the 1880s. Nor is McKinsey the biggest consultancy company in the world – Andersen Consulting dwarfs it in terms of revenues and numbers of consultants (but not, significantly, in revenue per consultant). McKinsey is special because it likes to think of itself as the best and has developed a self-perpetuating aura that it is unquestionably the best. Marvin Bower was the creator of this organizational magic.

Notes

1   Huey, John, 'How McKinsey does it', *Fortune*, 1 November 1993.
2   Interview with author.
3   Byrne, John, 'The McKinsey mystique', *Business Week*, 20 September 1993.

4   Byrne, John, 'The McKinsey mystique', *BusinessWeek*, 20 September 1993.
5   Hecht, Françoise, 'The firm walks tall', *Eurobusiness*, February 1995.

Bibliography

The Will to Manage: Corporate success through programmed management, McGraw Hill, New York, 1966.
The Will to Lead: Running a business with a network of leaders, Harvard Business School Press, Cambridge, MA, 1997.

Dale Carnegie

"Take a chance! All life is a chance. The man who goes the furthest is generally the one who is willing to do and dare.**"**

Dale Carnegie

American consultant and author
1888–1955

Breakthrough ideas

Salesmanship, communication and motivation

Key book

How to Win Friends and Influence People

I n 1987, a Taiwanese consulting company brought **Dale Carnegie's** training programs to the country for the first time. Within eight years, 7000 students were graduating each year and the business was generating annual profits of $4 million. In 1997, over forty years after his death, Dale Carnegie (1888–1955) was still featuring on the bestseller lists in Germany. These two examples are testament to the enduring popularity of Carnegie's work and the truism, first noted by Robert Louis Stevenson, that everyone lives by selling something.

Carnegie was the first superstar of the self-help genre. Go forth with a smile on your face and a song in your heart and sell, sell, sell. His successors – whether they be Anthony Robbins or Stephen Covey – should occasionally doff their caps in Carnegie's direction. It is surely no coincidence that Covey studied American 'success litera-ture', of which Carnegie is a prime example, before coming up with *The Seven Habits of Highly Effective People*. Carnegie did much the same 50 years before and his principles have a similar homely ring to those of Covey.

First, Carnegie presented the 'fundamental techniques in han-dling people' – 'don't criticize, condemn or complain; give honest and sincere appreciation; and arouse in the other person an eager want'. To these he added six ways to make people like you – 'become genuinely interested in other people; smile; remember that a person's name is to that person the sweetest and most important sound in any language; be a good listener. Encourage others to talk about them-selves; talk in terms of the other person's interests; make the other person feel important – and do it sincerely.' (It is not known whether Groucho Marx was a fan of Carnegie's, but he provided similar ad-vice: 'Sincerity is the key to success. If you can fake that, you've got it made.')

Dale Carnegie mastered sincerity early on. Born on a Missouri farm, Carnegie (originally Carnegey) began his working life selling bacon, soap and lard for Armour & Company in south Omaha. He turned his sales territory into the company's national leader, but then went to New York to study at the American Academy of Dramatic Arts – he toured the country as Dr Harley in *Polly of the Circus*. Real-izing the limits of his acting potential, Carnegie returned to sales-manship – selling Packard automobiles. It was then that Carnegie persuaded the YMCA schools in New York to allow him to conduct courses in public speaking.

Carnegie's talks became highly successful. So successful, in fact, that he turned them into a string of books – *Public Speaking and Influencing Men in Business*; *How to Stop Worrying and Start Living*; *How to Enjoy Your Life and Your Job*; *How to Develop Self-Confidence and Influence People by Public Speaking*; and his perennial bestseller, *How to Win Friends and Influence People*, which has sold over 15 million copies.

Carnegie was a salesman extraordinaire. In his books, names were dropped, promises made. Up-beat and laden with sentiment, *How to Win Friends and Influence People* was a simple selling document – 'The rules we have set down here are not mere theories or guesswork. They work like magic. Incredible as it sounds, I have seen the application of these principles literally revolutionize the lives of many people.'

It is easy to sneer at Carnegie's work – in the same way as Covey can be dismissed. It is homespun wisdom adorned with commercial know-how. Like any great salesman, Carnegie knew which levers to pull and when. Appearances can be deceptive. It is difficult to sneer at the enduring popularity of Carnegie's books and his company's training programs. They continue to strike a chord with managers and aspiring managers, because they deal with the universal challenge of face-to-face communication. Carnegie was also notable in being the first to create a credible long-term business out of his ideas. In creating a flourishing business, Carnegie ensured that his name and ideas should continue to live on – and make money – after his death.

Bibliography

How to Stop Worrying and Start Living, Pocket Books, 1985.
How to Enjoy Your Life and Your Job, Pocket Books, 1986.
How to Win Friends and Influence People, Pocket Books, 1994.
How to Develop Self-Confidence and Influence People by Public Speaking, Pocket Books, 1995.

James Champy

James Champy

American consultant
Born 1942

Breakthrough idea

Reengineering

Key book

Reengineering the Corporation

J **ames Champy** (born 1942) co-founded the consultancy company CSC Index and was, along with Michael Hammer, the thinker behind the management phenomenon of the early 1990s, reengineering. Their book, *Reengineering the Corporation*, was a business blockbuster and, thanks to the popularity of reengineering, CSC became one of the largest consultancy companies in the world with revenues in excess of $500 million and over 2000 consultants worldwide. Revenues prior to the success of the book were $70 million.

With reengineering Champy and Hammer promised a revolution, but it is one which – except in a few instances – largely failed to materialize.

The basic idea behind reengineering was that organizations needed to identify their key processes and make them as lean and efficient as possible. Peripheral processes (and therefore peripheral people) needed to be discarded. Champy and Hammer defined reengineering as 'the fundamental rethinking and radical redesign of business processes to achieve dramatic improvements in critical measures of performance such as cost, quality, service and speed'.

To Champy and Hammer, reengineering was more than dealing with mere processes. They eschewed the popular phrase 'business process reengineering', regarding it as too limiting. In their view the scope and scale of reengineering went far beyond simply altering and refining processes. True reengineering was all-embracing, a recipe for a corporate revolution.

Indeed, Champy and Hammer advocated that companies equip themselves with a blank piece of paper and map out their processes. Having come up with a neatly engineered map of how their business should operate, companies could then attempt to translate the paper theory into concrete reality. The past was dismissed as history; the future was there to be shaped and coerced into the optimum shape.

The concept was simple. To some it was Frederick Taylor's Scientific Management applied at an organizational rather than an individual level. Little wonder perhaps that making reengineering happen proved immensely more difficult than Champy and Hammer suggested. As the world conspicuously failed to revolutionize itself, reengineering attracted vituperative criticism. 'It's just a new label for something that's been around for a while', said quality guru, Joseph Juran. 'If I want to be mean, I'd say we have situations where some people want to be on top of a hill. Alas, every hill has a king. What is more logical than to create a hill?'[1] Champy and Hammer's thirst for publicity and media attention did their businesses no harm at all. But it did not lead to them or their idea being universally admired and liked.

Though there was a degree of professional jealousy and sour grapes, a great deal of the criticism was justified. The first problem was that the blank piece of paper ignored the years, often decades, of cultural evolution which led to an organization doing something in a certain way. Such preconceptions and often justifiable habits were not easily discarded.

The second problem was that reengineering appeared inhumane. (It not only appeared so. In some cases, people were treated appallingly in the name of reengineering.) 'Reengineering calls loudly for action, but its philosophy is prosaic in the extreme ... Its focus is on corporate mechanics, not on vision or strategy,' observed one critic.[2] Reengineering, as the name suggested, owed more to visions of the corporation as a machine than a human, or humane, system.

The human side of reengineering proved its greatest stumbling block – 'Most reengineering efforts will fail or fall short of the mark because of the absence of trust – meaning respect for the individual, his or her goodwill, intelligence and native, but long shackled, curiosity', observed Tom Peters.[3] 'Champy and Hammer ignored the importance of people', says Peter Cohan, author of *The Technology Leaders* and a former CSC consultant. 'They were objects who handled processes. Depersonalization was one of their themes. It was a huge flaw.'[4]

Reengineering became a synonym for redundancy and downsizing. ('Reengineering didn't start out as a code word for mindless bloodshed', reflected Thomas Davenport, one of its original champions.) For this Champy and Hammer could not be entirely blamed. Often, companies which claimed to be reengineering – and there were plenty – were simply engaging in cost-cutting under the convenient guise of the fashionable theory. Downsizing appeared more publicly palatable if it was presented as implementing a leading edge concept.

The third obstacle which emerged was that corporations were not natural or even willing revolutionaries. Instead of casting the reengineering net widely they tended to reengineer the most readily accessible process and then leave it at that. Related to this, and the subject of Champy's sequel, *Reengineering Management*, reengineering usually failed to impinge on management. Not surprisingly, managers were all too willing to impose the rigors of a process-based view of the business on others, but often unwilling to inflict it upon themselves. 'Senior managers have been reengineering business processes with a passion, tearing down corporate structures that no longer can support the organization. Yet the practice of management has largely escaped demolition. If their jobs and styles are left largely intact, managers will eventually undermine the very structure of their rebuilt enterprises,' Champy noted in 1994 at the height of reengineering's popularity.[5] In response, he suggested reengineering management should tackle three key areas: managerial roles, managerial styles and managerial systems.

Champy's agenda for management echoed that of a number of other thinkers. The revolutionaries quickly merged with the masses. 'With fewer job descriptions and less hierarchy, managers must change the fundamentals of career development and compensation. With people in jobs for longer, compensation must be based more on the skills and knowledge they acquire, not on their position on the organization chart,' said Champy.[6] In retrospect, the mistake of reengineering was not to tackle reengineering management first.

As the corporate enthusiasm for reengineering diminished, the fortunes of Champy and CSC Index also grew more troubled. In 1995 *BusinessWeek* suggested that the authors of *The Discipline of Market Leaders*, two CSC consultants, had bought large numbers of their book to secure a place in the bestseller lists. Champy returned to the daily management of the company – a job he had left in 1992. In August 1996 Champy left CSC to join Perot Systems to lead its management consulting activities.

Notes

1   Byrne, John, 'Bidding farewell to a guru', *BusinessWeek*, 30 August 1993.

2   Lloyd, Tom, 'Giant with feet of clay', *Financial Times*, 5 December 1994.
3   Peters, Tom, 'Out of the ordinary', Syndicated column, 23 July 1993.
4   Interview with the author, December 1997.
5   Champy, James, 'Time to reengineer the manager', *Financial Times*, 14 January 1994.
6   Champy, James, 'Time to reengineer the manager', *Financial Times*, 14 January 1994.

Bibliography

Reengineering the Corporation (with Michael Hammer), HarperBusiness, New York, 1993.

Reengineering Management, HarperBusiness, New York, 1995.

Alfred Chandler

"Unless structure follows strategy, inefficiency results."

Alfred Chandler

American business historian
Born 1918

Breakthrough ideas

Relationship between strategy and structure
The multi-divisional firm

Key book

Strategy and Structure

Alfred Chandler (born 1918) is a Pulitzer Prize-winning business historian. After graduating from Harvard, he served in the US Navy before becoming, somewhat unusually, a historian at MIT in 1950. Later he became Professor of History at Johns Hopkins University. He has been Straus Professor of Business History at Harvard since 1971.

Chandler's hugely detailed research into US companies between 1850 and 1920 has formed the cornerstone of much of his work. In his 1990 book, *Scale and Scope,* for example, Chandler compared and contrasted the growth of the largest 200 companies in the US, the UK and Germany from the 1880s until the 1940s. In his earlier work, Chandler observed that organizational structures in companies such as Du Pont, Sears Roebuck, General Motors and Standard Oil were driven by the changing demands and pressures of the marketplace. He traced the market-driven proliferation of product lines in Du Pont and General Motors and concluded that this proliferation led to a shift from a functional, monolithic organizational form to a more loosely coupled divisional structure. (Interestingly, Chandler's family has historical connections with DuPont – and DuPont is, in fact, Chandler's middle name. At the time DuPont also controlled General Motors.)

Chandler was highly influential in the trend among large organizations for decentralization in the 1960s and 1970s. While in 1950 around 20 percent of *Fortune 500* corporations were decentralized; this had increased to 80 percent by 1970. In his classic book, *Strategy and Structure,* Chandler praised Alfred Sloan's decentralization of General Motors in the 1920s. He was later influential in the transformation of AT&T in the 1980s from what was in effect a production-based bureaucracy to a marketing organization.

Chandler argued that the chief advantage of the multi-divisional organization was that 'it clearly removed the executives responsible for the destiny of the entire enterprise from the more routine operational responsibilities and so gave them the time, information and even psychological commitment for long-term planning and appraisal'. Chandler has not followed the modern fashion for dismissing large organizations. Indeed he has challenged the conventional belief that small companies have a monopoly on innovation and dynamism.

While the multi-divisional form has largely fallen out of favor – among thinkers at least – another of Chandler's theories continues to raise the blood pressure of those who care about such things. Chandler defined strategy as 'the determination of the long-term goals and objectives of an enterprise, and the adoption of courses of action and the allocation of resources necessary for carrying out these goals'. He argued that strategy came before structure. Having developed the best possible strategy, companies could then determine the most appropriate organizational structure to achieve it. In the early sixties, this was speedily accepted as a fact of life – no-one had previously considered strategy in such terms.

More recently, Chandler's premise has been regularly questioned. 'I think he got it exactly wrong', says Tom Peters with typical forthrightness. 'For it is the structure of the organization that determines, over time, the choices that it makes about the markets it attacks.'[1] Others suggest that the entire process is far messier than Chandler suggested. In a perfect world, companies would hatch perfect strategies and then create neat structures and organizational maps. Reality, however, is a mess in which strategy and structure mix madly.

Contemporary strategist, Gary Hamel provides a more positive perspective on Chandler's insights. 'Those who dispute Chandler's thesis that structure follows strategy miss the point', Hamel argues. 'Of course, strategy and structure are inextricably intertwined. Chandler's point was that new challenges give rise to new structures. The challenges of size and complexity, coupled with advances in communications and techniques of management control produced divisionalization and decentralization. These same forces, several generations on, are now driving us towards new structural solutions – the *federated organization*, the multi-company coalition, and the virtual company. Few historians are prescient. Chandler was.'[2] Further plaudits come from *BusinessWeek*: 'In the history of business, BC stands for Before Chandler'.

Chandler's theories also contributed to the 'professionalization of management'. He traced the historical development of what he labeled 'the managerial revolution' fueled by the rise of oil-based energy, the development of the steel, chemical and engineering industries and a dramatic rise in the scale of production and the size of companies. Increases in scale, Chandler observed, led to business owners having to recruit a new breed of professional manager.

Chandler believes that the roles of the salaried manager and technician are vital, and talks of the 'visible hand' of management coordinating the flow of product to customers more efficiently than Adam Smith's 'invisible hand' of the market (see Chandler's 1977 book, *The Visible Hand*). The logical progression from this is that organizations and their managements require a planned economy rather than a capitalist free-for-all dominated by the unpredictable whims of market forces. In the more sedate times of the sixties, the lure of the visible hand proved highly persuasive.

Notes

1   Peters, Tom, *Liberation Management,* Alfred P Knopf, New York, 1992.
2   Crainer, Stuart, *The Ultimate Business Library,* Capstone, Oxford, 1997.

Bibliography

Strategy and Structure, MIT Press, Boston, MA, 1962.
The Visible Hand: The Managerial Revolution in American Business, Harvard University Press, Cambridge, MA, 1977.
Managerial Hierarchies (with Deams, H., eds), Harvard University Press, Cambridge, MA, 1980.
Scale and Scope: The Dynamics of Industrial Capitalism, Harvard University Press, Cambridge, MA, 1990.

W. Edwards Deming

"Profit in business comes from repeat customers, customers that boast about your product and service, and that bring friends with them."

W. Edwards Deming

American consultant and academic
1900–93

Breakthrough ideas

'Manage for quality'
The Fourteen Points

Key book

Out of the Crisis

W. **Edwards Deming** (1900–93) has a unique place among management theorists. He had an impact on industrial history in a way others only dream. Testament to his impact can be seen if you walk into the headquarters building of Toyota in Tokyo. The lobby features three portraits. One is of the company's founder. The second is of the company's current chairman. The third is of W. Edwards Deming.

Deming was born in Iowa and spent his childhood in Wyoming. He trained as an electrical engineer at the University of Wyoming and then received a PhD in mathematical physics from Yale in 1928. He worked as a civil servant in Washington at the Department of Agriculture. While working at the Department he invited the statistician, Walter Shewhart, to give a lecture. This proved an inspiration. In 1939 Deming became head statistician and mathematician for the US census. During World War II he championed the use of statistics to improve the quality of US production and, in 1945, joined the faculty of New York University as a Professor of Statistics.

Deming visited Japan for the first time in 1947 on the invitation of General MacArthur. He was to play a key role in the rebuilding of Japanese industry. In 1950 he gave a series of lectures to Japanese industrialists on 'quality control'. 'I told them that Japanese industry could develop in a short time. I told them they could invade the markets of the world – and have manufacturers screaming for protection in five years. I was, in 1950, the only man in Japan who believed that,' Deming later recalled.

In fact, Deming was probably the *only* man in the world to believe that Japanese industry could be revived. But, helped by him, revive it did in a quite miraculous way. During the fifties, Deming and the other American standard bearer of quality, Joseph Juran, conducted seminars and courses throughout Japan. Between 1950 and 1970 the Japanese Union of Scientists and Engineers taught statistical methods to 14,700 engineers and hundreds of others. The message – and the practice – spread.

The Japanese were highly receptive to Deming's message. His timing was right – the country was desperate and willing to try anything. But, much more importantly, Deming's message of teamwork and shared responsibility struck a chord with Japanese culture. Deming's emphasis on group rather than individual achievement enabled the Japanese to share ideas and responsibility, and promoted collective ownership in a way that the West found difficult to contemplate let alone understand.

Within Japan, Deming's impact was quickly recognized. He was awarded the Second Order of the Sacred Treasure and the Union of Japanese Scientists and Engineers instigated the annual Deming Prize in 1951.

Deming's message was that organizations needed to 'manage for quality'. To do so required focus on the customer – in 1950, for example, Deming was anticipating the 1990s fad for reengineering with his call to arms: 'Don't just make it and try to sell it. But redesign it and then again bring the process under control … with ever-increasing quality … The consumer is the most important part of the production line.' At the time such pronouncements would have been greeted with disdain or bemusement in the West where production lines ran at full speed and little thought was given to who would buy the products.

Instead of the quick fix, Deming called for dedication and hard work. His message was never tainted by hype or frivolity. 'Quality is not something you install like a new carpet or a set of bookshelves. You implant it. Quality is something you work at. It is a learning process,' said Deming. The West stuck with their new carpets; the Japanese learned.

Also difficult for the West to swallow was Deming's argument that responsibility for quality must be taken by senior managers as well as those on the factory floor. Only with senior management commitment could belief in and implementation of quality cascade down through the organization. Quality, in Deming's eyes, was not the preserve of the few but the responsibility of all. He repeatedly said that management was 90 percent of the problem. Given that the West was hell-bent on 'professionalizing' management, this was hardly a message likely to go down well.

These exhortations were backed by the use of statistical methods of quality control. These enabled business plans to be expanded to include clear quality goals.

While the Japanese transformed their economy and world perceptions of the quality of their products, Western managers flitted from one fad to the next. Deming was completely ignored. Eventually, discovery came in 1980 when NBC featured a TV program on the emergence of Japan as an industrial power ('If Japan can, why can't we?'). Suddenly, Western managers were seeking out every morsel of information they could find. By 1984 there were over 3000 quality circles in American companies and many thousands of others appearing throughout the Western world.

It seemed that the sudden rush of fame and glory had come too late. After all, Deming was in his eighties by the time he was feted in the West. Undaunted, he dedicated the rest of his life to preaching his quality gospel wherever people wanted to hear it – and sometimes where they didn't.

Deming's message was distilled down to his famed Fourteen Points:

1 Create constancy of purpose for improvement of product and service.
2 Adopt the new philosophy.
3 Cease dependence on inspection to achieve quality.
4 End the practice of awarding business on the basis of price tag alone. Instead, minimize total cost by working with a single supplier.
5 Improve constantly and forever every process for planning, production and service.
6 Institute training on the job.
7 Adopt and institute leadership.
8 Drive out fear.
9 Break down barriers between staff areas.
10 Eliminate slogans, exhortations and targets for the workforce.
11 Eliminate numerical quotas for the workforce and numerical goals for management.
12 Remove barriers that rob people of pride of workmanship. Eliminate the annual rating or merit system.
13 Institute a vigorous program of education and self-improvement for everyone.
14 Put everybody in the company to work to accomplish the transformation.

Deming's Fourteen Points have become the commandments of the quality movement. In his efforts to move quality out of the factory floor and onto the desk of every single executive, Deming re-created it as a philosophy of business and, for some, of life. 'Unfortunately, a system of totality insists, by definition, that it will solve everything', noted Christopher Reed in an obituary of Deming.[1]

Deming disciples – and there are many – would counter by pointing towards the achievements of Toyota. Move beyond the portraits in the lobby and you enter the company which best personifies Deming's theories. Toyota was the first to champion 'lean production' in the 1950s – the West discovered the idea nearly 40 years later. Explaining its genesis, *The Economist* noted: 'Lean production grew from Toyota's crusade against waste: the waste of time caused by having to repair faulty products and the waste of resources caused by keeping unnecessarily large stocks. It has three principles. One, to produce things only when they are needed – just in time rather than just in case. Two, to turn every body into a quality checker, responsible for correcting errors as they happen. Three, to think of a company in terms of a value stream that extends all the way from suppliers to customers, rather than as isolated products and processes.'[2]

Toyota is the living exemplar of Deming's theories. As working examples go, it remains impressive. Gary Hamel has pointed out that its Western competitors have simply followed what Toyota has done for the last 40 years. If Western car manufacturers had listened to W. Edwards Deming, the roles might have been reversed. If Western industry as a whole had listened, who knows what might have happened.

Notes

1   Reed, Christopher, 'A profit in his own country', *The Observer*, 9 January 1994.
2   'Lean and its limits', *The Economist*, 14 September 1996.

Bibliography

Quality, Productivity and Competitive Position, MIT Centre for Advanced Engineering Study, MIT, Cambridge, MA, 1982.
Out of the Crisis, Cambridge University Press, Cambridge, MA, 1988.

Peter Drucker

"Management will remain a basic and dominant institution perhaps as long as Western civilization itself survives."

Peter Drucker

American consultant and author
Born Austria 1909

Breakthrough ideas

Management *en masse* from management by objectives to managing knowledge workers

Key books

The Practice of Management
The Age of Discontinuity
Management: Tasks, Responsibilities, Practices
Adventures of a Bystander

Peter Ferdinand Drucker (born 1909) is the major management and business thinker of the century. Of that there is little question. 'In a field packed with egomaniacs and snake-oil merchants, he remains a genuinely original thinker', observed the *Economist*.[1] Prolific, even in his eighties, Drucker's work is all-encompassing. There is little that executives do, think or face that he has not written about.

Take the political fashion of the 1980s for privatization. It was Drucker who first introduced the idea of privatization – though he labeled it 'reprivatization'. This was energetically seized upon by politicians in the 1980s, though their interpretation of privatization went far beyond that envisaged by Drucker.

Alternatively, take the contemporary fixation with knowledge management. 'The knowledge worker sees himself just as another *professional*, no different from the lawyer, the teacher, the preacher, the doctor or the government servant of yesterday', wrote Drucker in his 1969 classic *The Age of Discontinuity*. 'He has the same education. He has more income, he has probably greater opportunities as well. He may well realize that he depends on the organization for access to income and opportunity, and that without the investment the organization has made – and a high investment at that – there would be no job for him, but he also realizes, and rightly so, that the organization equally depends on him.'[2]

Drucker was exploring the implications of knowledge being both power *and* ownership 30 years ago. If knowledge, rather than labor, was to be the new measure of economic society then Drucker argued that the fabric of capitalist society must change: 'The knowledge worker is both the true *capitalist* in the knowledge society and dependent on his job. Collectively the knowledge workers, the employed educated middle-class of today's society, own the means of production through pension funds, investment trusts, and so on.'

In *Managing on the Edge* (1990), Richard Pascale noted: 'Peter Drucker's book *The Age of Discontinuity* describes the commercial era in which we live'. Drucker has proved remarkably prescient time and time again.

Far sighted and always opinionated, Peter Drucker was born in Austria where his father, Adolph, was the chief economist in the Austrian civil service. (Freud had lectured in psychiatry to his mother.)

His early experiences in the Austria of the 1920s and 1930s proved highly influential. 'His background ... has done more than shape Mr Drucker's style. It has left him with a burning sense of the importance of management. He believes that poor management helped to plunge the Europe of his youth into disaster, and he fears that the scope for poor management is growing larger, as organizations become ever more complicated and interdependent,' noted the *Economist*.[3]

Drucker worked as a journalist in London, before moving to America in 1937. His first book, *Concept of the Corporation* (1946) was a groundbreaking examination of the intricate internal working of General Motors and revealed the auto-giant to be a labyrinthine social system rather than an economical machine. (In the UK the book was retitled *Big Business* as, Drucker explains, 'both Concept and Corporation [were] then considered vulgar Americanisms'.)

His books have emerged regularly ever since – and now total 29. Along the way he has coined phrases and championed concepts such as *Management By Objectives*. Many of his innovations have become accepted facts of managerial life. He has celebrated huge organizations and anticipated their demise. (This has led to suggestions of inconsistency – though this is a rather hollow criticism of a career spanning over 60 years.) His 1964 book *Managing for Results* was, Drucker says, the 'first book ever on what we now call strategy'; *The Effective Executive* (1966) was 'the first and still the only book on the behavior being a manger or executive requires'. (As Drucker's comments suggests he is well aware of his influence – 'Mr Drucker is not shy about reminding people of his contribution to management studies and some find him a touch dogmatic,' wrote *The Economist* with its customary delicacy.[4])

The coping stones of Drucker's work are two equally huge and brilliant books: *The Practice of Management* (1954) and *Management: Tasks, Responsibilities, Practices* (1973). Both are encyclopedic in their scope and fulsome in their historical perspectives. More than any other volumes they encapsulate the essence of management thinking and practice.

The genius of Drucker is that he has combined quantity and quality while ploughing a thoroughly idiosyncratic furrow. He has resolutely pursued his own interests, and the dictates of his considerable intellect, rather than the dictates of the dollar. In an age of thinkers as media personalities, Drucker refuses to be distracted. Disturbers of his Californian retreat receive a preprinted message assuring them that he 'greatly appreciates your kind interest, but is unable to: contribute articles or forewords; comment on manuscripts or books; take part in panels and symposia; join committees or boards of any kind; answer questionnaires; give interviews; and appear on radio or television'.

Drucker has not shunned the world. He is not J.D. Salinger. But he is focused – as he has observed: 'The single minded ones, the monomaniacs, are the only true achievers. The rest, the ones like me, have more fun; but they fritter themselves away. The monomaniacs carry out a *mission*; the rest of us have *interests*. Whenever anything is being accomplished, it is being done ... by a monomaniac with a mission.'

Drucker's book production has been supplemented by a somewhat low key career as an academic and some time consultant. He was Professor of Philosophy and Politics at Bennington College from 1942 until 1949 and then became a Professor of Management at New York University in 1950 – 'The first person anywhere in the world to have such a title and to teach such a subject', he proudly recalls. Since 1971, Drucker has been a Professor at Claremont Graduate School in California. He also lectures in oriental art, has an abiding passion for Jane Austen and has written two novels (less successful than his management books). As if to prove that he is multidimensional, in *Who's Who* Drucker lists mountaineering as one of his recreations.

Drucker considers himself as much a journalist as an academic or consultant. (One career option he has ruled out: 'I would be a very poor manager. Hopeless. And a company job would bore me to death.') His autobiography is entitled, *Adventures of a Bystander*, emphasizing his role as a journalistic recorder of trends steering clear of direct involvement. 'I have always been politically incorrect. I have never belonged to the outer circle, let alone the inner circle. No, I am an outsider and I am a loner. I have always done my own work,' he said in 1996, getting in a barbed comment on the propensity of academics to get others to do their research and writing. Drucker's formidable ire is particularly reserved for business schools. 'The business schools in the US, set up less than a century ago, have been preparing well-trained clerks', he has written. Drucker has repeatedly dismissed Harvard and notes that 'Only now in my very old age has academia been willing to accept me'.[5]

Drucker's greatest achievement lies in identifying management as a timeless, human discipline. It was used to build the Great Wall of China, to erect the Pyramids, to cross the oceans for the first time, to run armies. 'Management is tasks. Management is discipline. But management is also people,' he wrote. 'Every achievement of management is the achievement of a manager. Every failure is the failure of a manager. People manage, rather than *forces* or *facts*. The vision, dedication and integrity of managers determine whether there is management or mismanagement.'

Drucker puts the historical importance of management at our fingertips. But, though management is the universal science, this does not necessarily mean we are very good at it, or improving in our execution of it. 'Actually very little has changed so far. Most organizations are being run very much the way they were when I first started to study them. We have a lot of new tools, but not very many new ideas,' lamented Drucker in 1995.[6]

Drucker's first attempt at creating the managerial bible was *The Practice of Management* ('a fairly short book of fundamentals' according to him). He largely succeeded. The book is a masterly exposition on the first principles of management. There may not be many new ideas, but it still pays to understand the fundamentals. In one of the most quoted and memorable paragraphs in management literature, Drucker gets to the heart of the meaning of business life. 'There is only one valid definition of business purpose: to create a customer. Markets are not created by God, nature or economic forces, but by businessmen. The want they satisfy may have been felt by the customer before he was offered the means of satisfying it. It may indeed, like the want of food in a famine, have dominated the customer's life and filled all his waking moments. But it was a theoretical want before; only when the action of businessmen makes it an effective demand is there a customer, a market.'

Drucker also provided an evocatively simple insight into the nature and *raison d'être* of organizations: 'Organization is not an end in itself, but a means to an end of business performance and business results. Organization structure is an indispensable means, and the wrong structure will seriously impair business performance and may even destroy it ... The first question in discussing organization structure must be: What is our business and what should it be? Organization structure must be designed so as to make possible the attainment of the objectives of the business for five, ten, fifteen years hence.' With its examinations of GM, Ford and others, Drucker's audience and world view in *The Practice of Management* is resolutely that of the large corporation. The world has moved on (and so has Drucker).

In *The Practice of Management* and the equally enormous *Management: Tasks, Responsibilities and Practices* in 1973, Drucker established five basics of the managerial role: to set objectives; to organize; to motivate and communicate; to measure; and to develop people. 'The function which distinguishes the manager above all others is his educational one', he wrote. 'The one contribution he is uniquely expected to make is to give others vision and ability to perform. It is vision and moral responsibility that, in the last analysis, define the manager.' This morality is reflected in the five areas identified by Drucker 'in which practices are required to ensure the right spirit throughout management organization:

'1   There must be high performance requirements; no condoning of poor or mediocre performance; and rewards must be based on performance.
'2   Each management job must be a rewarding job in itself rather than just a step on the promotion ladder.
'3   There must be a rational and just promotion system.
'4   Management needs a 'charter' spelling out clearly who has the power to make 'life-and-death' decisions affecting a manager; and there should be some way for a manager to appeal to a higher court.
'5   In its appointments, management must demonstrate that it realizes that integrity is the one absolute requirement of a manager, the one quality that he has to being with him and cannot be expected to acquire later on.'

At the time, the idea from *The Practice of Management* which was seized upon was what became known as Management By Objectives (MBO). 'A manager's job should be based on a task to be performed in order to attain the company's objectives ... the manager should be directed and controlled by the objectives of performance rather than by his boss', Drucker wrote. Hijacked as yet another bright idea, MBO became a simplistic means of setting a corporate goal and heading towards it and bore little relation to Drucker's broader interpretation. (The entire MBO concept was developed most fruitfully by a number of others including George Odiorne and the UK's John Humble.)

Drucker identified 'seven new tasks' for the manager of the future. Given that these were laid down over 40 years ago, their prescience is astounding. Drucker wrote that tomorrow's managers must:

'1 Manage by objectives.
'2 Take more risks and for a longer period ahead.
'3 Be able to make strategic decisions.
'4 Be able to built an integrated team, each member of which is capable of managing and of measuring his own performance and results in relation to the common objectives.
'5 Be able to communicate information fast and clearly.
'6 Traditionally a manager has been expected to know one or more functions. This will no longer be enough. The manager of the future must be able to see the business as a whole and to integrate his function with it.
'7 Traditionally a manager has been expected to know a few products or one industry. This, too, will no longer be enough.'

Recent years have seen Drucker maintain his remarkable work rate. In particular, his energies have been focused on non-profit organizations. His ability to return to first principles and question the fundamentals remains undimmed. In *Managing in a Time of Great Change* (1995) he objected to the term manager – 'Manager has implications of subordinates' (he prefers to talk of executives) – and suggested 'To build achieving organizations, you must replace power with responsibility'. The call to take responsibility is a consistent thread throughout 60 years of productive work.

Drucker has also developed his thinking on the role of knowledge – most notably in his 1992 book, *Managing for the Future*, in which he observes: 'From now on the key is knowledge. The world is becoming not labor intensive, not materials intensive, not energy intensive, but knowledge intensive.'

Approaching the millennium, Drucker remains worth listening to. He peppers conversation with anecdotes, a stream of pertinent statistics and controversial opinions. For example, Drucker dismisses talk of balancing the US budget by 2003 as 'sheer nonsense', predicting that by then the US 'will be totally bankrupt' if current trends continue. In reality, Drucker believes people will need to work longer. He is aghast at people who choose early retirement – regarding it as 'a severe indictment of our organizations' – but maintains that by the time they reach 60 people should withdraw from decision-making positions.[7]

Drucker castigates managers for becoming obsessed with promotions and suggests that new forms of work need to be explored. He remains a trenchant realist. 'The first constant in the job of management is to make human strength effective and human weakness irrelevant,' he says. Forget the theorizing. Drucker can make corporate life appear understandable, though never easy. And, the bottom-line is never far away: 'Managers are accountable for results, period'.

Notes

1 'Good guru guide', *The Economist*, 25 December–7 January 1994.
2 Drucker, Peter, *The Age of Discontinuity*, Heinemann, London, 1969.
3 'Peter Drucker, salvationist', *The Economist*, 1 October 1994.
4 'Good guru guide', *The Economist*, 25 December 1993–7 January 1994.
5 Donkin, Richard, 'Interview with Peter Drucker', *Financial Times*, 14 June 1996.
6 'Managing in a time of great change', *Business Week On-line conference*, 14 December 1995.
7 Drucker, Peter, 'The shape of things to come', *Leader to Leader*, Premier issue.

Bibliography

Concept of the Corporation, John Day, New York, 1946.

The New Society, Heinemann, London, 1951.

The Practice of Management, Harper & Row, New York, 1954.

Managing for Results, Heinemann, London, 1964.

The Effective Executive, Harper & Row, New York, 1967.

The Age of Discontinuity, Heinemann, London, 1969.

Management: Tasks, Responsibilities, Practices, Harper & Row, New York, 1973.

Managing in Turbulent Times, Harper & Row, New York, 1980.

Innovation and Entrepreneurship, Heinemann, London, 1985.

The New Realities, Heinemann, London, 1989.

Managing the Nonprofit Organization, HarperCollins, 1990.

Managing for the Future, Dutton, 1992.

Post-Capitalist Society, Harper, New York, 1993.

Managing in Times of Great Change, Butterworth Heinemann, Oxford, 1995.

Adventures of a Bystander, John Wiley, New York, 1998 (originally published in 1978).

Henri Fayol

"To manage is to forecast and plan, to organize, to command, to co-ordinate and to control."

Henri Fayol

French engineer and manager
1841–1925

Breakthrough ideas

The functional principle
Principles of management

Key book

General and Industrial Management

Europe has produced precious few original management thinkers. It is surprising therefore that the achievements and insights of the Frenchman **Henri Fayol** (1841–1925) are granted so little recognition.

Fayol was educated in Lyon, France and at the National School of Mines in St Etienne. In 1860 he graduated as a mining engineer and joined the French mining company, Commentry-Fourchamboult-Décazeville. Fayol spent his entire working career with the company and was its managing director between 1888 and 1918.

Fayol also developed an increasingly successful parallel career as a theorist. In 1900 he delivered a speech at a mining conference. When he gave a developed version of his ideas at a 1908 conference, 2000 copies were immediately reprinted to satisfy demand. By 1925, 15,000 copies had been printed and a book was published.

During that time Fayol produced the 'functional principle', the first rational approach to the organization of enterprise. His studies led to lectures at the Ecole Supérieure de la Guerre. While retired, Fayol set up a Center of Administrative Studies and examined the performance of a government department. (This led to his uncomplimentary report, 'L'Incapacité Administrative de l'Etat – les Postes et Télégraphes'.)

Fayol was important for two reasons. First, he placed management at center stage. Frederick Taylor's Scientific Management emasculated the working man, but still treated managers as stopwatch holding supervisors. Even among Taylor's managers, initiative, imagination and humanity were in short supply – or so he hoped and planned.

Fayol emerged from a similar background in heavy industry. His conclusions, however, were that management was critical and universal. 'Management plays a very important part in the government of undertakings; of all undertakings, large or small, industrial, commercial, political, religious or any other', he wrote. It was not until 1954, and Drucker's *The Practice of Management*, that anyone else made such a bold pronouncement in management's favor.

The second contribution of Fayol was to ponder the question of how best a company could be organized. (Again, this was something

Taylor had ignored.) In doing so, Fayol took a far broader perspective than anyone else had previously done. Fayol concluded: 'All activities to which industrial undertakings give rise can be divided into the following six groups'. The six functions which he identified were: technical activities; commercial activities; financial activities; security activities; accounting activities; and managerial activities.

'The management function is quite distinct from the other five essential functions', noted Fayol. Such functional separations have dominated the way companies have been managed throughout the twentieth century. It may be fashionable to talk of an end to functional mindsets and of free-flowing organizations, but Fayol's functional model largely remains.

Fayol also provided a pithy definition of the role of management: 'To manage is to forecast and plan, to organize, to command, to co-ordinate and to control'. Implicit in this was that managers can and should be trained in the basic disciplines demanded by their profession.

Fayol's methods were later exposed by Drucker who observed: 'If used beyond the limits of Fayol's model, functional structure becomes costly in terms of time and effort'.[1] While this is undoubtedly true, Fayol's observations and conclusions were important. He talked of 'ten yearly forecasts ... revised every five years' – one of the first instances of business planning in practice – and wrote: 'The maxim, "managing means looking ahead", gives some idea of the importance attached to planning in the business world, and it is true that if foresight is not the whole of management at least it is an essential part of it'.

In many respects Henri Fayol was the first *management* thinker. While others concentrated on the workman and the mechanics of performance, he focused on the role of management and the essential skills required of managers. His conclusions were accurate descriptions of the roles undertaken by managers and the structure of organizations for decades beyond Fayol's life. Yet their direct impact was marginal. No Fayol doctrine emerged in the same way as Taylorism. (In a thoroughly Anglo-Saxon industry, the lack of an English translation of his work didn't help.)

Notes

1 Quoted in 'The corporate sages', *Business*, September 1988.

Bibliography

General and Industrial Management, Pitman, London, 1949.

Mary Parker Follett

"Idealism and realism meet in the actual."

Mary Parker Follett

American political scientist
1868–1933

Breakthrough ideas

Integration
Sharing of responsibility

Key book

Dynamic Administration

T he canon of management literature and the list of management thinkers is dominated by men. The exceptions to this are substantial thinkers. None more so than the American political scientist, **Mary Parker Follett** (1868–1933).

Generally ignored, Follett was decades ahead of her time. She was discussing issues such as teamworking and responsibility (now reborn as empowerment) in the first decades of the twentieth century. Follett was a female, liberal humanist in an era dominated by reactionary males intent on mechanizing the world of business.

The breadth and humanity of her work was a refreshing counter to the dehumanized visions of Taylor and others. 'We should remember that we can never wholly separate the human from the mechanical sides,' warned Follett in *Dynamic Administration*.[1] 'The study of human relations in business and the study of the technology of operating are bound up together.'

Born in Quincy, Massachusetts, Mary Parker Follett attended Thayer Academy and the Society for the Collegiate Instruction of Women in Cambridge, Massachusetts (now part of Harvard University). She also studied at Newnham College, Cambridge in the UK and in Paris. Her first published work was *The Speaker of the House of Representatives* (1896), which she wrote while still a student.

Follett's career was largely spent in social work though her books appeared regularly – *The New State* (1918), an influential description of Follett's brand of dynamic democracy, and *Creative Experience* (1924), Follett's first business-oriented book. In her later years she was in great demand as a lecturer. After the death of her long-time partner, Isobel Briggs in 1926, she moved to London.

The simple thrust of Follett's thinking was that people were central to any business activity – or, indeed, to any other activity. 'I think we should undepartmentalize our thinking in regard to every problem that comes to us,' said Follett. 'I do not think that we have psychological and ethical and economic problems. We have human problems, with psychological, ethical and economical aspects, and as many others as you like.'

In particular, Follett explored conflict. She argued that as conflict is a fact of life 'we should, I think, use it to work for us'. Follett pointed out three ways of dealing with confrontation: domination, compromise or integration. The latter, she concluded, is the only positive way forward. This can be achieved by first 'uncovering' the real conflict and then taking 'the demands of both sides and breaking them up into their constituent parts'. 'Our outlook is narrowed, our activity is restricted, our chances of business success largely diminished when our thinking is constrained within the limits of what has been called an either-or situation. We should never allow ourselves to be bullied by an "either-or". There is often the possibility of something better than either of two given alternatives,' Follett wrote.

Follett advocated giving greater responsibility to people – at a time when the mechanical might of mass production was at its height. 'Responsibility is the great developer of men', she wrote. How many modern CEOs would mouth the same sentiments but still be unable to put them into practice?

There was also a modern ring to Follett's advice on leadership: 'The most successful leader of all is one who sees another picture not yet actualized'. Follett saw the leader's tasks as co-ordination, defining the purpose of the business and anticipation – 'We look to the leader to open up new paths, new opportunities'. Follett suggested that a leader was someone who saw the whole rather than the particular, organized the experiences of the group, offered a vision of the future and trained followers to become leaders.

Indeed, Follett was an early advocate of management training and that leadership could be taught. 'The theory has been of personal domination, but study the political leaders, the party bosses, and notice how often they have gained their positions by their ability to bring into harmonious relation men of antagonistic temperaments, their ability to reconcile conflicting interests, their ability to make a working unit out of many diverse elements.'

Follett's work was largely neglected in the West. Peter Drucker, now an admirer, recalls that when he was seeking out management literature in the 1940s, no-one even mentioned Follett's name. Once again, however, a Western thinker was honored in Japan, which even boasts a Follett Society. Her work has now been brought to a wider audience through the British academic Pauline Graham – in 1994, Graham edited *Mary Parker Follett: Prophet of Management*, a compendium of Follett's writings with commentaries from a host of contemporary figures including Kanter, Drucker and Mintzberg.[2]

Notes

1 Follett, Mary Parker, *Dynamic Administration* (eds Fox, Elliot and Urwick, Lyndall), Harper & Bros, New York, 1941.
2 Graham, Pauline (ed.), *Mary Parker Follett: Prophet of Management*, Harvard Business School Press, Cambridge, MA, 1995.

Bibliography

The New State: Group Organization – The Solution of Popular Government, Longman, London, 1918.
Creative Experience, Longman, London, 1924.
Dynamic Administration, Harper & Brothers, New York, 1941.
Freedom and Coordination, Pitman, London, 1949.

Henry Ford

"I have no use for a motor car which has more spark plugs than a cow has teats."

Henry Ford

American car maker
1863–1947

Breakthrough ideas

Mass production

Key book

My Life and Work

T | he standard view of **Henry Ford** (1863–1947) is that he was the first exponent of mass production. While this is true, there was a great deal more to the career, personality and achievements of the car maker.

Ford was originally a boy racer. After spending time as a machinist's apprentice, a watch repairer and a mechanic, he built his first car in 1896. Quickly he became convinced of the commercial potential and started his own company in 1903. (There was nothing unusual in this – between 1900 and 1908 over 500 American companies were set up to make cars.) Ford's first car, was the Model A. After a year, he was selling 600 a month. In 1908, Ford's Model T was born. Through innovative use of new mass production techniques, between 1908 and 1927 Ford produced 15 million Model Ts. At that time, Ford's factory at Highland Park, Michigan was the biggest in the world – over 14,000 people worked on the 57-acre site. And it was to the world Ford looked. He was quick to establish international operations – Ford's first overseas sales branch was opened in France in 1908 and, in 1911, Ford began making cars in the UK.

In 1919 Ford resigned as the company's President with his son, Edsel, taking over. By then the Ford company was making a car a minute. In 1923 annual sales peaked at 2,120,898. At the time, Ford's market share was in excess of 57 percent.

Henry Ford developed mass production not because he blindly believed in the most advanced production methods. He was no clone of Frederick Taylor. (In fact, the unique Ford was no clone of anyone.) Ford believed in mass production because it meant he could make cars which people could afford. And this, with staggering success, is what he achieved. At one point the company had cash reserves of $1 billion. (This did not stop Ford from maintaining: 'A business that makes nothing but money is a poor kind of business'.)

In 1907, Ford professed his aim was to 'build a motor car for the great multitude … It will be so low in price that no man making a good salary will be unable to own one – and enjoy with his family the blessing of hours of pleasure in God's great open spaces … everybody will be able to afford one, and everyone will have one. The horse will have disappeared from our highways, the automobile will be taken for granted'. Ford's commitment to lowering prices cannot be doubted. Between 1908 and 1916 he reduced prices by 58 per-cent – at a time when demand was such that he could easily have raised prices.

The paradox of Ford was that by thinking of the consumer first and production second his was a triumph of marketing as much as of production methods. Though the two were inextricably linked, he is usually associated with the latter rather than the former.

Ford's masterly piece of marketing lay in his intuitive realization that the mass car market existed – it just remained for him to provide the products the market wanted. Model Ts were black, straightfor-ward and affordable. The corollary of this was to prove Ford's nem-esis. Reasonably priced cars demanded mass production methods and costs could only be lowered through increased efficiency and standardization so that more cars could be produced. Ford followed this strategy through with characteristic thoroughness. General Mo-tors chief, Alfred Sloan, noted: 'Mr Ford's assembly line automobile production, high minimum wage, and low-priced car were revolu-tionary and stand among the greatest contributions to our industrial culture. His basic conception of one car in one utility model at an ever lower price was what the market, especially the farm market, needed at the time.'

Ford stuck rigidly to his policy. Having given the market what it wanted, he presumed that more of the same was also what it re-quired. He was reputed to have kicked a slightly modified Model T to pieces such was his commitment to the unadulterated version. When other manufacturers added extras, Ford kept it simple and dramatically lost ground. The company's reliance on the Model T nearly drove it to self-destruction.

The reasons why were explained by Ted Levitt in his article 'Mar-keting myopia' which re-evaluated Ford from a marketing perspec-tive. 'Mass production industries are impelled by a great drive to produce all they can. The prospect of steeply declining unit costs as output rises is more than most companies can usually resist. The profit possibilities look spectacular. All effort focuses on production. The result is that marketing gets neglected,' Levitt wrote. Finally, there is concentration on the product as this lends itself to measure-ment and analysis.

In terms of management, Ford was an atheist with attitude. In the same way as Ford didn't believe in Models Ts in different colors with fins and extras, he didn't believe in management. 'Fundamental to Henry Ford's misrule was a systematic, deliberate and conscious attempt to run the billion-dollar business without managers. The secret police that spied on all Ford executives served to inform Henry Ford of any attempt on the part of one of his executives to make a decision,' noted Peter Drucker in *The Practice of Management*.[1]

As a result, production, in the Ford company's huge plant, was based round strict functional divides – demarcations. Ford believed in people getting on with their jobs and not raising their heads above functional parapets. He didn't want engineers talking to salespeople, or people making decisions without his say so.

The methods used by Ford were grim and unforgiving. 'How come when I want a pair of hands I get a human being as well,' he complained. Ford will never be celebrated for his humanity or people management skills. Among his many innovations was a single human one: Ford introduced the $5 wage for his workers which, at the time, was around twice the average for the industry. Skeptics suggest that the only reason he did this was so that his workers could buy Model Ts of their own.

Notes

1   Drucker, Peter F., *The Practice of Management*, Harper & Row, New York, 1954.

Bibliography

My Life and Work, Doubleday, Page & Co, New York, 1923.

Harold Geneen

"The very fact that you go over the progression of those numbers week after week, month after month, means that you have strengthened your memory and your familiarity with them so that you retain in your mind a vivid composite picture of what is going on in your company."

Harold Geneen

American executive
1910–97

Breakthrough ideas

Management by facts and analysis

Key books

Managing
The Synergy Myth

A formidable mythology has built up around the career and management style of **Harold Geneen** (1910–1997). Born in Bournemouth on England's genteel south coast, Geneen became the archetypal bullish American executive; the 'legendary conglomerateur' according to *Business Week*; a remorselessly driven workaholic who believed that analytical rigor could – and surely would – conquer all. 'Trust is not earned by being a nice guy. It comes with character and competence. I say you must be a person of character, one willing to be responsible for people – their lives and their hopes,' wrote Geneen in one of his final articles.[1]

Geneen allowed for no frivolity and, even in his late eighties, worked a ten-hour day at his office in New York's Waldorf-Astoria Hotel running Gunther International, a company he bought into in 1992. Geneen combined hard work and an apparently slavish devotion to figures – 'Putting deals together beats spending every day playing golf', he once said.

Behind the mythology, Harold Geneen qualified as an accountant after studying at night schools. He then began climbing the executive career ladder working at American Can, Bell & Howell, Jones & Laughlin and finally Raytheon. This company was taken over by ITT, which had started life in 1920 as a Caribbean telephone company. Geneen joined the board of ITT in 1959 and set about turning the company into the world's greatest conglomerate.

His basic organizational strategy was that diversification was a source of strength. There was nothing half-hearted in Geneen's pursuit of diversity. Under Geneen, ITT bought companies as addictively as Imelda Marcos once bought shoes. ITT's spending spree amounted to 350 companies and included Avis Rent-A-Car, Sheraton Hotels, Continental Baking and Levitt & Sons among many others. By 1970 ITT was composed of 400 separate companies operating in 70 countries.

The ragbag collection of names was a managerial nightmare. Keeping the growing array of companies in check was a complex series of financial checks and targets. Geneen managed them with intense vigor. Few other executives could have done so, but he brought a unique single-mindedness to the task. As part of his formula, every month over 50 executives flew to Brussels to spend four days poring over the figures. 'I want no surprises,' announced Geneen. He hoped to make people 'as predictable and controllable as the capital resources they must manage'. While others would have watched as the deck of cards fell to the ground, Geneen kept adding more cards, while managing to know the pressures and stresses each was under.

Facts were the lifeblood of the expanding ITT – and executives sweated blood in their pursuit. 'The highest art of professional management requires the literal ability to *smell* a *real fact* from all others – and, moreover, to have the temerity, intellectual curiosity, guts and/ or plain impoliteness, if necessary, to be sure that what you do have is indeed what we will call an *unshakeable fact*', said Geneen.

His managerial approach was candidly explained by ITT in its 1971 annual report: 'More than 200 days a year are devoted to management meetings at various organizational levels throughout the world. In these meetings in New York, Brussels, Hong Kong, Buenos Aires, decisions are made based on logic – the business logic that results in making decisions which are almost inevitable because all the facts on which the decisions must be based are available. The function of the planning and the meetings is to force the logic out into the open where its value and need are seen by all.'

By sheer force of personality, Geneen's approach worked. (More cynically, you could say that ITT was a success in the parameters created by Geneen.) Between 1959 and 1977, ITT's sales went from $765 million to nearly $28 billion. Earnings went from $29 million to $562 million and earnings per share rose from $1 to $4.20. Geneen stepped down as chief executive in 1977 and as chairman in 1979.

ITT rapidly disintegrated following Geneen's departure. Indeed, the writing was on the wall before that – the company's profits fell in 1974 and 1975. 'Running a conglomerate requires working harder than most people want to work and taking more risks that most people want to take', said Geneen. His followers were unable to sustain his uniquely driven working style. The underside of ITT was exposed – it had worked with the CIA in Chile and been involved in offering bribes. The deck of cards tumbled.

To Geneen, the fall in ITT's fortunes simply served to validate his methods and philosophy. 'After I left, the company veered on to a new course, emphasizing consolidation rather than growth ... Often,

I have felt the stab of frustration and regret, wondering what might have been,' he reflected in his 1997 book, *The Synergy Myth*.[2] It was curiously fitting that in the month of Harold Geneen's death, ITT was taken over.

Notes

1   Geneen, Harold, 'Inspire confidence and trust', *Management General*, 1997.
2   Geneen, Harold, *The Synergy Myth*, St Martin's Press, 1997.

Bibliography

Managing (with Alvin Moscow), Doubleday, 1984.
The Synergy Myth, St Martin's Press, 1997.

Sumantra Ghoshal

"Companies that succeed are driven by internal ambition. Stock price doesn't drive them. Ambition and values drive them. You have to create tension between reality and aspirations.**"**

Sumantra Ghoshal

Indian academic
Born 1948

Breakthrough ideas

Globalization and corporate structure

Key books

Managing Across Borders
The Individualized Corporation

W ith his film star cheekbones, piercing eyes, hawkish intensity and intellectual brilliance, **Sumantra Ghoshal** (born 1948) is an intimidating figure. Working along with Harvard Business School's Christopher Bartlett, he has become one of the most sought-after intellectuals in the business world.

Ghoshal first came to prominence with the book *Managing Across Borders* (1989) which was one of the boldest and most accurate pronouncements of the arrival of a new era of global competition and truly global organizations. The 1997 book, *The Individualized Corporation*, marked a further step forward in the thinking of Ghoshal and Bartlett. Ghoshal joined London Business School in 1994 and was formerly Professor of Business Policy at INSEAD and a visiting professor at MIT's Sloan School.

Ghoshal has mapped and recorded the death of a variety of corporate truisms. He insists that his questions have remained the same, but the answers have changed – 'I am a plain vanilla strategy guy. What does strategy mean is where I started.'

Bartlett and Ghoshal, unlike others, suggest that new, revitalizing, organizational forms can – and are – emerging. Crucial to this is the recognition that multinational corporations from different regions of the world have their own management heritages, each with a distinctive source of competitive advantage.

The first multinational form identified by Bartlett and Ghoshal is the **multinational** or multidomestic firm. Its strength lies in a high degree of local responsiveness. It is a decentralized federation of local firms (such as Unilever or Philips) linked together by a web of personal controls (expatriates from the home country firm who occupy key positions abroad).

The second is the **global** firm, typified by US corporations such as Ford earlier this century and Japanese enterprises such as Matsushita. Its strengths are scale efficiencies and cost advantages. Global scale facilities, often centralized in the home country, produce standardized products, while overseas operations are considered as delivery pipelines to tap into global market opportunities. There is tight control of strategic decisions, resources and information by the global hub.

The **international** firm is the third type. Its competitive strength is its ability to transfer knowledge and expertise to overseas environments that are less advanced. It is a co-ordinated federation of local firms, controlled by sophisticated management systems and corporate staffs. The attitude of the parent company tends to be parochial, fostered by the superior know-how at the center.

Bartlett and Ghoshal argue that global competition is forcing many of these firms to shift to a fourth model, which they call the **transnational**. This firm has to combine local responsiveness with global efficiency and the ability to transfer know-how – better, cheaper, and faster.

The transnational firm is a network of specialized or differentiated units, with attention paid to managing integrative linkages between local firms as well as with the center. The subsidiary becomes a distinctive asset rather than simply an arm of the parent company. Manufacturing and technology development are located wherever it makes sense, but there is an explicit focus on leveraging local know-how in order to exploit worldwide opportunities.

Ghoshal and Bartlett not surprisingly conclude that, in the flux of global businesses, historical solutions are no longer applicable. They point to the difficulties in managing growth through acquisitions and the dangerously high level of diversity in businesses which have acquired companies indiscriminately in the quest for growth. They have also declared as obsolete the assumption of independence among different businesses, technologies and geographic markets which is central to the design of most divisionalized corporations. Such independence, they say, actively works against the prime need: integration and the creation of 'a coherent system for value delivery'.

The demise of the divisionalized corporation – as exemplified by Alfred Sloan's General Motors – lies at the heart of Ghoshal and Bartlett's work during the late eighties and early nineties.

Today's reality, as described by Ghoshal, is harsh: 'You cannot manage third generation strategies through second generation organizations with first generation managers'.[1] Even the perspectives from 'successful' companies appear bleak. 'Talk of transformation and you get the same examples,' he says. 'Toshiba in Asia Pacific, ABB, GE. If you listen to managers of those companies you will detect great skepticism about achieving victory. The battle ahead is far more complex.'

Despite such a damning critique of corporate reality, Ghoshal is not totally discouraged. 'Look at today and compare it to years ago. The quality of the strategic debate and discussion has improved by an order of magnitude,' he says. 'Third generation strategies are sophisticated and multi-dimensional. The real problem lies in managers themselves. Managers are driven by an earlier model. The real challenge is how to develop and maintain managers to operate in the new type of organization.'

The shift in emphasis in Ghoshal's work is from the cool detachment of strategy to the heated complexities of people. While *Managing Across Borders* was concerned with bridging the gap between strategies and organizations, Ghoshal and Bartlett's sequel, *The Individualized Corporation,* moved from the elegance of strategy to the messiness of humanity.

One of the phenomena Ghoshal has examined is the illusion of success which surrounds some organizations like a well-burnished halo. 'Satisfactory under-performance is a far greater problem than a crisis', he says pointing to the example of Westinghouse which is now one-seventh the size of GE in revenue terms. 'Over 20 years, three generations of top management have presided over the massive decline of a top US corporation,' says Ghoshal. 'Yet, 80 per cent of the time the company was thought to be doing well. Westinghouse CEOs were very competent and committed. They'd risen through the ranks and did the right things. Yet they presided over massive decline.'

The explanation he gives for this delusion of grandeur is that few companies have an ability for self-renewal. 'You cannot renew a company without revitalizing its people. Top management has always said this. After a decade of restructuring and downsizing, top management now believes it. Having come to believe it, what does it really mean?'

Ghoshal contends that revitalizing people is fundamentally about changing people. The trouble is that adults don't change their basic attitudes unless they encounter personal tragedy. Things that happen at work rarely make such an impact. If organizations are to revitalize people, they must change the context of what they create around people.

'The oppressive atmosphere in most large companies resembles downtown Calcutta in summer', says Ghoshal. 'We intellectualize a lot in management. But if you walk into a factory or a unit, within the first 15 minutes you get a smell of the place.'

Vague and elusive though 'smell' sounds, Ghoshal – no touchy-feely idealist – believes that it can be nurtured. 'Smell can be created and maintained – look at 3M. Ultimately the job of the manager is to get ordinary people to create extraordinary results.'

To do so requires a paradoxical combination of what Ghoshal labels stretch and discipline. As an example of this in practice he cites Intel: 'At Intel there is constructive confrontation. It is demanded that you explain your point of view. The flip side is that at the end of a meeting a decision is made and you have to commit to it. Stretch and discipline are the yin and yang of business.'

These factors do not render attention to strategy, structure and systems obsolete. Businesses can still be run by strict attention to this blessed corporate trinity. These are, in Ghoshal's eyes, the legacy of the corporate engineer, Alfred Sloan, and the meat and drink of business school programs. They are necessary, but Ghoshal adds a warning: 'Sloan created a new management doctrine. Sloan's doctrine has been wonderful but the problem is that it inevitably ends up creating downtown Calcutta in summer.'

The way out of the smog is through purpose ('the company is also a social institution'); process ('the organization as a set of roles and relationships'); and people ('helping individuals to become the best they can be'). Undoubtedly these factors are less hard and robust than the three Ss, but Ghoshal believes they are the way forward.

Notes

1   International Management Symposium, London Business School, 11 November 1997.

Bibliography

Managing Across Borders (with Christopher Bartlett), Harvard Business School Press, Boston, MA, 1989.
The Individualized Corporation (with Christopher Bartlett), Harvard Business School Press, Boston, MA, 1997.

Gary Hamel

"A company surrenders today's businesses when it gets smaller faster than it gets better. A company surrenders tomorrow's businesses when it gets better without getting different.**"**

Gary Hamel

American academic and consultant
Born 1954

Breakthrough ideas

Strategic intent
Core competencies
Strategic architecture
Industry foresight

Key book

Competing for the Future

n 1978 **Gary Hamel** (born 1954) left his job as a hospital administrator and went to the University of Michigan to study for a PhD in International Business. At Michigan, Hamel met his eventual mentor, C.K. Prahalad. 'We shared a deep dissatisfaction with the mechanistic way strategy was carried out', Hamel recalls.[1] Twenty years on, Hamel has established himself at the vanguard of contemporary thinking on strategy. Hard hitting, opinionated and rigorously rational, Hamel summarizes the challenge of the 1990s, in a typically earthy phrase, as 'separating the shit from the shinola, the hype from the reality and the timeless from the transient.'

Hamel talks in eminently quotable shorthand. Challenge follows challenge; question is added to question. 'Go to any company and ask when was the last time someone in their twenties spent time with the board teaching them something they didn't know. For many it is inconceivable, yet companies will pay millions of dollars for the opinions of McKinsey's bright 29-year old. What about their own 29-year olds?'

As well as being visiting professor of strategic and international management at London Business School, California-based Hamel is a consultant to major companies and chairman of Strategos, a world-wide strategic consulting company. His reputation has burgeoned as a result of a series of acclaimed articles in the *Harvard Business Review* – including 'Strategic intent'; 'Competing with core competencies'; and 'The core competence of the corporation' – as well as the popularity of the bestselling, *Competing for the Future*. (All of these were co-written with Prahalad.)

Along the way, Hamel has created a new vocabulary for strategy which includes strategic intent, strategic architecture, industry foresight (rather than vision) and core competencies. (Hamel and Prahalad define core competencies as 'the collective learning in the organization, especially how to co-ordinate diverse production skills and integrate multiple streams of technologies' and call on organizations to see themselves as a portfolio of core competencies as opposed to business units. The former are geared to growing 'opportunity share' wherever that may be; the latter narrowly focused on market share and more of the same.) Instead of talking about strategy or planning, they advocate that companies should talk of *strategizing* and ask 'What are the fundamental preconditions for developing complex, variegated, robust strategies?'

The need for new perspectives on strategy is forcefully put by Hamel. 'I am a professor of strategy and often times I am ashamed to admit it because there is a dirty secret: we only know a great strategy when we see one. In business schools we teach them and pin them to the wall like specimens. Most of our smart students raise their hands and say wait a minute was that luck or foresight? They're partly right. We don't have a theory of strategy creation. There is no foundation beneath the multi-billion dollar strategy industry. Strategy is lucky foresight. It comes from a serendipitous cocktail,' he says.[2]

The trouble is we have sought to explain strategy by a series of simplistic frameworks. 'We have an enormous appetite for simplicity. We like to believe we can break strategy down to Five Forces or Seven Ss. But you can't. Strategy is extraordinarily emotional and demanding. It is not a ritual or a once-a-year exercise, though that is what it has become. We have set the bar too low,' says Hamel. As a result, managers are bogged down in the nitty-gritty of the present – spending less than three percent of their time looking to the future.

The reinvention of strategy occurs against the backdrop of an environment in which success has never been more important and tenuous. If Bill Gates says that Microsoft is always two years away from failure, what hope can there be for the rest of us? Hamel admits that the circumstances under which strategy is created have changed. 'In many companies you see institutional entropy. How do you teach individuals to be enemies of entropy? It is like being a map maker in an earthquake zone. We are talking about products entering a market which is emerging and changing. How do you create strategy in the absence of a map?'

First, he says, you need to challenge traditional assumptions. The entire thrust of Hamel's argument is that complacency and cynicism are endemic. 'Dilbert is the bestselling business book of all time. It is cynical about management. Never has there been so much cynicism.' It is only by challenging convention that change will happen. 'Taking risks, breaking the rules, and being a maverick have always been important, but today they are more crucial than ever. We live in a discontinuous world – one where digitization, deregulation and globalization are profoundly reshaping the industrial landscape,' he says.[3]

Hamel argues that there are three kinds of companies. First are, 'the real makers', companies such as British Airways and Xerox. They are the aristocracy; well managed, consistent high achievers. Second, says Hamel, are the takers, 'peasants who only keep what the Lord doesn't want'. This group typically have around 15 percent market share – such as Kodak in the copier business or Avis – 'Avis' slogan *We try harder* enshrined the peasantry in its mission statement. 'Harder doesn't get you anywhere', says Hamel dismissively.

Third are the breakers, industrial revolutionaries. These are companies Hamel believes are creating the new wealth – and include the likes of Starbucks in the coffee business. 'Companies should be asking themselves, who is going to capture the new wealth in your industry?' he says.

When Hamel talks of change, he is not considering tinkering at the edges. 'The primary agenda is to be the architect of industry transformation not simply corporate transformation', he says. Companies which view change as an internal matter are liable to be left behind. Instead they need to look outside of their industry boundaries. Hamel calculates that if you want to see the future coming, 80 percent of the learning will take place outside company boundaries. This is not something companies are very good at. 'The good news is that companies in most industries are blind in the same way,' says Hamel. 'There is no inevitability about the future. There is no proprietary data about the future. The goal is to imagine what you can make happen.'

He argues that there are four preconditions for wealth creating strategies. First, a company must have 'new passions'. People inside the organization must care deeply about the future. Strategy has to rediscover passion.

Second, wealth creation requires 'new voices'. In many companies Hamel observes 'a lack of genetic diversity. Young people are largely disenfranchised from discussions of strategy. We need a hierarchy of imagination, not experience. Among the people who work on strategy in organizations and the theorists, a huge proportion, perhaps 95 percent, are economists and engineers who share a mechanistic view of strategy. Where are the theologists, the anthropologists to give broader and fresher insights?'

Third, Hamel calls for 'new conversations'. Instead of having the same five people talking to the same five people for the fifth year in a row, more people need to become involved in the process of strategy creation.

Finally, there is a need for 'new perspectives' – 'You cannot make people any smarter but you can give them new lenses,' says Hamel. 'Only non-linear strategies will create new wealth.'

There are, of course, other options. Many will continue to ignore Hamel's call for a revolution. It is the easy route. 'There is a lot of talk about creating wealth for shareholders. It is not a hard thing to do. Just find a 60-year-old CEO and set a 65-year-old retirement age and then guarantee a salary based on the share price growing.' The trouble is that it is here, at the stock option packed top of the organization, that change needs to begin. 'What we need is not visionaries but activists. We need antidotes to Dilbert,' Hamel proclaims. 'Revolutionaries always challenge the orthodoxies of the incumbent. We believe change has to start at the top, but how often does revolution begin with the monarch?'

Notes

1   Byrne, John, 'Three of the busiest new strategists', *Business Week*, 26 August 1996.
2   International Management Symposium, London Business School, 11 November 1997.
3   Hamel, Gary, 'Killer strategies that makes shareholders rich', *Fortune*, 23 June 1997.

Bibliography

Competing for the Future (with CK Prahalad), Harvard University Press, Cambridge, MA, 1994.
Competence-Based Competition (editors Hamel and Aimé Heene), John Wiley, New York, 1995.

Charles Handy

"Only one firm can be the industry leader, only one country top economically, there are richer or more successful neighbors to compare ourselves with. Competition is healthy, maybe even essential, but there has to be more to life than winning or we should nearly all be losers."

Charles Handy

Irish academic and author
Born 1932

Breakthrough ideas

Shamrock and federal organizations
Future of work

Key books

Understanding Organizations
The Age of Unreason
The Empty Raincoat (aka *The Age of Paradox*)

Charles Handy (born 1932) is a bestselling writer and broadcaster. In his quiet and undemonstrative way, Handy has established himself as one of the most mainstream and important of business thinkers. His work is accessible and popular. Because of this it is dismissed by some – 'He has an unerring tendency to state the obvious, which is ironically one of his strengths', noted one magazine.[1] Yet Handy has brought major questions about the future of work and of society onto the corporate and personal agenda.

Irish-born, Charles Handy worked for Shell until 1972 when he left to teach at London Business School. He spent time at MIT where he came into contact with many of the leading lights in the human relations school of thinking including Ed Schein.

Handy's early academic career was conventional. His first book, *Understanding Organizations* (1976), gives little hint of the wide-ranging social and philosophical nature of his later work. It is a comprehensive and readable primer of organizational theory, which was written as much to clarify Handy's own perspectives on the subject. From there Handy moved on to the more typically idiosyncratic *Gods of Management* (1978). The Gods identified by Handy were Apollo (order and rules); Athena (task-oriented); Dionysus (individualistic); and Zeus (one dominant leader).

It was in 1989 with the publication of *The Age of Unreason* that Handy's thinking made a great leap forward. The age of unreason, which Handy predicts, is 'a time when what we used to take for granted may no longer hold true, when the future, in so many areas, is there to be shaped, by us and for us; a time when the only prediction that will hold true is that no predictions will hold. A time therefore for bold imaginings in private life as well as public, for thinking the unlikely and doing the unreasonable'.

Suddenly the world mapped out by Handy became an uncertain and dangerous one. The future will be one of 'discontinuous change' (a phrase which has now entered the mainstream). The path through time, with society slowly, naturally and radically improving on a steady course, is a thing of the past. The blinkers have to be removed. Handy tells the story of the Peruvian Indians who saw invading ships on the horizon. Having no knowledge of such things, they discounted them as a freak of the weather. They settled for their sense of continuity.

In order to adapt to a society in which mysterious invaders are perpetually on the horizon, the way people think will have to change fundamentally. This is where Handy begins to offer challenges to his audience. We all accept his arguments that things are changing, but not necessarily that we ourselves need to change. 'We are all prisoners of our past. It is hard to think of things except in the way we have always thought of them. But that solves no problems and seldom changes anything,' says Handy. He points out that people who have thought unconventionally, 'unreasonably', have had the most profound impact on twentieth-century living. Freud, Marx and Einstein succeeded through 'discontinuous' (or what Handy labels 'upside down') thinking.

In practice, Handy believes that certain forms of organization will become dominant. These are the type of organization most readily associated with service industries. First and most famously, what he calls 'the shamrock organization' – 'a form of organization based around a core of essential executives and workers supported by outside contractors and part-time help'. The consequence of such an organizational form is that organizations in the future are likely to resemble the way consultancy firms, advertising agencies and professional partnerships are currently structured.

The second emergent structure identified by Handy is the federal one. It is not, he points out, another word for decentralization. He provides a blueprint for federal organizations in which the central function co-ordinates, influences, advises and suggests. It does not dictate terms or short-term decisions. The center is, however, concerned with long-term strategy. It is 'at the middle of things and is not a polite word for the top or even for head office'.

The third type of organization Handy anticipates is what he calls 'the Triple I'. The three 'Is' are Information, Intelligence and Ideas. In such organizations the demands on personnel management are large. Explains Handy: 'The wise organization already knows that their smart people are not to be easily defined as workers or as managers but as individuals, as specialist, as professional or executives, or as leader (the older terms of manager and worker are dropping out of use), and that they and it need also to be obsessed with the pursuit of learning if they are going to keep up with the pace of change.'

Discontinuity demands new organizations, new people to run them with new skills, capacities and career patterns. No one will be able to work simply as a manager; organizations will demand much more.

As organizations change in the age of unreason so, Handy predicts, will other aspects of our lives. Less time will be spent at work – 50,000 hours in a lifetime rather than the present figure of around 100,000. Handy does not predict, as people did in the 1970s, an enlightened age of leisure. Instead he challenges people to spend more time thinking about what they want to do. Time will not simply be divided between work and play – there could be 'portfolios' which spilt time between fee work (where you sell time); gift work (for neighbors or charities), study (keeping up-to-date with your work) and homework and leisure.

Handy continues to champion the 'federal' organization, 'an old idea whose time may have come'. The federal organization allows units and divisions individual independence while preserving corporate unity. Through federalism Handy believes the modern company can bridge some of the paradoxes it continually faces – such as the need to be simultaneously global and local.

Handy also continues gently to pose awkward questions. We must consider what sort of jobs, what sort of companies, what sort of capitalism, what sort of society, what sort of education and what sort of life we want. And, more worryingly, there are no easy answers; perhaps there are no bold generic answers at all.

Handy has reached his own conclusions. He says he has made his last speech to a large audience. He now sets a limit to his audiences of 12, reflecting that 'enough is enough'. Handy has become a one-man case study of the new world of work he so successfully and humanely commentates on. At a personal level, he appears to have the answers. Whether these can be translated into answers for others remains the question and the challenge.

Notes

1   'Good guru guide', *Business Age*, 1 November 1995.

Bibliography

Understanding Organizations, Penguin Books, London, 1976.

The Future of Work, Basil Blackwell, Oxford, 1984.

Gods of Management, Business Books, London, 1986.

The Making of Managers (with John Constable), Longman, London, 1988.

The Age of Unreason, Business Books, London, 1989.

Inside Organizations: 21 Ideas for Managers, BBC Books, London 1990.

Waiting for the Mountain to Move and other reflections on life, Arrow, London, 1991.

The Empty Raincoat, Hutchinson, London, 1994.

Beyond Certainty: The changing world of organizations, Century, London, 1995.

The Hungry Spirit, Hutchinson, London, 1997.

Bruce Henderson

"Darwin is probably a better guide to business competition than economists are."

Bruce Henderson

Australian engineer and consultant
1915–92

Breakthrough ideas

Growth/share matrix
Learning curve

I n the business world, models have traditionally been the domain of economists and strategists who develop understanding by building models of the way the world works. While managers may rely on experience to predict how their business will respond to their actions, strategists and economists rely on their models which are amalgams of many different experiences. Models assume that the distilled mass of experience will enable people to make accurate decisions.

Models synthesize and persuade. Models are reassuring. If a model suggests a distribution of a certain kind, you know what you are looking for. It is like having a map – you just have to ensure it is the right map for the area. In his book, *Sensemaking in Organizations*, Karl Weick cites the example of a Hungarian army platoon lost in the Alps. One soldier discovered a map in his pocket and that helped get the troops to safety. The map was for a different area of the Alps. 'Once people begin to act, they generate tangible outcomes (which) help them discover what is occurring … and what should be done next', says Weick. Models reassure – even if they are completely wrong.

The man who brought business models into the mainstream was the Australian, **Bruce Henderson** (1915–92). Henderson was an engineer who worked as a strategic planner for General Electric. He then joined the management consultancy, Arthur D Little. In 1963, Henderson announced that he was leaving to set up his own consultancy, the Boston Consulting Group.

In the early 1960s management consulting was beginning to be established as a profession in its own right. BCG is regarded by some as the first pure strategy consultancy. It quickly became a great success. Within five years BCG was in the top group of consulting firms – where it has largely remained. It has been called 'the most idea driven major consultancy in the world'.

The first model discovered – or re-discovered in this case – by Henderson was something of an antique. In the 1920s, an obscure company called Curtiss Aircraft came up with the concept of the 'learning curve', which also became known as the 'experience curve'. This posited that unit costs declined as cumulative production increased because of the acquisition of experience. This had been applied solely to manufacturing. Henderson applied it to strategy rather than production and found that it still worked and provided a useful practical tool.

The model for which Henderson and BCG are best known is the Growth/Share Matrix. It measures market growth and relative market share for all the businesses in a particular firm. The hypothesis of this particular framework is that companies with higher market share and growth are more profitable. The further to the left a business is on the BCG Matrix, the stronger a company should be.

BCG then superimposed on the matrix a theory of cash management which included a hierarchy of uses of cash, numbered from 1 to 4 in their order of priority. Richard Koch explained them in his *Financial Times Guide to Strategy*:

1   The most effective use of cash is to defend cash cows. They should not need to use cash very often, but if investment in a new factory or technology is required, it should be made without question.

2   The next call on cash should normally be stars. These will need a great deal of investment to hold (or gain) relative market share.

3   The trouble potentially begins with BCG's third priority, to take money from cash cows and invest in question-marks.

4   The lowest priority was investment in dogs, which BCG said should be minimal or even negative, if they were run for cash.

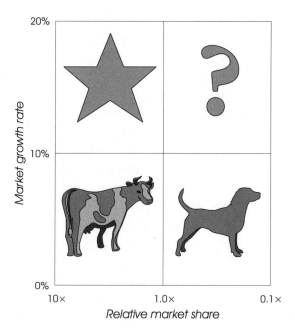

'Bruce weaved it all together in a coherent philosophy of business that highlighted more clearly than ever before the compelling importance of market leadership, a low cost position, selectivity in business, and looking at cash flows,' says Koch. 'He was ahead of his time in seeing the threat to American business posed both by Japan and by America's (and Britain's) obsession with return on investment, which he roundly condemned.'[1]

Notes

1   Koch, Richard, *Financial Times Guide to Strategy*, FT/Pitman, London, 1995.

Frederick Herzberg

"My theories have tended to emphasize strategies for keeping the sane sane.**"**

Frederick Herzberg

American clinical psychologist
Born 1923

Breakthrough ideas

Hygiene and motivation factors
KITA motivational theory

Key book

The Motivation to Work

I t is astonishing how little time is spent by management researchers actually talking to people in real situations. Frederick Taylor watched people and measured their performance. He wouldn't have dreamed of asking for their opinion. The Hawthorne experiments treated the people involved as pawns. Few have treated people in organizations as interesting or even worthy of examination. The strategist Henry Mintzberg is a notable exception to this and so too is **Frederick Herzberg** (born 1923). In the late 1950s, as part of their research, the clinical psychologist Herzberg and his colleagues asked 203 Pittsburgh engineers and accountants about their jobs and what pleased and displeased them.

This was hardly a miraculously original approach. But Herzberg's conclusions were. He separated the motivational elements of work into two categories – those serving people's animal needs (hygiene factors) and those meeting uniquely human needs (motivation factors). 'Hygiene operates to remove health hazards from the environment of man. It is not a curative; it is, rather, a preventative ... Similarly, when there are deleterious factors in the context of the job, they serve to bring about poor job attitudes. Improvements in these factors of hygiene will serve to remove the impediments to positive job attitudes,' wrote Herzberg and his co-authors in their 1959 book, *The Motivation to Work*.

Hygiene factors – also labeled maintenance factors – were determined to include supervision, inter-personal relations, physical working conditions, salary, company policies and administrative practices, benefits, and job security. 'When these factors deteriorate to a level below that which the employee considers acceptable, then job dissatisfaction ensues,' observed Herzberg. Hygiene alone is insufficient to provide the 'motivation to work'. Indeed, Herzberg argued that the factors which provide satisfaction are quite different from those leading to dissatisfaction.

True motivation, said Herzberg, comes from achievement, personal development, job satisfaction and recognition. The aim should be to motivate people through the job itself rather than through rewards or pressure.

Herzberg went on to broaden his research base. This further confirmed his conclusion that hygiene factors are the principal creator of unhappiness in work and motivational factors are the route to satisfaction.

The roots of Herzberg's fascination with motivation lay in his experiences when he served in the Second World War and was posted to Dachau concentration camp after its liberation. Not surprisingly, this proved a powerful experience. 'The central core of my work steams from Second World War experiences in Dachau Concentration Camp, where I realized that a society goes insane when the sane are driven insane. As a psychologist, I believe that sanity requires as much professional attention to nourishing the humanistic content of character and ethics as to showing compassion for differences in personality. The insane also require care and compassion but their insane actions should never be reinforced by ethically neutral strategies.'

On his return to the US, Herzberg studied at the University of Pittsburgh and worked for the US Public Health Service as a clinical psychologist. (His first love and subject of study was history – 'I went to the psychology department to understand people so I could understand history', he says.) He was subsequently Professor of Management at the University of Utah.

After the success of *The Motivation to Work*, there was a hiatus until Herzberg returned to the fray with the publication of an influential article in the *Harvard Business Review* in 1968. The article, 'One More Time: How Do You Motivate Employees?', has sold over one million copies in reprints making it the *Review*'s most popular article ever. Herzberg asked: 'What is the simplest, surest, and most direct way of getting someone to do something? Ask? But if the person responds that he or she does not want to do it, then that calls for psychological consultation to determine the reasons for such obstinacy. Tell the person? The response shows that he or she does not understand you, and now an expert in communication methods has to be brought in to show you how to get through. Give the person a monetary incentive? I do not need to remind the reader of the complexity and difficulty involved in setting up and administering an incentive system. Show the person? This means a costly training program. We need a simple way.' The article introduced the helpful motivational acronym KITA (kick in the ass) and argued: 'If you have someone on a job, use him. If you can't use him get rid of him.' Herzberg said that KITA came in three categories: negative physical;

negative psychological and positive. The latter was the preferred method for genuine motivation.

Herzberg has also coined the, now popular, phrase 'job enrichment'. He believes that business organizations could be an enormous force for good, provided they liberate both themselves and their people from the thrall of numbers, and get on with creative expansion of individuals' roles within them.

Herzberg's work has had a considerable effect on the rewards and remuneration packages offered by corporations. Increasingly, there is a trend towards 'cafeteria' benefits in which people can choose from a range of options. In effect, they can select the elements which they recognize as providing their own motivation to work.

Similarly, the current emphasis on self-development, career management and self-managed learning can be seen as having evolved from Herzberg's insights. Ultimately, motivation comes from within the individual rather than being created by the organization according to some formula.

'Pay-for-performance, employee stock ownership plans, end-of-year bonuses – too many organizations seem to believe that the only motivation to work is an economic one', says Gary Hamel. 'Treating knowledge assets like Skinnerian rats is hardly the way to get the best out of people. Herzberg offered a substantially more subtle approach – one that still has much to recommend it.'

Bibliography

The Motivation to Work (with Mausner, B., and Snyderman, B.), Wiley, New York, 1959.

Geert Hofstede

"Management within a society is very much constrained by its cultural context, because it is impossible to co-ordinate the actions of people without a deep understanding of their values, beliefs and expressions."

Geert Hofstede

Dutch psychologist
Born 1928

Breakthrough ideas

Cultural management

Key book

Culture's Consequences

A ccording to *The Economist,* **Geert Hofstede** (born 1928) 'more or less invented [cultural diversity] as a management subject'. Few would deny that this is the case. The Dutch academic has exerted considerable influence over thinking on the human and cultural implications of globalization. Indeed, in the social science citation index reviewing 1400 journals, Hofstede was one of the most cited thinkers, ahead of such luminaries as Kant, Wittgenstein, Derrida, Mill and Keynes.

In Hofstede's hands, culture becomes the crux of business. He defines it as 'the collective programming of the mind which distinguishes the members of one group or category of people from another'. Hofstede describes its power in almost lyrical terms: 'Culture consists of the patterns of thinking that parents transfer to their children, teachers to their students, friends to their friends, leaders to their followers, and followers to their leaders. Culture is reflected in the meanings people attach to various aspects of life; their ways of looking at the world and their role in it; their values- that is, in what they consider as *good* and as *evil*; their collective beliefs – what they consider as *true* and as *false*; their artistic expressions – what they consider as *beautiful* and *ugly*. Culture, although basically resident in people's minds, becomes crystallized in the institutions and tangible products of a society, which reinforce the mental programs in their turn.'

Hofstede's conclusions are based on huge amounts of research. His seminal work on cross-cultural management, *Culture's Consequences,* involved over 100,000 surveys from over 60 countries. Fons Trompenaars, who follows in Hofstede's footsteps as a Dutch cultural expert, adopts a similarly obsessive approach to questionnaires. The sheer size of Hofstede's research base leads to perennial questions about how manageable and useful it can be.

One of the fruits of Hofstede's research into national values and practices was his five-dimensional model. Hofstede concluded that there was a structure in to cultural differences between countries. Each society faces some similar problems, but solutions differ from one society to another. Hofstede identified five basic characteristics that distinguish national cultures. These dimensions are:

- **Power distance** – the extent to which the less powerful members of institutions and organizations expect and accept that power is unequally distributed.
- **Individualism** – in some societies the ties between individuals are loose while in others there is greater collectivism and strong cohesive groups. According to Hofstede's measurements, the US scores 91 out of 100 for individualism. At the other end of the scale, Guatemala scores six.
- **Masculinity** – how distinct are social gender roles?
- **Uncertainty avoidance** – the extent to which society members feel threatened by uncertain or unknown situations.
- **Long-term orientation** – the extent to which a society exhibits a pragmatic future-oriented perspective.

Hofstede was greatly influenced by his wartime experiences in occupied Holland. He trained as a mechanical engineer and wrote his doctoral thesis on 'The game of budget control'. Along the way he metamorphosed from an engineer into a psychologist and completed a PhD in social psychology. He spent time working in factories as a foreman and plant manager; was chief psychologist on the international staff of IBM; and joined IMEDE, the Swiss business school in 1971. He has also worked at the European Institute for Advanced Studies in Management in Brussels and at the University of Limburg in Maastricht where he is now Emeritus Professor of Organizational Anthropology and International Management. He is founding director of the Institute for Research on Intercultural Co-operation at the University of Limburg.

Bibliography

Uncommon Sense About Organizations: Cases, studies and field observations, Sage Publications, 1997.

Cultures and Organizations: Software of the mind, McGraw Hill, New York, 1995.

Culture's Consequences: International differences in work-related values, Sage Publications, 1984.

Game of Budget Control, Garland Publishing, 1984.

European Contributions to Organizational Theory (with M. Sami Kassem), Longwood Press, 1976.

Elliott Jaques

"I'm completely convinced of the necessity of encouraging everybody to accept the maximum amount of personal responsibility, and allowing them to have a say in every problem in which they can help."

Elliott Jaques

Canadian psychologist
Born 1917

Breakthrough ideas

Time span of discretion
Industrial democracy

Key book

A General Theory of Bureaucracy

lliott Jaques (born 1917), the Canadian-born psychologist has ploughed an idiosyncratic furrow throughout his
career. His work is based on exhaustive research and has
generally been ignored by the mass managerial market. He
was one of the founders of the Tavistock Institute of Human Relations in London. Jaques worked at Brunel University in the UK and
later at George Washington University.

Jaques is best known for his involvement in an extensive study of
industrial democracy in practice at the UK's Glacier Metal Company between 1948 and 1965. The experiment was driven forward
by the vision and political ideas of the company's chairman and managing director, Wilfred Brown. Brown served in the Labour government of Harold Wilson and later became Lord Brown. He died in
1985.

Glacier introduced a number of highly progressive changes in
working practices. A works council was introduced. This was far removed from the usually toothless attempts at worker representation.
Indeed, no change of company policy was allowed unless all members of the works council agreed. Any single person on the council
had a veto. Contrary to what experts and observers anticipated, the
company did not grind to an immediate halt. Other innovations at
Glacier included the abolition of 'clocking on', the traditional means
of recording whether someone had turned up for work.

The emphasis was on granting people responsibility and of understanding the dynamics of group working. 'I'm completely convinced of the necessity of encouraging everybody to accept the maximum amount of personal responsibility, and allowing them to have a
say in every problem in which they can help', said Jaques. He was
brought into the project as a facilitator, though his role was more
expansive than that. 'We spent the first month just having widespread
discussions through the company and gradually we worked through
things', is how Jaques remembers his introduction.[1]

The Glacier research led to Jaques' 1951 book *The Changing
Culture of a Factory*. 'The project itself produced none of the successors we had anticipated. It was a decade ahead of any form of organizational development,' said Eric Trist. What the experiment did successfully highlight was the redundancy of conventional organization
charts; the potential power of corporate culture (a concept then barely

understood) and the potential benefits of running organizations in a fair and mutually beneficial way.

Later, in *The General Theory of Bureaucracy* (1976), Jaques presented his theory of the value of work. This was ornate, but aimed to clarify something Jaques had observed during his research: 'The manifest picture of bureaucratic organization is a confusing one. There appears to be no rhyme or reason for the structures that are developed, in number of levels, in titling, or even in the meaning to be attached to the manager-subordinate linkage.'

His solution was labeled the *time span of discretion*, which contended that levels of management should be based on how long it was before their decisions could be checked, and that people should be paid in accordance with that time. This meant that managers were measured by the long-term impact of their decisions.

The site of the Glacier factory in Alperton is now a supermarket car park. Jaques remains convinced of the merits of Glacier's approach and is roundly dismissive of current managerial fashions: 'The consultants and the gurus and so on continue to play around with these fantasy fads; empowerment and self-managed teams, and now it's competency theory and God knows what. It goes on and on. I think it's the same issue as why modern natural science hadn't developed until the seventeenth century and the answer is that they hadn't as they were ensconced in alchemy. I think the major point we're talking about now, and Wilfred [Brown] was deeply aware of this, was the need for a scientifically based approach, and that we've not achieved. The field consultancy and gurus and so on is very much like alchemy; no concepts, no rigorous definition and just waffle and fiddling around.'[2]

Notes

1   'Here comes the boss', BBC Radio Four, 1 August 1997.
2   'Here comes the boss', BBC Radio Four, 1 August 1997.

Bibliography

The Changing Culture of a Factory, Tavistock, London, 1951.
A General Theory of Bureaucracy, John Wiley, New York, 1976.
Free Enterprise, Fair Employment, Crane Russak & Co, 1982.
Requisite Organization (2nd edn), Cason Hall & Co, 1996.

Joseph M. Juran

"In broad terms, quality planning consists of developing the products and processes required to meet customers' needs."

Joseph Juran

American consultant
Born 1904

Breakthrough ideas

Managing for quality

Key book

Quality Control Handbook

A s a very old man, the bow-tie wearing **Joseph M. Juran** (born 1904) became an unlikely part of the guru showbiz set. His pre-retirement tour in 1994 was entitled 'Last word' and included the souvenirs usually associated with rock concerts – autographed pictures, bow-tie paperweights. For Juran, the wheel had turned full circle.

Trained as an electrical engineer, Juran worked for Western Electric in the 1920s and then AT&T. In 1953, he made his first visit to Japan on the invitation of the Japanese Federation of Economic Associations and the Japanese Union of Scientists and Engineers. For two months Juran observed Japanese practices and trained managers and engineers in what he called 'managing for quality'.

Juran's weighty *Quality Control Handbook* was published in 1951. Juran was awarded the Second Class Order of the Sacred Treasure by the Emperor of Japan – the highest honor for a non-Japanese citizen – for 'the development of quality control in Japan and the facilitation of US and Japanese friendship'.

For the next quarter of a century, the Romanian-born Juran gave seminars on the subject of quality throughout the world. Meanwhile, Western companies continued to assume that the Japanese were low-quality imitators. Western managers mastered their financial models. Then, at the beginning of the 1980s, the world woke up to what Juran had spent his career talking about: quality. From being peripheral, Juran and his Juran Institute found themselves near the epicenter of an explosion of interest.

Juran's quality philosophy is built around a quality trilogy: quality planning, quality management and quality implementation. While Juran is critical of W. Edwards Deming as being overly reliant on statistics, his own approach is based on the forbiddingly entitled Company-Wide Quality Management (CWQM) which aims to create a means of disseminating quality to all.

Juran insists that quality cannot be delegated and was an early exponent of what has come to be known as empowerment: for him quality has to be the goal of each employee, individually and in teams, through self-supervision.

His approach is less mechanistic than Deming and places greater stress on human relations (though Deming adherents disagree with this interpretation).

Juran places quality in a historical perspective. Manufacturing products to design specifications and then inspecting them for defects to protect the buyer, he points out, was something the Egyptians had mastered 5000 years previously when building the pyramids. Similarly, the ancient Chinese had set up a separate department of the central government to establish quality standards and maintain them. Juran's message – most accessibly encapsulated in his book, *Planning for Quality* – is that quality is nothing new. This is a simple, but daunting message. If quality is so elemental and elementary why had it become ignored in the West? Juran's unwillingness to gild his straightforward message is attractive to some, but has made the communication of his ideas less successful than he would have liked.

Where Juran is innovative is in his belief that there is more to quality than specification and rigorous testing for defects. The human side of quality is regarded as critical. The origins of Juran's thoughts can be traced to his time at Western Electric. Juran analyzed the large number of tiny circuit breakers routinely scrapped by the company. Instead of waiting at the end of a production line to count the defective products, Juran looked at the manufacturing process as a whole. He came up with a solution and offered it to his bosses. They were not impressed and told Juran that this wasn't his job: 'We're the inspection department and our job is to look at these things after they are made and find the bad ones. Making them right in the first place is the job of the production department.'

In response, Juran developed his all-embracing theories of what quality should entail. 'In broad terms, quality planning consists of developing the products and processes required to meet the customers' needs. More specifically, quality planning comprises the following basic activities:

- identify the customers and their needs
- develop a product that responds to those needs
- develop a process able to produce that product.'

Quality planning, says Juran, can be produced through 'a road map ... an invariable sequence of steps. These are:

- identify who are the customers
- determine the needs of those customers
- translate those needs into our language
- develop a product that can respond to those needs
- optimize the product features so as to meet our needs as well as customers' needs
- develop a process that is able to produce the product
- optimize the process
- prove that the process can produce the product under operating conditions
- transfer the process to the operating forces.'

As with so many other recipes for quality, Juran's is more far reaching and difficult to achieve than a list of bullet-points can ever suggest.

Bibliography

Managerial Breakthrough, McGraw Hill, New York, 1964.
Juran on Planning for Quality, Free Press, New York, 1988.

Rosabeth Moss Kanter

"Thinkers, makers and traders are the DNA of the world class company.**"**

Rosabeth Moss Kanter

American academic and consultant
Born 1943

Breakthrough ideas

Empowerment
The post-entrepreneurial firm

Key books

Change Masters
World Class

T he United States' managerial tradition tends to remain centered on a corporate perspective. Corporate giants, such as General Motors, IBM, Ford and GE, create and nurture their own mythology and culture. However, there is also a very strong American humanistic tradition which puts individuals at the center of its world view. **Rosabeth Moss Kanter** (born 1943) belongs solidly in this second camp. Her perspective is resolutely humane. Her success, however, is based on the corporate application and basis of her thinking. For someone who tends to the utopian, Kanter is a diligent and persuasive commentator on industrial reality. Her standards are informed. Her opinions are backed to the hilt by research. The idealistic bent of her thinking is tempered by and grounded in reality. She may talk about 'soft' issues, but she takes no prisoners – 'I was really at the cutting edge of new management theory, but it wasn't just a fad. My writings offer enduring lessons.'[1]

Kanter, an isolated female figure in any gathering of management thinkers, graduated from Bryn Mawr and has a PhD from the University of Michigan. She taught at Brandeis and Harvard Universities (1967–77) and at Yale (1977–86). She has also been a Fellow in Law and Social Sciences and a visiting scholar at Harvard Law School. She is now Class of 1960 Professor of Business Administration at Harvard Business School. Moss Kanter is the former editor of the *Harvard Business Review* (1989–92) and co-founded the consulting company Goodmeasure in 1977 – she is now its chair.

Rosabeth Moss Kanter began her career as a sociologist before the transformation into international business guru. In her earlier incarnation she examined utopian communities. 'Most management gurus learn their craft by taking MBAs and serving time in business schools or consultancies. Rosabeth Moss Kanter learnt hers hanging around in the counter-culture, rubbing shoulders with the sort of gurus who believe in founding communes rather than re-inventing corporations,' observed one magazine.[2]

Her first book, *Men and Women of the Corporation* (1977) looked at the innermost working of an organization. It was a premature epitaph for corporate man and corporate America before downsizing and technology hit home.

The sociologist within Kanter remains strong. 'Kanter-the-guru still studies her subject with a sociologist's eye, treating the corporation not so much as a micro-economy, concerned with turning inputs into outputs, but as a mini-society, bent on shaping individuals to collective ends,' says *The Economist*.[3]

Moving on from her intricate examination of corporate life, Kanter has mapped out the potential for a more people-based corporate world. This is driven by smaller organizations, or at least less monolithic organizations. She introduced the concept of the post-entrepreneurial firm which manages to combine the traditional strengths of a large organization with the flexible speed of a smaller organization.

Key to this is the entire idea of innovation. This has been a recurrent theme of Kanter's since her first really successful book, *Change Masters* – sub-titled 'Innovation and entrepreneurship in the American corporation'. In the book she defines change masters as 'those people and organizations adept at the art of anticipating the need for, and of leading, productive change'. At the opposite end to the change masters are the 'change resisters' intent on reining in innovation.

Change is fundamentally concerned with innovation (or 'newstreams' in Kanter-speak). The key to developing and sustaining innovation is, says Kanter, an 'integrative' approach rather than a 'segmentalist' one. (This has distinct echoes of the theories of that other female management theorist, Mary Parker Follett, whose work Kanter admires.) American woes are firmly placed at the door of 'the quiet suffocation of the entrepreneurial spirit in segmentalist companies'.

'Three new sets of skills are required to manage effectively in such integrative, innovation-stimulating environments', writes Kanter. 'First are *power skills* – skills in persuading others to invest information, support, and resources in new initiatives driven by an *entrepreneur*. Second is the ability to manage the problems associated with the greater use of teams and employee participation. And third is an understanding of how change is designed and constructed in an organization – how the microchanges introduced by individual innovators relate to macrochanges or strategic reorientations.' (Kanter also has a talent for jargon – she has forwarded the case for 'employability' among other sins against language purity.)

Kanter was partly responsible for the rise in interest – if not the practice – of empowerment. 'The degree to which the opportunity to use power effectively is granted to or withheld from individuals is one operative difference between those companies which stagnate and those which innovate', she says. Recently she has expressed grave doubts about whether the corporate hype about the subject goes anywhere near matching reality – 'Managers may say they're empowering employees, for instance, but how many are really doing it?'[4]

She has also championed the broader social responsibilities of organizations. 'I think we're going to see multinationals playing a very different role, needing to be good corporate citizens because the regions in which they operate will draw them into a wider range of activities', she predicts.[5]

More recently, Kanter has been carrying out research into globalization and cross-boundary management. She is researching the dynamics of cross-border partnership and alliances as well as the local impact of the global economy.

Notes

1   Griffith, Victoria, 'It's a people thing', *Financial Times*, 24 July 1997.
2   'Moss Kanter, corporate sociologist', *The Economist*, 15 October 1994.
3   'Moss Kanter, corporate sociologist', *The Economist*, 15 October 1994.
4   Griffith, Victoria, 'It's a people thing', *Financial Times*, 24 July 1997.
5   Quoted in Dickson, Tim, 'An interview with Rosabeth Moss Kanter', *Financial Times*, 17 May 1996.

Bibliography

Men and Women of the Corporation, Basic Books, New York, 1977.
The Change Masters, Simon & Schuster, New York, 1983.
When Giants Learn to Dance, Simon & Schuster, London, 1989.
The Challenge of Organizational Change (with Stein, B.; & Jick, T.D.), Free Press, New York, 1992.
World Class: Thriving locally in the global economy, Simon & Schuster, New York, 1995.
Rosabeth Moss Kanter on the Frontiers of Management, Harvard Business School Press, Boston, MA, 1997.

"Good companies will meet needs; great companies will create markets."

Philip Kotler

American academic
Born 1931

Breakthrough ideas

Recognition of marketing as a central business function

Key book

Marketing Management

Philip Kotler (b. 1931) is a Chicagoan whose influence on the subject of marketing is matched only by his productiveness. The author of countless books, translated into over 20 languages, he is also the author of over 100 articles. While championing the role of marketing over 30 years, Kotler has coined phrases such as 'mega marketing', 'demarketing' and 'social marketing'. His books include the definitive textbook on the subject, *Marketing Management* (now in its eighth edition).

Kotler was a student at DePaul University from 1948 until 1950. Subsequently, he received his Master's degree in economics from the University of Chicago and a PhD from MIT. At Chicago he was taught by Milton Friedman and at MIT by Paul Samuelson – 'I concluded that if those two great minds couldn't agree on economic issues, I probably wasn't going to make a difference in that field', says Kotler. 'At the same time, I was attracted to very tangible problems that economists don't deal with, such as: how much do you spend on advertising? What's a sensibly sized sales force? How do you really set prices intelligently? I got into the mindset of a market.'[1]

Kotler did his postdoctoral work in mathematics at Harvard University and in behavioral science at the University of Chicago. Kotler worked as an analyst for Westinghouse in Pittsburgh and was then an assistant professor at Chicago's Roosevelt University from 1957 until 1961. He then joined Northwestern University becoming professor of marketing in 1969.

He has a penchant for useful definitions. 'When I am asked to define marketing in the briefest possible way I say marketing is meeting needs profitably. A lot of us meet needs – but businesses are set up to do it profitably. Marketing is the homework that you do to hit the mark that satisfies those needs exactly. When you do that job, there isn't much selling work to do because the word gets out from delighted customers that this is a wonderful solution to our problems.'[2]

Elsewhere, Kotler has defined marketing as 'a social and managerial process by which individuals and groups obtain what they need and want through creating, offering, and exchanging products of value with others'. He went on to explain the concept of a market as consisting 'of all the potential customers sharing a particular need or want who might be willing and able to engage in exchange to satisfy that need or want'. Marketing management therefore 'is the process of planning and executing the conception, pricing, promotion, and distribution of goods, services, and ideas to create exchanges with target groups that satisfy customer and organizational objectives'.

Kotler also provides a useful definition of a product as 'anything that can be offered to a market for attention, acquisition, use, or consumption that might satisfy a want or need'. He says that a product has five levels: the core benefit ('Marketers must see themselves as benefit providers'); the generic product; the expected product (the normal expectations the customer has of the product); the augmented product (the additional services or benefits added to the product) and, finally, the potential product ('all of the augmentations and transformations that this product might ultimately undergo in the future').

He has also explored what he labels 'customer delivered value' – defined as 'the difference between total customer value and total customer cost. And total customer value is the bundle of benefits customers expect from a given product or service.' Total customer value is made up of product value, service value, personnel value and image value. Total customer cost is made up of monetary price, time cost, energy cost and psychic cost. The two are combined to produce customer delivered value. ('Satisfying is silent. When you satisfy the customer you haven't created any noise, any dedication, any devotion – so now we say, you have to try and delight the customer. You don't just do it, you enjoy it,' says Kotler.)

Among Kotler's innovations have been 'demarketing' – which Kotler coined with Sydney J. Levy. This is the idea that an element of marketing is to dissuade customers from desiring a particular product or service. In the 1970s, Kotler also originated 'social marketing' with Gerald Zaltman. This explained the use of marketing in the dissemination of socially useful ideas.

But Kotler's most enduring achievement is to have marketed his chosen subject so successfully. 'Before he came on the scene, marketing writing and teaching was largely a matter of describing marketing functions, Kotler brought to marketing thinking and writing an analytical orientation and made it an acceptable academic discipline,' says Warwick University's Peter Doyle.[3]

Kotler has also written the marketing bible, *Marketing Management*, which celebrates and redefines marketing with each new edition. 'The marketing discipline is redeveloping its assumptions, concepts, skills, tools, and systems for making sound business decisions', writes Kotler in the most recent edition. 'Marketers must know when to cultivate large markets and when to niche; when to launch new brands and when to extend existing brand names; when to push products through distribution and when to pull them through distribution; when to protect the domestic market and when to penetrate aggressively into foreign markets; when to add more benefits to the offer and when to reduce the price; and when to expand and when to contract their budgets for salesforce, advertising, and other marketing tools.'

The central shift that Kotler has described is from 'transaction oriented' marketing to 'relationship marketing'. 'Good customers are an asset which, when well managed and served, will return a handsome lifetime income stream to the company. In the intensely competitive marketplace, the company's first order of business is to retain customer loyalty through continually satisfying their needs in a superior way,' says Kotler.

In order to become marketing-oriented, Kotler believes organizations encounter three common hurdles:

1   **Organized resistance** – entrenched functional behavior tends to oppose increased emphasis on marketing as it is seen as undermining functional power bases.
2   **Slow learning** – most companies are only capable of slowly embracing the marketing concept. In the banking industry, Kotler says that marketing has passed through five stages. In the first marketing was regarded as sales promotion and publicity. Then it was taken to be smiling and providing a friendly atmosphere. Banks moved on to segmentation and innovation, and then regarded marketing as positioning. Finally, they came to see marketing as marketing analysis, planning and control.
3   **Fast forgetting** – companies which embrace marketing concepts tend, over time, to lose touch with core marketing principles. Various US companies have sought to establish their products in Europe with little knowledge of the differences in the marketplace.

Yet these obstacles must be overcome. Kotler regards marketing as the essence of business and more. 'Good companies will meet needs; great companies will create markets', he writes. 'Market leadership is gained by envisioning new products, services, lifestyles, and ways to raise living standards. There is a vast difference between companies that offer me-too products and those that create new product and service values not even imagined by the marketplace. Ultimately, marketing at its best is about value creation and raising the world's living standards.'

Notes

1 Litchfield, Randall, 'Why we buy', *Canadian Business*, February 1994.
2 Mazur, Laura, 'Silent satisfaction', source unknown.
3 Rines, Michael, 'Philip Kotler guru of marketing', *Marketing*, November 1977.

Bibliography

Marketing Management: Analysis, Planning and Control, Prentice Hall, Englewood Cliffs, NJ, 1967 (9th edn 1997).
Marketing Decision Making: A Model Building Approach, Holt, Rinehart & Winston, New York, 1971 (Later revised in 1983 and in 1992, re-published by Prentice Hall under the title *Marketing Models* with co-authors Garry L. Lilien and K. Sridhar Moorthy).
Readings in Marketing Management, Prentice Hall, Englewood Cliffs, NJ, 1972 (Re-titled *Marketing Management and Strategy* for 1983 revised edition).
Simulation in the Social and Administrative Sciences (with Harold Guetzkow and Randall L. Schultz), Prentice Hall, Englewood Cliffs, NJ, 1972.
Creating Social Change (with Gerald Zaltman and Ira Kaufman), Holt, Rinehart and Winston, New York, 1972.
Marketing for Nonprofit Organizations, Prentice Hall, Englewood Cliffs, NJ, 1975 (Re-titled *Strategic Marketing for Nonprofit Organizations* with Alan Andreasen as co-author).
Principles of Marketing, Prentice Hall, Englewood Cliffs, NJ, 1980 (7th edition, 1996).

Cases and Readings for Marketing for Nonprofit Organizations (with OC Ferrell and Charles lamb), Prentice Hall, Englewood Cliffs, NJ, 1983 (later re-named *Strategic Marketing for Nonprofit Organizations: Cases and Readings*).

Marketing Essentials, Prentice Hall, Englewood Cliffs, NJ, 1984.

Marketing – An introduction, Prentice Hall, Englewood Cliffs, NJ, 1987.

Marketing Professional Services (with Paul N. Bloom), Prentice Hall, Englewood Cliffs, NJ, 1984.

Strategic Marketing for Educational Institutions (with Karen Fox), Prentice Hall, Englewood Cliffs, NJ, 1985.

The New Competition: What Theory Z Didn't Talk About – Marketing (with Liam Fahey and Somkid Jatusripitak), Prentice Hall, Englewood Cliffs, NJ, 1985.

Marketing for Health Care Organizations (with Roberta N. Clarke), Prentice Hall, Englewood Cliffs, NJ, 1987.

High Visibility (with Irving Rein and Martin Stoller), Dodd, Mead & Co, New York, 1987.

Social Marketing: Strategies for Changing Public behavior (with Eduardo Roberto), Free Press, New York, 1989.

Marketing for Congregations: Choosing to Serve People More Effectively (with Norman Shawchuck, Bruce Wrenn and Gustave Rath), Abingdon Press, Nashville, TN, 1992.

Marketing Places: Attracting Investment, Industry and Tourism to Cities, States and Nations (with Donald H. Haider and Irving Rein), Free Press, New York, 1993.

Marketing for Hospitality and Tourism (with John Bowen and James makens), Prentice Hall, Englewood Cliffs, NJ,1996.

Standing Room Only: Strategies for Marketing the Performing Arts (with Joanne Scheff), Harvard Business School Press, Boston, MA, 1997.

The Marketing of Nations: A Strategic Approach to Building National Wealth (with Somkid Jatusripitak and Suvit Maesincee), Free Press, New York, 1997.

Museum Strategies and Marketing: Designing the Mission, Building Audiences, Increasing Financial Resources (with Neil Kotler), Jossey-Bass, San Francisco, CA, 1998.

Ted Levitt

"If you are not thinking customer, you are not thinking.**"**

Ted Levitt

American academic
Born 1925

Breakthrough ideas

Marketing
Globalization

Key books

Innovation in Marketing
The Marketing Imagination

T he July/August 1960 issue of the *Harvard Business Review* launched the career of **Ted Levitt** (born 1925). It included his article entitled 'Marketing myopia' which, totally unexpectedly, brought marketing back onto the corporate agenda. 'Marketing myopia' has sold over 500,000 reprints and has entered a select group of articles that have genuinely changed perceptions.[1]

The article propelled the German-born Levitt to prominence. It was, he admits, a lucky break. In 1975 he reflected: *'Marketing myopia* was not intended as analysis or even prescription; it was intended as manifesto. Nor was it a new idea – Peter F Drucker, JB McKitterick, Wroe Alderson, John Howard, and Neil Borden had each done more original and balanced work on *the marketing concept*. My scheme, however, tied marketing more closely to the inner orbit of business policy.'[2]

Drucker had argued that, since the role of business was to create customers, its only two essential functions were marketing and innovation. In 1954 he wrote: 'Marketing is not a function, it is the whole business seen from the customer's point of view'. As markets have matured and become more competitive, especially during the 1990s, this 40-year-old concept has become increasingly widely accepted.

In 'Marketing myopia' Levitt argued that the central preoccupation of corporations should be with satisfying customers rather than simply producing goods. Companies should be marketing-led rather than production-led and the lead must come from the chief executive and senior management – 'Management must think of itself not as producing products but as providing customer-creating value satisfactions.' (In his ability to coin new management jargon, as well as his thinking, Levitt was ahead of his time.)

At the time of Levitt's article, the fact that companies were production-led was not open to question. Henry Ford's success in mass production had fueled the belief that low-cost production was the key to business success. Ford persisted in his belief that he knew what customers wanted, long after they had decided otherwise. (Even so, Levitt saluted Ford's marketing prowess, arguing that the mass production techniques he used were a means to a marketing end rather than an end in themselves.)

Levitt observed that production-led thinking inevitably led to narrow perspectives. He argued that companies must broaden their view of the nature of their business. Otherwise their customers will soon be forgotten. 'The railroads are in trouble today not because the need was filled by others … but because it was not filled by the railroads themselves', wrote Levitt. 'They let others take customers away from them because they assumed themselves to be in the railroad business rather than in the transportation business. The reason they defined their industry wrong was because they were railroad-oriented instead of transportation-oriented; they were product-oriented instead of customer-oriented.' The railroad business was constrained, in Levitt's view, by a lack of willingness to expand its horizons.

Levitt went on to level similar criticisms at other industries. The film industry failed to respond to the growth of television because it regarded itself as being in the business of making movies rather than providing entertainment.

Growth, wrote Levitt, can never be taken for granted – 'In truth, there is no such thing as a growth industry'. Growth is not a matter of being in a particular industry, but in being perceptive enough to spot where future growth may lie. History, said Levitt, is filled with companies which fall into 'undetected decay' usually for a number of reasons. First, they assume that the growth in their particular market will continue so long as the population grows in size and wealth. Second is the belief that a product cannot be surpassed. Third, there is a tendency to place faith in the ability of improved production techniques to deliver lower costs and therefore higher profits.

In 'Marketing myopia' Levitt also made a telling distinction between the tasks of selling and marketing. 'Selling concerns itself with the tricks and techniques of getting people to exchange their cash for your product. It is not concerned with the values that the exchange is all about. And it does not, as marketing invariably does, view the entire business process as consisting of a tightly integrated effort to discover, create, arouse, and satisfy customer needs,' he writes. This was picked up again in the 1980s when marketing underwent a resurgence and companies began to heed Levitt's view that they were overly oriented towards production.

Levitt's article and his subsequent work pushed marketing to center stage. Indeed, in some cases it led to what Levitt labeled 'marketing mania', with companies 'obsessively responsive to every fleeting whim of the customer'. The main thrust of the article has stood the test of time ('I'd do it again and in the same way', commented Levitt in 1975).

Levitt spent all his career at Harvard Business School and was editor of the *Harvard Business Review* for four years. He consistently revealed a reliable antennae for business trends. He attributed this to his voracious curiosity: 'I go into factories, stores and look out the window and ask why? Why are they doing that? Why are things this way and not that? You ask questions and pretty soon you come up with answers.'

Levitt's other major insight was on the emergence of globalization. In the same way as he had done with 'Marketing myopia', Levitt signaled the emergence of a major movement and then withdrew to watch it ignite. 'The world is becoming a common marketplace in which people – no matter where they live – desire the same products and lifestyles. Global companies must forget the idiosyncratic differences between countries and cultures and instead concentrate on satisfying universal drives,' he said.

Notes

1   Other career-enhancing HBR articles include Robert Hayes and William Abernathy's 'Managing our way to economic decline'; Frederick Herzberg's 'One more time how do you motivate employees?'; and Hamel and Prahalad's 'The core competence of the corporation'.
2   Levitt, Ted, 'Marketing myopia 1975: retrospective commentary', *Harvard Business Review*, September–October 1975.

Bibliography

Innovation in Marketing, McGraw Hill, New York, 1962.
The Marketing Mode, McGraw Hill, New York, 1969.
The Marketing Imagination, Free Press, New York, 1983.
Thinking About Management, Free Press, New York, 1991.

Kurt Lewin

"Nothing is so practical as a good theory."

Kurt Lewin

German-born American psychologist
1890–1947

Breakthrough ideas

T-groups
Field theory

Key book

A Dynamic Theory of Personality

Kurt Lewin (1890–1947) was a German-born psychologist. He was Professor of Philosophy and Psychology at Berlin University until 1932 when he fled from the Nazis to America. He was then Professor of Child Psychology at the Child Welfare Research Station in Iowa until 1944. Prior to his death from a heart attack, he worked at MIT – with Douglas McGregor among others – founding a research center for group dynamics.

In the 1940s Lewin carried out research at boys' clubs in Iowa City. Groups of boys were given leaders with different leadership styles and the ways in which the groups responded and worked was recorded by Lewin and his colleagues. This research found that the more democratic groups worked most effectively. This hardly seems a staggering conclusion but, in an era still dominated by Scientific Management, corporate dictatorship was the order of the day.

In 1946 Lewin was called into a troubled area of Connecticut to help create better relations between the black and Jewish communities. Here it was found that bringing together groups of people was a very powerful means of exposing areas of conflict. The groups were christened 'T-Groups' (the T stood for training).

The theory underlying T-Groups and the Lewin model of change was that behavior patterns need to be 'unfrozen' before they can be changed and then 'refrozen'. T-Groups were a means of making this happen.

Keen to take the idea forward, Lewin began making plans with his associates to establish a 'cultural island' where T-Groups could be examined more closely. A suitable location – an old school in Bethel, Maine – was identified shortly before Lewin's premature death. The National Training Laboratories for Group Dynamics were established in Bethel and proved highly influential. An entire generation of human relations specialists became involved. These included Warren Bennis, Douglas McGregor, Robert Blake, Chris Argyris and Ed Schein. 'NTL crackled with intellectual energy and the heady sense that some major discovery about the real nature of groups was taking place', recalls Warren Bennis, going on to pay tribute to Lewin's colleagues Ronald Lippitt, Kenneth Benne and Leland Bradford who turned NTL into a reality.[1]

Lewin also originated 'field theory'. A field was defined as 'the totality of coexisting facts which are conceived of as mutually interdependent'[2] and field theory had three basic principles:

- behavior is a function of the field that exists at the time the behavior occurs
- analysis begins with the situation as a whole from which are differentiated the component parts
- the concrete person in a concrete situation can be represented mathematically.

Lewin's premature death robbed the human relations movement of its central figure. While the NTL had an impact on a large number of people, this was dissipated as they moved off to institutions throughout the world. Indeed, the NTL's legacy was most fully explored thousands of miles away at the Tavistock Institute in London.

Notes

1   Bennis, Warren, *An Invented Life*, Addison-Wesley, Wokingham, 1993.
2   Lewin, Kurt, *Field Theory in Social Science* (ed. Cartwright, D.), Harper & Row, New York, 1951.

Bibliography

A Dynamic Theory of Personality, McGraw Hill, New York, 1935.
Principles of Topological Psychology, McGraw Hill, New York, 1936.
Resolving Social Conflicts: Selected Papers on Group Dynamics (ed. Gertrude Lewin), Harper & Row, New York, 1948.
Field Theory in Social Science: Selected Theoretical Papers (ed. D. Cartwright), Harper & Row, New York, 1951.

Douglas McGregor

"The motivation, the potential for development, the capacity for assuming responsibility ... are all present in people. Management does not put them there."

Douglas McGregor

American academic
1906–64

Breakthrough ideas

Motivational theories X and Y

Key book

The Human Side of Enterprise

ven though he died over 30 years ago, **Douglas McGregor** (1906–64) remains one of the most influential thinkers in the sphere of human relations. 'McGregor had a gift of getting toward the zone of understanding that would truly affect practitioners', says Warren Bennis, a student and protégé of McGregor. 'Doug was not a great scholar, but he had that quality of unbridled lucidity for taking what was then referred to as behavioral science research and employing it in a way that it would really have resonance for practitioners.'[1]

Detroit-born, McGregor was the son of a clergyman. He graduated from the City College of Detroit (now Wayne University) in 1932. He then went on to Harvard to study for a PhD. Following his PhD McGregor worked at Harvard as an instructor and tutor in social psychology. He then moved to MIT as an assistant professor of psychology. In 1948 he became President of Antioch College in Yellow Springs, Ohio. Antioch was renowned as a progressive liberal college. Warren Bennis remembers McGregor's arrival, 'broad-grinned and tweedy from MIT'. In 1954, McGregor returned to MIT as a Professor of Management. He became Sloan Fellows Professor of Industrial Management in 1962.

At MIT, McGregor attracted some of the emerging generation of thinkers to work with him, including Warren Bennis and Ed Schein. At the time Ed Schein joined MIT in 1956, McGregor's reputation was rapidly growing. 'McGregor was my mentor at MIT', says Schein. 'I think he has always been misunderstood. He observed that the more efficient manager tends to be the one who values and trusts people upfront. The ineffective manager is cynical and mistrusts people. The inference from this was that McGregor was HR-oriented. But he was stating a fact of life rather than a prescription. In the process people began to attribute participative approaches to McGregor. Yet, lots of Theory Y managers were autocrats. They did trust people, but they were still autocrats. Plenty of Theory X managers were participative and screwed everything up. In fact, McGregor never took a position on how participatory leaders should be.'[2]

As Schein suggests, McGregor remains best known for his division of motivational theory into Theory X and Theory Y. (These were the centerpiece of his 1960 classic, *The Human Side of Enterprise*.)

Theory X was traditional carrot and stick thinking built on 'the assumption of the mediocrity of the masses'. This assumed that workers were inherently lazy, needed to be supervised and motivated, and regarded work as a necessary evil to provide money. The premises of Theory X, wrote McGregor, were '(1) that the average human has an inherent dislike of work and will avoid it if he can (2) that people therefore need to be coerced, controlled, directed, and threatened with punishment to get them to put forward adequate effort toward the organization's ends and (3) that the typical human prefers to be directed, wants to avoid responsibility, has relatively little ambition, and wants security above all'.

McGregor lamented that Theory X 'materially influences managerial strategy in a wide sector of American industry', and observed 'if there is a single assumption that pervades conventional organizational theory it is that authority is the central, indispensable means of managerial control'.

'The human side of enterprise today is fashioned from propositions and beliefs such as these', wrote McGregor, before going on to conclude that 'this behavior is not a consequence of man's inherent nature. It is a consequence rather of the nature of industrial organizations, of management philosophy, policy, and practice.' It is not people who have made organizations, but organizations which have transformed the perspectives, aspirations and behavior of people.

The other extreme was described by McGregor as Theory Y, based on the principle that people want and need to work. If this was the case, then organizations needed to develop the individual's commitment to its objectives, and then to liberate his or her abilities on behalf of those objectives. McGregor described the assumptions behind Theory Y: '(1) that the expenditure of physical and mental effort in work is as natural as in play or rest – the typical human doesn't inherently dislike work; (2) external control and threat of punishment are not the only means for bringing about effort toward a company's ends; (3) commitment to objectives is a function of the rewards associated with their achievement – the most important of such rewards is the satisfaction of ego and can be the direct product of effort directed toward an organization's purposes; (4) the average human being learns, under the right conditions, not only to accept but to seek responsibility; and (5) the capacity to exercise a relatively high degree of imagination, ingenuity, and creativity in the solution of organizational problems is widely, not narrowly, distributed in the population.'

Theories X and Y were not simplistic stereotypes. McGregor was realistic: 'It is no more possible to create an organization today which will be a full, effective application of this theory than it was to build an atomic power plant in 1945. There are many formidable obstacles to overcome.'

It is worth noting that Theory Y was more than mere theorizing. In the early 1950s, McGregor helped design a Proctor & Gamble plant in Georgia. Built on the Theory Y model with self-managing teams its performance soon surpassed other P&G plants.

McGregor also examined the process of acquiring new skills and identified four kinds of learning relevant for managers: intellectual knowledge; manual skills; problem-solving skills; and social interaction. The last element was, said McGregor, outside the confines of normal teaching and learning methods. 'We normally get little feedback of real value concerning the impact of our behavior on others. If they don't behave as we desire, it is easy to blame their stupidity, their adjustment, their peculiarities. Above all, it isn't considered good taste to give this kind of feedback in most social settings. Instead, it is discussed by our colleagues when we are not present to learn about it.' McGregor recommended the use of T-Groups, then in their early stages, in which group participation was used to help people extend their insights in their own and other people's behavior.

The common complaint against McGregor's Theories X and Y is that they are mutually exclusive, two incompatible ends of an endless spectrum. To counter this, before he died in 1964, McGregor was developing Theory Z, a theory which synthesized the organizational and personal imperatives. The concept of Theory Z was later seized upon by William Ouchi (see Appendix). In his book of the same name, he analyzed Japanese working methods. Here, he found fertile ground for many of the ideas McGregor was proposing for Theory Z – lifetime employment, concern for employees including their social life, informal control, decisions made by consensus, slow promotion, excellent transmittal of information from top to bottom and bottom to top with the help of middle management, commitment to the firm and high concern for quality.

While Theories X and Y dominate McGregor's legacy, his work deserves recognition for its impact on human relations as a whole. His ambition remains as relevant today: 'If we can learn how to realize the potential for elaboration inherent in the human resources of industry, we will provide a model for governments and nations which mankind sorely needs.'

Notes

1   'Profile of Warren Bennis', *Organization Frontier*, 93/3.
2   Interview with the author, June 1997.

Bibliography

The Human Side of Enterprise, McGraw Hill, New York, 1960.

Nicolo Machiavelli

"A Prince ought to have no other aim or thought, nor select anything else for his study, than war and its rules and discipline; for this is the sole art that belongs to him who rules."

Nicolo Machiavelli

Florentine diplomat and author
1469–1527

Breakthrough ideas

Power and leadership

Key book

The Prince

P ower is a fact of corporate life. 'Adversarial power relationships work only if you never have to see or work with the
bastards again', says Peter Drucker.

'Managers have been brought up on a diet of power,
divide and rule. They have been preoccupied with authority rather
than making things happen,' notes Charles Handy. 'Powerlessness is
a state of mind. If you think you're powerless, you are,' concludes
Tom Peters. While virtually everyone has expressed an opinion on
power, its patron saint is uncontested: the Florentine diplomat and
author **Nicolo Machiavelli** (1469–1527). His is the last word on
the subject. 'Whoever is the cause of another becoming powerful, is
ruined himself; for that power is produced by him either through
craft or force; and both of these are suspected by the one who has
been raised to power', said Machiavelli.

Nicolo Machiavelli served as an official in the Florentine government. During 14 years as Secretary of the Second Chancery, he
became known as the 'Florentine secretary' and served on nearly 30
foreign missions. His work brought him into contact with some of
Europe's most influential ministers and government representatives.
His chief diplomatic triumph occurred when Florence obtained the
surrender of Pisa.

Machiavelli's career came to an end in 1512 when the Medicis
returned to power. He was then exiled from the city and later ac-
cused of being involved in a plot against the government. For this he
was imprisoned and tortured on the rack. He then retired to a farm
outside Florence and began a successful writing career, with books
on politics as well as plays and a history of Florence. 'The most influential business strategist ever born, Machiavelli was a useless businessman', is how the magazine, *Business Age* summed his career up.[1]

Machiavelli's bible on power is *The Prince*. Within it, embedded
beneath details of Alexander VI's tribulations, lie a ready supply of
aphorisms and insights which are, perhaps sadly, as appropriate to
many of today's managers and organizations as they were half a millennium ago. (Indeed, Antony Jay's 1970 book, *Management and
Machiavelli* developed the comparisons.)

Machiavelli portrayed a world of cunning, intrigue and brutal
opportunism. 'I believe also that he will be successful who directs his

actions according to the spirit of the time, and that he whose actions do not accord with the time will not be successful', he wrote. 'Because men are seen, in affairs that lead to the end which every man has before him, namely, glory and riches, to get there by various methods; one with caution, another with haste; one by force, another by skill; one by patience, another by its opposite; and each one succeeds in reaching the goal by a different method.' If it works, do it.

'It is unnecessary for a prince to have all the good qualities I have enumerated, but it is very necessary to appear to have them,' Machiavelli advised, adding the suggestion that it is useful 'to be a great pretender and dissembler'. But Machiavelli went beyond such helpful presentational hints. Like all great self-improvement writers, he offered something for everyone. Take Machiavelli on managing change: 'There is nothing more difficult to take in hand, more perilous to conduct, or more uncertain in its success, than to take the lead in the introduction of a new order of things'. Or on sustaining motivation: 'He ought above all things to keep his men well-organized and drilled, to follow incessantly the chase'.

Machiavelli even had advice for executives acquiring companies in other countries: 'But when states are acquired in a country differing in language, customs, or laws, there are difficulties, and good fortune and great energy are needed to hold them, and one of the greatest and most real helps would be that he who has acquired them should go and reside there ... Because if one is on the spot, disorders are seen as they spring up, and one can quickly remedy them; but if one is not at hand, they are heard of only when they are great, and then one can no longer remedy them.' Executives throughout the world will be able to identify with Machiavelli's analysis.

There was even talk of what would now be called empowerment in Machiavelli's work – 'The Masses are more knowing and more Constant than is a Prince' is the title of one of his Discourses which concludes 'government by the populace is better than government by princes'.

Machiavelli was at his best in discussing leadership. Success, he said, was not down to luck or genius, but 'happy shrewdness'. Machiavelli also examined the perils facing the self-made leader when he (the thought of a 'she' would have been impossible for him to contemplate) reached the dizzy heights: 'Those who solely by good fortune become princes from being private citizens have little trouble in rising, but much in keeping atop; they have not any difficulties on the way up, because they fly, but they have many when they reach the summit.'

Above all, Machiavelli was the champion of leadership through cunning and intrigue, the triumph of force over reason. An admirer of Borgia, Machiavelli had a dismal view of human nature. Unfortunately, as he sagely pointed out, history has repeatedly proved that a combination of being armed to the teeth and devious is more likely to allow you to achieve your objectives. It is all very well being good, said Machiavelli, but the leader 'should know how to enter into evil when necessity commands'.

Notes

1   'The good guru guide', *Business Age*, 1 November 1995.

Bibliography

The Prince, Penguin, London, 1967.

Abraham Maslow

"It seems clear to me that in an enterprise, if everybody concerned is absolutely clear about the goals and objectives and far purposes of the organization, practically all other questions then become simple technical questions of fitting means to the ends. But it is also true that to the extent that these far goals are confused as conflicting or ambivalent or only partially understood, then all the discussions of techniques and methods and means in the world will be of little use."

Abraham Maslow

American behavioral psychologist
1908–70

Breakthrough ideas

Hierarchy of needs

Key books

Motivation and Personality
Eupsychian Management

T he behavioral psychologist **Abraham Maslow** (1908–70) was a member of the Human Relations School of the late 1950s. Born in Brooklyn, he trained at the University of Wisconsin. After receiving his PhD in 1934 he worked as a research fellow at Teachers College of Columbia University. He also spent some time studying primates – one of his earliest papers was on primate behavior in the Bronx Park Zoo. Between 1937 and 1951, he was an associate professor at Brooklyn College. Also, during this time, between 1945 and 1947, he was plant manager at the Maslow Cooperage Corporation in Pleasanton, California. In 1951 he moved to Brandeis University to become professor of social psychology and department chairman.

Maslow is best known for his 'hierarchy of needs' – a concept which was first published by Maslow in 1943. In this, he argued that there was an ascending scale of needs which need to be understood if people are to be motivated.

The hierarchy parallels the human life cycle. First are the fundamental physiological needs of warmth, shelter and food. 'It is quite true that man lives by bread alone – when there is no bread. But what happens to man's desires when there is plenty of bread and when his belly is chronically filled?' Maslow asked.

Once basic physiological needs are met, others emerge to dominate. 'If the physiological needs are relatively well gratified, there then emerges a new set of needs, which we may categorize roughly as the safety needs', wrote Maslow in *Motivation and Personality*. 'A man, in this state, if it is extreme enough and chronic enough, may be characterized as living almost for safety alone.'[1]

Next on the hierarchy are social or love needs, and ego, or self-esteem, needs. Ultimately, as man moves up the scale, with each need being satisfied comes what Maslow labeled 'self-actualization', the individual achieves their own personal potential. 'A musician must make music, an artist must paint, a poet must write, if he is to be ultimately at peace with himself. What a man be, he must be,' said Maslow.

While the hierarchy of needs provides a rational framework for motivation, its flaw lies in the nature of humanity. Man always wants more. When asked what salary they would be comfortable with, people routinely – no matter what their income – name a figure which is around twice their current income.

After presenting his hierarchy of needs, Maslow went on to study self-actualization in greater depth. He studied 48 people he considered to be self-actualized. These included Thomas Jefferson, Albert Einstein, Abraham Lincoln and, slightly less obviously, Eleanor Roosevelt. Maslow found that they tended to share some of 12 characteristics: they perceived reality accurately; accepted themselves, others and nature; they lived spontaneous, simple and natural lives; they were problem-centered; liked privacy and detachment; didn't take life for granted; had mystical or peak experiences; had a social interest; profound interpersonal relationships; little racial, religious or social prejudice; were creative; and were resistant to having ideas or cultures thrust upon them.

Maslow took his work further following his experiences in the summer of 1962 when he spent time with a Californian electronics company, Non-Linear Systems. While working there he kept a diary which was published as *Eupsychian Management* (1965). This described Maslow's ideas on 'enlightened management'. Maslow created the word 'Eupsychian' to describe 'the culture that would be generated by 1,000 self-actualizing people on some sheltered island where they would not be interfered with'.

Maslow's work can be regarded as utopian, but it was undoubtedly a powerful argument for more inclusive and humane thinking to be applied in the workplace. 'The more influence and power you give to someone else in the team situation, the more you have yourself', he said. 'It is well to treat working people as if they were type Theory Y human beings ... because this is the path to success of any kind whatsoever, including financial success.'

Notes

1   Maslow, Abraham, *Motivation and Personality*, Harper & Row, New York, 1954.

Bibliography

Motivation and Personality, Harper & Row, New York, 1954 (third edition, Harper & Row, 1987).

Towards a Psychology of Being (second edition), Van Nostrand Reinhold, New York, 1982.

The Journals of Abraham Maslow, Brooks/Cole, Monterey, CA, 1979.

Eupsychian Management, Irwin-Dorsey, Homewood, IL, 1965 (re-published as *Maslow on Management*, John Wiley, New York, 1998).

Konosuke Matsushita

"We are going to win and the industrial West is going to lose out; there's not much you can do about it because the reasons for your failure are within yourselves."

Konosuke Matsushita

Japanese industrialist
1894–1989

Breakthrough ideas

Customer service
The entrepreneurial corporate giant

Key book

Not For Bread Alone

F or Western managers one of the most chilling passages in management literature must be that when **Konosuke Matsushita** (1894–1989) mapped out why the West was destined to lose and the Japanese were inevitably going to emerge victorious in the battle for industrial supremacy. Matsushita spoke from a position of remarkable strength. His story tells of one of the most impressive industrial achievements of the twentieth century.

Matsushita was brought up in poverty in a small village near Wakayama. He had seven brothers and sisters. His once relatively prosperous family lived in straitened circumstances after his father lost money betting on commodities. He left school in 1904 and was apprenticed to a maker of charcoal grills. Matsushita later worked his way up to become an inspector in the Osaka Electric Light Company and, in 1917, founded his own company, Matsushita Electric.

Matsushita's first product was a plug adapter. He had suggested the idea to his previous employer but they had shown no interest – this was hardly surprising as Matsushita had little idea of how to actually make the product. It took Matsushita and four others four months to figure out how to make the adapter. No-one bought them.

Matsushita's first break was an order to made insulator plates. The order was delivered on time and was high quality. Matsushita began to make money. He then developed an innovative bicycle light. Again retailers were unimpressed. Then Matsushita had his salesmen leave a switched on light in each shop. This simple product demonstration impressed and the business took off. By 1932 Matsushita had over 1000 employees, ten factories and 280 patents.

During World War II he made ships and planes as part of the Japanese war effort – even though he had no experience in either area. In 1958 Matsushita Electric was given an award for the quality of its factory operations and, in 1990, Matsushita bought MCA, a year after Sony bought Columbia Pictures. This is a cruelly abbreviated version of how Matsushita created a $42 billion revenue business from nothing. He also created one of the world's most successful brands, Panasonic, and amassed a personal fortune of $3 billion.

Matsushita's success story contains a huge number of managerial lessons (analyzed in John Kotter's 1997 book, *Matsushita Leader-*

ship). First, Matsushita understood customer service before anyone in the West had even thought about it. 'Don't sell customers goods that they are attracted to. Sell them goods that will benefit them,' he said. 'After-sales service is more important than assistance before sales. It is through such service that one gets permanent customers.'

Second, Matsushita – who admired Henry Ford – emphasized efficient production and quality products. 'To be out of stock is due to carelessness. If this happens, apologize to the customers, ask for their address and tell them that you will deliver the goods immediately.'

The third factor in Matsushita's success was pure entrepreneurialism. He took risks and backed his beliefs at every stage. The classic example of this is the development of the video cassette. Matsushita developed VHS video and licensed the technology. Sony developed Betamax which was immeasurably better and failed to license the technology. The world standard is VHS and Betamax is consigned to history.

Finally, Matsushita advocated business with a conscience. This was manifested in his paternalistic employment practices. During a recession early in its life the company did not make any people redundant. This cemented loyalty. 'It's not enough to work conscientiously. No matter what kind of job, you should think of yourself as being completely in charge of and responsible for your own work,' he said, going on to describe how he approached his work – 'Big things and little things are my job. Middle-level arrangements can be delegated.' He also explained the role of the leader in more cryptic style – 'The tail trails the head. If the head moves fast, the tail will keep up the same pace. If the head is sluggish, the tail will droop.'

Matsushita mapped out the broader spiritual aims he believed a business should have. Profit was not enough. 'The mission of a manufacturer should be to overcome poverty, to relieve society as a whole from misery, and bring it wealth.' Matsushita's 'basic management objective', coined in 1929, said: 'Recognizing our responsibilities as industrialists, we will devote ourselves to the progress and development of society and the well-being of people through our business activities, thereby enhancing the quality of life throughout the world'.

And failure to make a profit was regarded by him as 'a sort of crime against society. We take society's capital, we take their people, we take their materials, yet without a good profit, we are using precious resources that could be better used elsewhere.'

To Matsushita business was demanding, serious and crucial: 'Business, we know, is now so complex and difficult, the survival of firms so hazardous in an environment increasingly unpredictable, competitive and fraught with danger, that their continued existence depends on the day-to-day mobilization of every ounce of intelligence.'

Bibliography

Not For Bread Alone, Berkeley Publishing, 1994.

Elton Mayo

"So long as commerce specializes in business methods which take no account of human nature and social motives, so long may we expect strikes and sabotage to be the ordinary accompaniment of industry."

Elton Mayo

Australian
1880–1949

Breakthrough ideas

Motivation and teamworking

Key book

The Human Problems of an Industrial Civilization

T he Australian **Elton Mayo** (1880–1949) had an interestingly diverse career though he remains best known – if known at all – for his contribution to the famous Hawthorne experiments into motivation.

The Hawthorne Studies were carried out at Western Electric's Chicago plant between 1927 and 1932. The studies offered important insights into the motivation of workers. It was found, for example, that changes in working conditions led to increased output – even if the changes weren't obviously for the betterment of working conditions.

The Hawthorne experiments were celebrated as a major event. Their significance lay not so much in their results and discoveries, though these were clearly important, but in the statement they made – whatever the dictates of mass production and Scientific Management, people and their motivation were critical to the success of any business; and in their legacy – the Human Relations school of thinkers which emerged in the 1940s and 1950s.

The experiments were carried out in the Relay Assembling Test Room of Western Electric's Hawthorne Works. Mayo was not the only academic involved in the project. The experiments were also written about by a variety of others including Harvard's Fritz Roethlisberger and William Dickson.

The researchers were interested in exploring the links between morale and output. Five women workers were removed to a test room and observed as they worked. The research initially restricted itself to physical and technical variables. Sociological factors were not expected to be of any significance. The results proved otherwise. Removed from their colleagues, the morale of the guinea pigs improved. By virtue of their selection, the women felt that more attention was being paid to them. They felt chosen, and so responded positively. The second important fact which emerged was that the feeling of belonging to a cohesive group led to an increase in productivity. 'The desire to stand well with one's fellows, the so-called human instinct of association, easily outweighs the merely individual interest and the logic of reasoning upon which so many spurious principles of management are based,' commented Mayo.

Mayo's route to becoming involved in the Hawthorne experiments was circuitous. The early part of his career was spent in a variety of places and occupations. He underwent medical training in London and Edinburgh; spent time in Africa; worked in an Adelaide printing company and taught at Queensland University. He also worked on psychoanalysing sufferers of shell shock after World War I.[1] Mayo arrived in the United States in 1923 and worked at the University of Pennsylvania before joining Harvard. It was at Harvard that Mayo cemented his long-term contribution to business thinking.

Mayo's belief that the humanity needed to be restored to the workplace struck a chord at a time when the dehumanizing side of mass production was beginning to be more fully appreciated. 'So long as commerce specializes in business methods which take no account of human nature and social motives, so long may we expect strikes and sabotage to be the ordinary accompaniment of industry', Mayo noted. He championed the case for teamworking and for improved communications between management and the workforce. The Hawthorne research revealed informal organizations between groups as a potentially powerful force which companies could utilize or ignore.

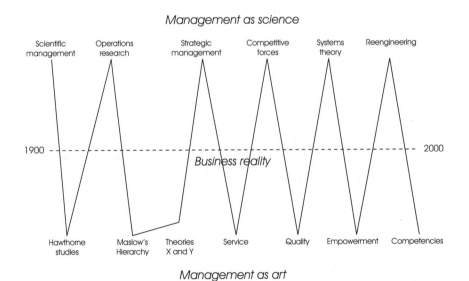

Management – art or science?

While Mayo offered a humanistic view of the workplace, it was still one which assumed that the behavior of workers was dictated by the 'logic of sentiment' while that of the bosses was by the 'logic of cost and efficiency'. A Japanese manager, quoted in Richard Pascale's *Managing on the Edge*, made an important observation: 'There is nothing wrong with the findings. But the Hawthorne experiments look at human behavior from the wrong perspective. Your thinking needs to build from the idea of empowering workers, placing responsibility closest to where the knowledge resides, using consistently honored values to draw the separate individuals together. The Hawthorne experiments imply smug superiority, parent-to-child assumptions. This is not a true understanding.'

Even so, Mayo's work and that of his fellow Hawthorne researchers, redressed the balance in management theorizing. The scientific bias of earlier researchers was put into a new perspective. This is part of a cyclical pattern as management theorizing swings from science to humanity or art. The yin and yang of thinking have rarely mixed. The humanists (from Mary Parker Follett, Mayo, Douglas McGregor, and Abraham Maslow to Charles Handy and Tom Peters) have shared little or no common ground with the scientists (Frederick Taylor, Alfred P Sloan, Igor Ansoff, Alfred Chandler, Michael Porter and contemporary gurus of reengineering). Mayo's work served as a foundation for all who followed on the humanist side of the divide.

Notes

1   War time has provided a range of influences on management thinkers: Frederick Herzberg was deeply affected by the Dachau concentration camp; Ed Schein studied the brainwashing of prisoners of war during the Korean War; Tom Peters served in Vietnam.

Bibliography

Human Problems of an Industrial Civilization, Macmillan, New York, 1933.
Social Problems of an Industrial Civilization, Harvard University Press, Cambridge, MA, 1945.

Henry Mintzberg

"Management is a curious phenomenon. It is generously paid, enormously influential, and significantly devoid of common sense."

Henry Mintzberg

Canadian academic
Born 1939

Breakthrough ideas

Strategy as craft
Roles of managers
Management education

Key books

The Nature of Managerial Work
The Rise and Fall of Strategic Planning

H **enry Mintzberg** (born 1939) is one of the most interesting of management thinkers. Eschewing the guru seminar-trail, he forges a unique intellectual path.

Among his latest adventures is a global management program which aims to be the next generation MBA. Mintzberg is a long-term critic of MBA programs (despite teaching at McGill in Canada and INSEAD). 'The idea that you can take smart but inexperienced 25 year-olds who have never managed anything or anybody and turn them into effective managers via two years of classroom training is ludicrous', he says.[1]

The resulting Master's Program involves five business schools from around the world and is built around five mind-sets: the reflective mind-set; the analytic mind-set; the worldly mind-set; the collaborative mind-set and the catalytic mind-set. The traditional functional divides are dispensed with. Instead of running separate courses on marketing and finance the subjects are interwoven. Mintzberg argues that management should be less 'specialist-driven', regarding the role of managers as integration.

Mintzberg reserves his sternest criticism for the power of Wall Street and financiers over American business. 'These are the people most distant from the ones who make, sell, use, and service a product, but because they have the financial training they control a company', he says going on to note that successes such as Jack Welch and Andy Grove are engineers by training, willing to gets their hands dirty.

Mintzberg is also an engineer and reality is never far away in his work. Though it is characterized by studious academic research, Mintzberg continually injects an undercurrent of common sense and a willingness to be opinionated. While some researchers are carried away into the oblivion of academic jargon, Mintzberg never leaves reality far behind. The quirky, original and perplexing nature of reality is always there.

Mintzberg is a great debunker of received wisdom. He collects typographical errors and aphorisms and is cheerfully quotable – 'Great organizations, once created, don't need great leaders'; 'Delayering can be defined as the process by which people who barely know what's going on get rid of those who do'; 'The trouble with most strategies are chief executives who believe themselves to be strategists. Great strategists are either creative or generous. We have too few of either type'; 'Buzzwords are the problem, not the solution. Hot techniques dazzle us, then fizzle'; 'It is time to close down conventional MBA programs. We should be developing real managers, not pretending to create them in the classroom.'

Mintzberg is Professor of Management at McGill University, Montreal and Professor of Organization at INSEAD in Fontainebleau, France. He graduated in mechanical engineering from McGill University in 1961 and completed a general arts degree in the evenings. Between 1961 and 1963, Mintzberg worked in the operational research branch of Canadian Railways before going onto MIT's Sloan School from where he has a PhD in management.

Mintzberg's PhD thesis was titled 'The manager at work – determining his activities, roles and programs by structured observation'. It formed the basis of his first book, *The Nature of Managerial Work*. This involved Minztberg – in true engineering fashion – examining how managers worked. Not surprisingly, managers did not do what they liked to think they did.

Instead of spending time contemplating the long-term, Mintzberg found that managers were slaves to the moment, moving from task to task with every move dogged by another diversion, another call. The median time spent on any one issue was a mere nine minutes. Mintzberg identified the characteristics of the manager at work:

- performs a great quantity of work at an unrelenting pace
- undertakes activities marked by variety, brevity and fragmentation
- has a preference for issues which are current, specific and non-routine
- prefers verbal rather than written means of communication
- acts within a web of internal and external contacts
- is subject to heavy constraints but can exert some control over the work.

From these observations, Mintzberg identified the manager's 'work roles' as:

- **Interpersonal roles**
  - Figurehead: representing the organization/unit to outsiders
  - Leader: motivating subordinates, unifying effort
  - Liaiser: maintaining lateral contacts.
- **Informational roles**
  - Monitor: of information flows
  - Disseminator: of information to subordinates
  - Spokesman: transmission of information to outsiders.
- **Decisional roles**
  - Entrepreneur: initiator and designer of change
  - Disturbance handler: handling non-routine events
  - Resource allocator: deciding who gets what and who will do what
  - Negotiator: negotiating.

Mintzberg's approach to other areas he has researched has been similar. Instead of accepting what he is told, he takes the mechanism apart to see how it works. Nowhere has he done this more successfully than in the field of strategy. Mintzberg's work on strategy, in particular his ideas of 'emergent strategy' and 'grass-roots strategy making', has been highly influential.

In particular, Mintzberg has long been a critic of formulae and analysis-driven strategic planning. He defines planning as 'a formalized system for codifying, elaborating and operationalizing the strategies which companies already have'. In contrast, strategy is either an 'emergent' pattern or a deliberate 'perspective'. Mintzberg argues that strategy cannot be planned. While planning is concerned with analysis, strategy making is concerned with synthesis. Today's planners are not redundant but are only valuable as strategy finders, analysts and catalysts. They are supporters of line managers, forever questioning rather than providing automatic answers. Their most effective role is in unearthing 'fledgling strategies in unexpected pockets of the organization so that consideration can be given to (expanding) them'.

Mintzberg identifies three central pitfalls to today's strategy planning practices.

First, the assumption that discontinuities can be predicated. Forecasting techniques are limited by the fact that they tend to assume that the future will resemble the past. This gives artificial reassurance and creates strategies which are liable to disintegrate as they are overtaken by events.

He points out that our passion for planning mostly flourishes during stable times such as in the 1960s. Confronted by a new world order, planners are left seeking to re-create a long-forgotten past.

Second, that planners are detached from the reality of the organization. Mintzberg is critical of the 'assumption of detachment'. 'If the system does the thinking,' he writes, 'the thought must be detached from the action, strategy from operations (and) ostensible thinkers from doers ... It is this disassociation of thinking from acting that lies close to the root of (strategic planning's) problem.'

Planners have traditionally been obsessed with gathering hard data on their industry, markets, competitors. Soft data – networks of contacts, talking with customers, suppliers and employees, using intuition and using the grapevine – have all but been ignored.

Mintzberg points out that much of what is considered 'hard' data is often anything but. There is a 'soft underbelly of hard data', typified by the fallacy of 'measuring what's measurable'. The results are limiting, for example a pronounced tendency 'to favor cost leadership strategies (emphasizing operating efficiencies, which are generally measurable) over product-leadership strategies (emphasizing innovative design or high quality, which tends to be less measurable)'.

To gain real and useful understanding of an organization's competitive situation soft data needs to be dynamically integrated into the planning process. 'Strategy-making is an immensely complex process involving the most sophisticated, subtle and at times subconscious of human cognitive and social processes', writes Mintzberg. 'While hard data may inform the intellect, it is largely soft data that generate wisdom. They may be difficult to "analyze", but they are indispensable for synthesis – the key to strategy making.'

The third and final flaw identified by Mintzberg is the assumption that strategy making can be formalized. The left side of the brain has dominated strategy formulation with its emphasis on logic and analysis. Overly structured, this creates a narrow range of options. Alternatives which do not fit into the pre-determined structure are ignored. The right side of the brain needs to become part of the process with its emphasis on intuition and creativity. 'Planning by its very nature', concludes Mintzberg, 'defines and preserves catego-ries. Creativity, by its very nature, creates categories or rearranges established ones. This is why strategic planning can neither provide creativity, nor deal with it when it emerges by other means.' Mold-breaking strategies 'grow initially like weeds, they are not cultivated like tomatoes in a hothouse ... (They) can take root in all kinds of places'.

Strategy-making, as presented by Mintzberg, has the following characteristics:

- Derived from synthesis.
- Informal and visionary, rather than programmed and formal-ized.
- Relies on divergent thinking, intuition and using the subcon-scious. This leads to outbursts of creativity as new discoveries are made.
- Irregular, unexpected, *ad hoc*, instinctive. It upsets stable pat-terns.
- Managers are adaptive information manipulators, opportun-ists, rather than aloof conductors.
- Done in time of instability characterized by discontinuous change.
- Results from an approach which takes in broad perspectives and is therefore visionary, and involves a variety of actors ca-pable of experimenting and then integrating.

By championing the role of creativity in strategy creation and in pro-viding carefully researched rebuttals of formulaic approaches to man-agement, Mintzberg has provided new insights into strategy. 'The real challenge in crafting strategy lies in detecting their subtle discontinuities that may undermine a business in the future', he says. 'And for that there is no technique, no program, just a sharp mind in touch with the situation.'

Notes

1   Mintzberg, Henry, 'The new management mind-set', *Leader to Leader*, Spring 1997.

Bibliography

The Nature of Managerial Work, Harper & Row, New York, 1973.

The Structuring of Organizations, Prentice-Hall, Englewood Cliffs, NJ, 1979.

Structures In Fives: Designing Effective Organizations, Prentice-Hall, Englewood Cliffs, NJ, 1983 (this is an expurgated version of the above).

Power In and Around Organizations, Prentice Hall, Englewood Cliffs, NJ, 1983.

Mintzberg on Management: Inside Our Strange World of Organizations, Free Press, New York, 1989.

The Strategy Process: Concepts, Contexts, Cases (with J.B. Quinn), 2nd edition, Prentice Hall, Englewood Cliffs, NJ, 1991.

The Rise and Fall of Strategic Planning, Prentice Hall International, Hemel Hempstead, 1994.

Akito Morita

"American managers are too little concerned about their workers."

Akito Morita

Japanese businessman
Born 1921

Breakthrough ideas

Japanese management

Key book

Made in Japan

Akito Morita (born 1921) was the co-founder of Sony and the best known of the new wave of Japanese businessmen who rose to prominence in the West in the 1980s.

Akito Morita was an officer in the Japanese Navy during World War II. Trained as a physicist and scientist, Morita could have followed family tradition and gone into sake production. (He refers to himself as 'the first son and fifteenth generation heir to one of Japan's finest and oldest sake-brewing families'.) Instead, he founded a company with Masaru Ibuka (1908–97) immediately after the end of the war.

Ibuka was the technical expert; Morita the salesman. The company, was christened Tokyo Tsushin Kogyo KK (Tokyo Telecommunications Engineering Corporation). Not a good name to put on a product, Morita later ruminated. Initially, the company made radio parts and a rice cooker, among other things. Its rice cooker was unreliable.

In 1949 the company developed magnetic recording tape and, in 1950, sold the first tape recorder in Japan. In 1957 the company produced a pocket sized radio and a year later renamed itself Sony (*sonus* is Latin for sound). In 1960 it produced the first transistor TV in the world.

And increasingly the world was Sony's market. Its combination of smaller and smaller products at the leading edge of technology proved irresistible. In 1961 Sony Corporation of American was the first Japanese company to be listed on Wall Street and, in 1989, Sony bought Columbia Pictures so that by 1991 it had more foreigners on its 135,000 payroll than Japanese.

Morita became famous as the acceptable face of Japanese industry. Sophisticated and entrepreneurial, he did not fit the Western stereotype. (He also advocated a more assertive Japanese approach in *The Japan That Can Say No* which he wrote with a Japanese politician, Ishihara Shintaro.)

In 1993 Morita resigned as Sony chairman after suffering a cerebral hemorrhage playing tennis. In the same year, the company wrote off $3.2 billion for its movie operations – the major misadventure in its history. Even so, the modern Sony is a $37 billion company.

Morita and Sony's story parallels the rebirth of Japan as an industrial power. 'We in the free world can do great things. We proved it in Japan by changing the image of Made in Japan from something shoddy to something fine,' says Morita. When Sony was first attempting to make inroads into Western markets it cannot be forgotten that Japanese products were sneered at as being of the lowest quality. Surmounting that obstacle was a substantial business achievement.

Morita and Sony's gift was to invent new markets. Describing what he called Sony's 'pioneer spirit', Morita said: 'Sony is a pioneer and never intends to follow others. Through progress, Sony wants to serve the whole world. It shall be always a seeker of the unknown ... Sony has a principle of respecting and encouraging one's ability ... and always tries to bring out the best in a person. This is the vital force of Sony.' While companies such as Matsushita were inspired followers, Sony set a cracking pace with product after product, innovation after innovation.

Sony brought the world the hand-held video camera, the first home video recorder and the floppy disc. The blemishes on its record were the Betamax video format, which it failed to license, and color television systems.

Its most famous success was the brainchild of Morita, the Walkman. The evolution of this now ubiquitous product is the stuff of corporate legend. Morita noticed that young people liked listening to music wherever they went. He put two and two together and made a Walkman. 'I do not believe that any amount of market research could have told us that it would have been successful', he said adding the rider – 'The public does not know what is possible, we do'.

Such brilliant marketing was no mere accident. 'If you go through life convinced that your way is always best, all the new ideas in the world will pass you by', says Morita who argues that analysis and education do not necessarily get you to the best business decisions. 'You can be totally rational with a machine. But if you work with people, sometimes logic often has to take a backseat to understanding,' he says. Morita is also the author of *Never Mind School Records*.

Apart from his marketing prowess, Morita has emphasized the cultural differences in Japanese attitudes towards work. 'Never break another man's rice bowl', he advises and observes: 'Japanese people tend to be much better adjusted to the notion of work, any kind of work, as honorable'. Management is regarded by Morita as where the buck stops and starts: 'If we face a recession, we should not lay off employees; the company should sacrifice a profit. It's management's risk and management's responsibility. Employees are not guilty; why should they suffer?'

Bibliography

Made in Japan (with Edwin M. Reingold and Mitsuko Shimonura), Dutton, New York, 1986.

John Naisbitt

"The most reliable way to anticipate the future is by understanding the present."

John Naisbitt

American futurologist
Born 1930

Breakthrough ideas

Restructurings

Key books

Megatrends

John Naisbitt (born 1930) worked as an executive with IBM and Eastman Kodak, and has been a distinguished international fellow at the Institute of Strategic and International Studies in Kuala Lumpar. He is a futurologist whose books have sold in their millions. Naisbitt was educated at Cornell. Indeed, at one time Cornell could boast the top three authors in the bestseller lists as alumni – Naisbitt with his *Megatrends*, Kenneth Blanchard with *The One Minute Manager* and Tom Peters with *In Search of Excellence*.

The book that really established Naisbitt as someone worth listening to was the 1982 publication of *Megatrends*. It has sold over eight million copies and Naisbitt has also produced *Megatrends Asia*. In *Megatrends*, Naisbitt identified ten 'critical restructurings'. While some have proved accurate predictions of what has happened in intervening years, others have proved less accurate:

- 'Although we continue to think we live in an industrial society, we have in fact changed to an economy based on the creation and distribution of information.' This has become accepted and is now a hackneyed truism. In the early 1980s, however, traditional issues, such as production methods, still held sway. Naisbitt was ahead of the game. The technological possibilities in information exchange and transfer were contemplated by a small group in West coast laboratories.
- 'We are moving in the dual directions of high tech/high touch, matching each new technology with a compensatory human response.' This is a theme Naisbitt has returned to and developed in more recent years. 'The acceleration of technological progress has created an urgent need for a counter ballast – for high touch experiences. Heart transplants have led to new interest in family doctors and neighborhood clinics; jet airplanes have resulted in more face-to-face meetings. High touch is about getting back to a human scale,' he says. 'All change is local and bottom-up ... If you keep track of local events, you can see the shifting patterns. Also, remember that high-tech/high-touch isn't an either/or decision. You can't stop technological progress, but by the same token, you can hardly go wrong with a high-touch response. Give out your home phone number. Send a hand-

written letter. FedEx has all the reliability and efficiency of modern electronics, but its success is built on a form of high touch: hand delivery.'

- 'No longer do we have the luxury of operating within an isolated, self-sufficient, national economic system; we must now acknowledge that we are part of a global economy. We have begun to let go of the idea that the US is and must remain the world's industrial leader as we move on to other tasks.' Naisbitt was right to identify the emergence of globalization as a powerful force. His perception of a change in America's perception of itself is open to doubt. Naisbitt has gone onto explore what he calls the 'global paradox', which he believes is that 'The bigger the world economy, the more powerful its smallest player'.

- 'We are restructuring from a society run by short-term considerations and rewards in favor of dealing with things in much longer-term time frames.' There is little evidence, some 16 years on, that this trend has become a reality.

- 'In cities and states, in small organizations and subdivisions, we have rediscovered the ability to act innovatively and to achieve results – from the bottom up.' Naisbitt anticipated the fashion in the late eighties and early nineties for empowerment with responsibility being spread more evenly throughout organizations rather than centered on a coterie of managers.

- 'We are shifting from institutional help to more self-reliance in all aspects of our lives.' Trends in working patterns, such as employability, suggest that this is becoming the case for a select few professionals with marketable skills.

- 'We are discovering that the framework of representative democracy has become obsolete in an era of instantaneously shared information.' Alvin Toffler was suggesting this in his 1970 book *Future Shock,* though there are few signs of reform.

- 'We are giving up our dependence on hierarchical structures in favor of informal networks. This will be especially important to the business community.' This has become one of the great trends of the last decade as networks are developed in a bewildering variety of ways – with suppliers, between competitors, internally, globally. Technology has enabled networks never previously anticipated – with important repercussions. 'When everyone hears about everything at the same time, everyone else hears about it, and we all know that. Instantly. But we still have the same old system. So … we're going through a big period of correction,' says Naisbitt.[1] Linked to this is the entire question of speed which Naisbitt identified early on as a competitive weapon – 'Economies of scale are giving way to economies of scope, finding the right size for synergy, market flexibility, and above all, speed', he says in *The Global Paradox*.

- 'More Americans are living in the South and West leaving behind the old industrial cities of the North.' In the era of Silicon Valley *et al.* this is stating the obvious, but in the 1980s it was less so.
- 'From a narrow either/or society with a limited range of personal choices, we are exploding into a free-wheeling multiple option society.' To this, Naisbitt could have added the caveat that this society would offer multiple options but only for a few.

Aside from these trends, Naisbitt has championed the role of small business in generating the wealth of the future. 'Small companies, right down to the individual, can beat big bureaucratic companies ten out of ten times. Unless big companies reconstitute themselves as a collection of small companies, they will just continue to go out of business. It's the small companies who are creating the global company,' he says.[2]

Notes

1   Interview with John Naisbitt, *Star Tribune*, November 1996.
2   Gibson, Rowan (editor), *Rethinking the Future*, Nicholas Brealey, London, 1996.

Bibliography

Megatrends, Warner Books, 1984.
Global Paradox, William Morrow & Co., New York, 1994.

Kenichi Ohmae

"In strategic thinking, one first seeks a clear understanding of the particular character of each element of a situation and then makes the fullest possible use of human brain power to restructure the elements in the most advantageous way."

Kenichi Ohmae

Japanese consultant and author
Born 1943

Breakthrough ideas

Strategy and key factors for success
Japanese business thinking
Impact of globalization on nations

Key books

The Mind of the Strategist
The Borderless World

W hen **Kenichi Ohmae** (born 1943) left the consulting firm McKinsey to stand for the governorship of Tokyo in 1995, the firm's departure announcement noted Ohmae was 'a great consultant, a compelling speaker, an incredibly prolific writer, a musician and a motorcyclist'. While the significance of the latter accomplishment is difficult to determine, there is no doubting Ohmae's credentials as a modern Renassiance man. It is reputed that Ohmae's comment on his departure was that it was simply a question of changing clients to all of Japan.

Modesty would ill suit Ohmae's qualifications and credentials. Even among the brilliant minds of McKinsey he stood out. Ohmae is a graduate of Waseda University, the Tokyo Institute of Technology, and has a PhD in nuclear engineering from Massachusetts Institute of Technology. He is also a talented flautist and some time advisor to the former Japanese Prime Minster Nakasone. Ohmae joined McKinsey in 1972, becoming managing director of its Tokyo office. McKinsey Americanized him as 'Ken' but the ambitions of his thinking remained resolutely global.

Indeed, Ohmae's book *The Borderless World* concluded with a 'Declaration of Interdependence toward the world' signed by Ohmae and McKinsey's Fred Gluck and Herbert Henzler. It was immodestly noted below that 'this statement ... is one we each embrace and believe to be the best possible course for all countries and governments to follow'. In the declaration, the trio contended that the role of central governments must change to 'allow individuals access to the best and cheapest goods and services from anywhere in the world; help corporations provide stable and rewarding jobs anywhere in the world regardless of the corporation's national identity; coordinate activities with other governments to minimize conflicts arising from narrow interests; and avoid abrupt changes in economic and social fundamentals.' It called on governments to 'deal collectively with traditionally parochial affairs' including taxation.

Away from such bold pronouncements, Ohmae's work is important for two reasons. First, he revealed the truth behind Japanese strategy-making to an expectant Western audience. He demonstrated that the Japanese were human after all – at the time, Western managers were beginning to wonder. Second, Ohmae has explored the ramifications of globalization more extensively than virtually any other thinker.

Ohmae's first contribution was to explode simplistic Western myths about Japanese management. Forget company songs and lifetime employment, there was more to Japanese management than that. Most notably there was the Japanese art of strategic thinking. This, said Ohmae, is 'basically creative and intuitive and rational' – though none of these characteristics were evident in the usual Western stereotype of Japanese management. Peters and Waterman, McKinsey colleagues, quoted Ohmae in *In Search of Excellence*: 'Most Japanese companies don't even have a reasonable organization chart. Nobody knows how Honda is organized, except that it uses lots of project teams and is quite flexible ... Innovation typically occurs at the interface, requiring multiple disciplines. Thus, the flexible Japanese organization has now, especially, become an asset.'[1]

In 1982, when *In Search of Excellence* was published, Ohmae's *The Mind of the Strategist* also reached America – though it had been published in Japan in 1975. Ohmae pointed out that unlike large US corporations, Japanese businesses tend not to have large strategic planning staffs. Instead they often have a single, naturally talented strategist with 'an idiosyncratic mode of thinking in which company, customers, and competition merge in a dynamic interaction out of which a comprehensive set of objectives and plans for action eventually crystallizes'.

Ohmae also noted that the customer was at the heart of the Japanese approach to strategy and key to corporate values. 'In the construction of any business strategy, three main players must be taken into account: the corporation itself, the customer, and the competition. Each of these "strategic three Cs" is a living entity with its own interests and objectives. We shall call them, collectively, the "strategic triangle",' he said. 'Seen in the context of the strategic triangle, the job of the strategist is to achieve superior performance, relative to competition, in the key factors for success of the business. At the same time, the strategist must be sure that his strategy properly matches the strengths of the corporation with the needs of a clearly defined market. Positive matching of the needs and objectives of the two parties involved is required for a lasting good relationship; without it, the corporation's long-term viability may be at stake.'

The central thrust of Ohmae's arguments was that strategy as epitomized by the Japanese approach is irrational and non-linear. (Previously, the Japanese had been feted in the West for the brilliance of their rationality and the far-sighted remorselessness of their thinking.) 'Phenomena and events in the real world do not always fit a linear model. Hence the most reliable means of dissecting a situation into its constituent parts and reassembling them in the desired pattern is not a step-by-step methodology such as systems analysis. Rather, it is that ultimate non-linear thinking tool, the human brain. True strategic thinking thus contrasts sharply with the conventional mechanical systems approach based on linear thinking. But it also contrasts with the approach that stakes everything on intuition, reaching conclusions without any real breakdown or analysis.'

Ohmae went on to suggest that an effective business strategy 'is one, by which a company can gain significant ground on its competitors at an acceptable cost to itself'. This can be achieved in four ways: by focusing on the key factors for success (KFSs); by building on relative superiority; through pursuing aggressive initiatives; and the final route to an effective strategy is through utilizing strategic degrees of freedom. By this, Ohmae means that the company can focus upon innovation in areas which are 'untouched by competitors'.

The second area which Ohmae has greatly influenced is that of globalization. In *Triad Power* (1985), he suggested that the route to global competitiveness is to establish a presence in each area of the Triad (United States; Japan and the Pacific; Europe). Also, companies must utilize the three Cs of commitment, creativity and competitiveness.

To Ohmae, countries are mere governmental creations. In the Interlinked Economy (also made up of the Triad) consumers are not driven to purchase things through nationalistic sentiments – no matter what politicians suggest or say. 'At the cash register, you don't care about country of origin or country of residence. You don't think about employment figures or trade deficits,' Ohmae wrote. This, he argues, also applies to industrial consumers.

Ohmae has since gone on to explore the role of nations still further and now suggests that we have reached a time when 'the end of the nation state' is imminent.

Globalization and strategy continue to be at the heart of Ohmae's recent work. 'The essence of business strategy is offering better value to customers than the competition, in the most cost-effective and sustainable way,' Ohmae writes. 'But today, thousands of competitors from every corner of the world are able to serve customers well. To develop effective strategy, we as leaders have to understand what's happening in the rest of the world, and reshape our organization to respond accordingly. No leader can hope to guide an enterprise into the future without understanding the commercial, political and social impact of the global economy.'[2]

Ohmae believes that the global economy is the result of a number of forces. First, there are booming regional economies. Instead of talking about countries as economic units, we need to begin thinking in terms of regions. To Ohmae, the question is whether to invest in Catalonia, Wales, Alsace-Lorraine rather than Spain, the UK or France.

The second factor is the much reported growth in new media and information technology. Ohmae points out that full utilization of technology requires 'new laws, policies and relationships among business, government, individuals and communities'. There is more to technology than sitting in the same place doing the same things quicker.

The third factor is the rise of universal, consumer cultures. Technology and the global dominance of certain products mean that we are all Californians now. The obvious corollary of this is that there are huge economies of scale to be made. Global standards 'lay the groundwork for enormous generation of wealth'. Though Ohmae adds that small companies can still succeed by imaginatively nipping at the heels of their larger competitors.

To meet these challenges, Ohmae suggests that corporate leaders should concentrate on building networks. 'We have to learn to share, sort and synthesise information, rather than simply direct the work of others. We have to rethink our basic approach to decision making, risk taking and organizational strategy. And we have to create meaning and uphold values in flatter, more disciplined enterprises,' Ohmae concludes. We will, it seems, have to forget the past in order to create the future.

Notes

1   Peters, Tom, and Waterman, Robert, *In Search of Excellence*, Harper & Row, New York, 1982.
2   Ohmae, Kenichi, 'Strategy in a world without borders', *Leader to Leader*, Winter 1998.

Bibliography

The Mind of the Strategist, McGraw Hill, New York, 1982.
Triad Power: The Coming Shape of Global Competition, Free Press, New York, 1985.
The Borderless World, William Collins, London, 1990.
The Evolving Global Economy (editor) Harvard Business School Press, Boston, MA, 1995.
The End of the Nation State, HarperCollins, London, 1995.

David Packard

"You shouldn't gloat about anything you've done; you ought to keep going and try to find something better to do."

David Packard

American executive
1912–96

Breakthrough ideas

MBWA
Employee involvement

Key book

The HP Way

W hen they were assembling their list of 'excellent' companies in the late 1970s, Tom Peters and Robert Waterman included Hewlett-Packard. It was one of their least controversial choices. Similarly, when Jerry Porras and James Collins wrote *Built to Last*, their celebration of long-lived companies, there was no doubt that Hewlett-Packard was worthy of inclusion. In 1985, *Fortune* ranked Hewlett-Packard as one of the two most highly admired companies in America. The company is ranked similarly in virtually every other poll on well-managed companies or ones which would be good to work for. Hewlett-Packard has pulled off an unusual double: it is admired and successful.

David Packard (1912–96) was one half of the partnership which created one of the business and management benchmarks of the century. In 1937, with a mere $538 and a rented garage in Palo Alto, Bill Hewlett and David Packard created one of the most successful corporations in the world. The two had met while students at nearby Stanford. Their ambitions were typical of many young people starting a business. 'We thought we would have a job for ourselves. That's all we thought about in the beginning,' said Packard. 'We hadn't the slightest idea of building a big company.' The garage was the birthplace of Silicon Valley.

In their first year of business Hewlett and Packard achieved sales of $5100 with $1300 in profits. Hewlett-Packard's first success was a device for measuring sound waves which they sold to Walt Disney. An automatic lettuce thinner and a shock machine to help people lose weight followed. They also pondered on the market opportunities for automatic urinal flushers, bowling alley sensors and air conditioning equipment. The duo left the garage for good in 1940.

During wartime the business flourished, employing 144 people at its height. Immediately after the war, sales fell off – by half in 1946 alone. Undaunted, Hewlett and Packard hired technical talent. The business revived. By 1948, the company's sales were $2.1 million.

Their secret, said Hewlett and Packard, lay in the simplicity of their methods. 'Professors of management are devastated when I say we were successful because we had no plans. We just took on odd jobs,' said Hewlett. But their legacy is not the efficiency of their lettuce thinner or the quality of their urinal flusher, it lies in the culture of the company they created and the management style they used to run it, the H-P way.

From the very start, Hewlett-Packard worked to a few fundamental principles. It did not believe in long-term borrowing to secure the expansion of the business. Its recipe for growth was simply that its products needed to be leaders in their markets. It got on with the job. 'Our main task is to design, develop and manufacture the finest [electronic equipment] for the advancement of science and the welfare of humanity. We intend to devote ourselves to that task,' said Packard in a 1961 memo to employees.

The duo eschewed fashionable management theory. 'If I hear anybody talking about how big their share of the market is or what they're trying to do to increase their share of the market, I'm going to personally see that a black mark gets put in their personnel folder,' Packard said in a 1974 speech.

The company believed that people could be trusted and should always be treated with respect and dignity. 'We both felt fundamentally that people want to do a good job. They just need guidelines on how to do it,' said Packard.

H-P believed that management should be available and involved – Managing By Wandering About was the motto. Indeed, rather than the administrative suggestions of management, Packard preferred to talk of leadership.

If there was conflict, it had to be tackled through communication and consensus rather than confrontation.

'Their legacy, and the achievement that Packard was most proud of, is a management style based on openness and respect for the individual,' noted Louise Kehoe of the *Financial Times* in Packard's obituary.[1]

Hewlett-Packard was a company built on very simple ideas. While all about were turning into conglomerates, Hewlett and Packard kept their heads down and continued with their methods. When their divisions grew too big – and by that they meant around 1500 people – they split them up to ensure that they didn't spiral out of control.

They kept it simple. Nice guys built a nice company. They didn't do anything too risky or too outlandish. (Packard was skeptical about pocket calculators though, in the end, the company was an early entrant into the market.) They didn't bet the company on a big deal or get into debt. Indeed, in his research Richard Pascale identified 'terminal niceness' as a potential problem for the company. Being criticized for being too good could only happen in the business world.

For living up to their simple standards, Hewlett-Packard deserve acknowledgment.

Indeed, their values worked to save the company when times were hard. During the 1970s recession, Hewlett-Packard staff took a 10 percent pay cut and worked 10 percent less hours. If the company hadn't had a long-term commitment to employee stock ownership perhaps they wouldn't have been so keen to make sacrifices.

Commitment to people, clearly fostered commitment to the company. 'The most extraordinary trait at Hewlett-Packard is uniformity of commitment, the consistency of approach and attitude. Wherever you go in the HP empire, you find people talking product quality, feeling proud of their division's achievements in that area. HP people at all levels show boundless energy and enthusiasm,' observed Peters and Waterman in *In Search of Excellence*.

David Packard was also involved in politics. He was deputy defense secretary in the Nixon administration (1969–71) and also worked on a variety of government commissions. A devout Republican to the end, he supported George Bush against Bill Clinton and warned of being 'caught in the updraft of Bill Clinton's hot air balloon'.

Both Packard and Hewlett felt that Stanford engineering professor Frederick Terman had launched their careers. They gave donations of over $300 million to Stanford. Packard also gave $40 million to found the Monterey Bay Aquarium. It is estimated that his private family foundation has given $480 million to good causes.

Packard retired as chairman in 1993. On his death in 1996, the company had 100,000 employees in 120 countries with revenues of $31 billion.

Notes

1   Kehoe, Louise, 'Radical who built group with open management style', *Financial Times*, 28 March 1996.

Bibliography

The HP Way, HarperBusiness, New York, 1995.

Richard Pascale

"Managerial behavior is predicated on the assumption that we should rationally order the behavior of those we manage. That mindset needs to be challenged.**"**

Richard Pascale

American consultant and academic
Born 1938

Breakthrough ideas

Seven S framework
Japanese management
Corporate transformation

Key books

The Art of Japanese Management
Managing on the Edge

Richard Pascale (born 1938) first came to the attention of a large audience with the advent of the Seven S framework, one of the most renowned and debated management tools of the 1980s. The framework emerged from a series of meetings during June 1978 between Pascale, Anthony Athos, then of Harvard Business School, and the McKinsey consultants, Tom Peters and Robert Waterman who were already involved in the research which was to form the basis of *In Search of Excellence*.

The evolution of the Seven S framework provides an insight into the haphazard means by which many influential ideas see the light of day. Initially a meeting was arranged between the quartet. 'Athos said we needed an agenda for the five days otherwise we'd be driven round the bend by Peters – he's so energetic, such a scatter shot. Otherwise we wouldn't survive the five days,' Pascale recalls. 'Athos said he had given it some thought and said there was a guy at Harvard, Chuck Gibson, who had a scheme – strategy, structure and systems. He had developed these three Ss for Harvard's PMD Program of which he and Tony were in charge. So why didn't we start with strategy on Monday then move on to structure on Tuesday and systems on Wednesday. Athos said he had a couple of his own to add – superordinate goals and shared values. I was working on *The Art of Japanese Management* [published in 1981] so was interested in the idea of shared values. Athos insisted on superordinate goals and I contributed style. So we walked in with five of the Seven Ss.'[1]

Athos and Pascale persuaded Waterman and Peters to use alliteration. Peters and Pascale then suggested another variable was needed, one concerned with timing and implementation. Athos and Pascale proposed calling it 'sequencing'.

Julian Phillips of McKinsey who also joined the group, argued vigorously for replacing *sequencing* with *staff*. 'Since everyone was having trouble with sequencing it was easy to drop,' say Athos and Pascale. 'And since Peters was proposing that *people* and *power* needed somehow to be included (Athos was adding *aggregates of people* at Harvard), it was also possible to agree that staff was an addition which resolved various concerns, Thus, the final Seven S Framework came into being.'

The Seven Ss (strategy, structure, skills, staff, shared values, systems and style) are a kind of *aide memoire*, a useful memory jogger of what concerns organizations. The Seven S Framework gained a great deal of attention though, as a generic statement of the issues facing organizations, it was unremarkable. (Tom Peters himself initially thought it 'corny' – though Peters and Waterman used it a year later in *In Search of Excellence* – published a year after *The Art of Japanese Management*.) 'The framework is nothing more than seven important categories that managers pay attention to', Pascale later noted in *Managing on the Edge*. 'There is nothing sacred about the number seven. There could be six or eight Ss. The value of a framework such as the Seven Ss is that it imposes an interesting discipline on the researcher.'

From Pascale's perspective the Seven Ss presented a way into comparisons between US and Japanese management. Pascale and Athos concluded that the Japanese succeeded largely because of the attention they gave to the soft Ss – style, shared values, skills and staff. In contrast, the West remained preoccupied with the hard Ss of strategy, structure and systems. These conclusions formed the bedrock of *The Art of Japanese Management* (1981), which was one of the first business bestsellers.

At the time of the development of the Seven S framework, Pascale was a member of the faculty at Stanford's Graduate School of Business. He taught there for 20 years and his course on organizational survival was reputed to be the most popular on the Stanford MBA program. Pascale has since worked as an independent consultant. He has also been a White House Fellow, Special Assistant to the Secretary of Labor and Senior Staff of a White House Task Force reorganizing the President's executive office. He is also the author of *Managing on the Edge* (1990).

In addition to the Seven S framework, Pascale's work is significant for a number of reasons. First, he was among the first researchers to provide original insights into Japanese approaches to business and management. Working for the US's National Commission on Productivity, Pascale initially thought that lessons from Japan were limited for cultural reasons. He then decided more fertile ground lay in looking at Japanese companies in the US. His research eventually covered 34 companies over six years

The second area of Pascale's work which gained popular attention was that of vision. This was identified by he and Athos as one of the key components of Japanese management. Their championing of vision proved highly influential. Today, corporate visions are a fact of life though many fail to match the Japanese practice mapped out by Pascale and Athos in which visions are dynamic, vivifying *modus operandi* rather than pallid or generic statements of corporate intent.

The third element of Pascale's work are the related areas of corporate mortality and corporate transformation. In the late 1980s and 1990s, Pascale has drawn attention to the fragile foundations on which our grand corporate assumptions are made. *Managing on the Edge* begins with the line 'Nothing fails like success'. 'Great strengths are inevitably the root of weakness,' argued Pascale, pausing only to point out that from the *Fortune 500* of 1985 143 had departed five years later. Since then there have been various studies of corporate longevity – most notably Arie de Geus' *The Living Company* (1997).

Pascale contends that four factors 'drive stagnation and renewal in organizations':

1 **Fit** – pertains to an organization's internal consistency (unity)
2 **Split** – describes a variety of techniques for breaking a bigger organization into smaller units and providing them with a stronger sense of ownership and identity (plurality)
3 **Contend** – refers to a management process that harnesses (rather than suppresses) the contradictions that are inevitable by-products of organizations (duality)
4 **Transcend** – alerts us to the higher order of complexity that successfully managing the renewal process entails (vitality).

To overcome such inertia and survive in a turbulent climate requires a constant commitment to what Pascale labels 'corporate transformation'. Change, says Pascale, is a fact of business life. The trouble is we are ill-equipped to deal with it and our traditional approach to managing change is no longer applicable. 'The incremental approach to change is effective when what you want is more of what you've already got. Historically, that has been sufficient because our advantages of plentiful resources, geographical isolation, and absence of serious global competition defined a league in which we competed with ourselves and everyone played by the same rules.'

True transformation requires the involvement and commitment of all in the organization. The problem with programmes of change does not usually lie with the programmes themselves. Instead, their central limitation is that they are driven by and involve so few people.

Incorporating employees fully into the principal business challenges facing the company is the first 'intervention' required if companies are to thrive. The second is to lead the organization in a way which sharpens and maintains incorporation and 'constructive stress'. Finally, Pascale advocates instilling mental disciplines that will make people behave differently and then help them sustain their new behaviour. In the latter element, Pascale cites the work of the United States Army – in which a strong culture allows minds and behavior to be changed through rigorous and carefully thought through training.[2]

In particular, Pascale has examined the work of the Army's National Training Center in California. 'The Army's success stems from: every one of its soldiers having a shared and intricate understanding of what drives 'business results'; cultivating relentless discomfort with the status quo ... and establishing a standard of uncompromising straight talk that evokes cross-hierarchical feedback and introspection,' he says.[3]

The Center puts units of 3000–4000 people through a gruelling 14-day programme involving 600 instructors, 18-hour days, simulated battles and 'After Action Reviews' where, says Pascale, 'hardship and insight meet'. Pascale believes that what makes this intense training effective is its concentration on identifying the key tasks that drive success; the immersion of the teams in the tasks they encounter; the collection of hard data to avoid subjectivity and needless debate; the use of highly trained facilitators; and a fundamental belief in not criticizing people. Interestingly, the Center does not evaluate performance. Instead its onus is on how much each person can learn. The lessons for industry are important, says Pascale: only immersion in an environment of learning, constant questioning and openness can create a culture geared to transformation. (There is only one drawback in converting the Army's methods into the corporate world: cost – 'all it takes is 650,000 acres and a million dollars a day'.)

In his recent work, Pascale has coined the term agility to describe the combination of skills and thinking required of the organizations of the future. Pascale and his co-researchers believe that there are 'four indicators that tell us a great deal about how an organization is likely to perform and adapt'. These are power (do employees think they can have any influence on the course of events?); identity (to what extent do individuals identify with the organization as a whole, rather than with a narrow group); contention (is conflict brought out into the open and used as a learning tool); and learning (how does the organization deal with new ideas?).[4]

The trouble is that these four elements, under normal circumstances, tend to coagulate and the organization eventually stagnates. Pascale says that this can only be avoided if an organization pursues seven disciplines of agility – which range from the self-explanatory 'accountability in action' to the more elusive and painful 'course of relentless discomfort'.

Pascale's vision of the future is a troubling one. To survive companies must continually move on, using the agility engendered by their individuals and culture to ask questions, discuss the undiscussable and shake things up. Case studies of this in practice are few and far between.

Notes

1   Interview with the author, 23 July 1996.
2   Pascale, Richard, Millemann , Mark, and Gioja, Linda, 'Changing the way we change', *Harvard Business Review*, November/December 1997.
3   Pascale, Richard, 'Manoeuvres for the millennium', *Human Resources*, November/December 1996.
4   Golzen, Godfrey, 'The next big idea', *Human Resources*, March/April 1997.

Bibliography

The Art of Japanese Management (with Anthony Athos), Penguin, London, 1981.
Managing on the Edge, Viking, London, 1990.

Laurence J. Peter

"In an organization, each person rises to the level of his own incompetency."

Laurence Peter

Canadian author and educator
1919–90

Breakthrough ideas

Career mismanagement

Key book

The Peter Principle

T here is precious little to laugh about in the work and thoughts of management thinkers. The few exceptions therefore stand out as eccentric beacons of hope. There are perhaps three key mileposts of business humor which have mirrored changes in corporate life.

The first was Parkinson's Law. This was a brilliantly comic exposé of bureaucracy by the British academic C. Northcote Parkinson (see Appendix). It owed its inspiration to tortuous administration and the pointless shuffling of paper. Parkinson's Law was simply that work expands to fill the time available for its completion. As a result, companies grow without thinking of how much they are producing. Even if growth in numbers doesn't make them more money, companies grow and people become busier and busier. Parkinson observed that 'an official wants to multiply subordinates, not rivals' and 'officials make work for each other'.

Parkinson's Law took the logic of mass production and applied it to administration. You can measure and prescribe all you like but it is doomed to failure. Parkinson wryly and accurately debunked the notion of a particular task having an optimum time for completion. There were no rules – it depended on the person doing the job and their unique situation. 'An elderly lady of leisure can spend an entire day in writing and dispatching a postcard to her niece at Bognor Regis', wrote Parkinson. 'An hour will be spent in finding the postcard, another in hunting for spectacles, half-an-hour in a search for the address, an hour and a quarter in composition, and twenty minutes in deciding whether or not to take an umbrella when going to the pillar-box in the next street. The total effort which would occupy a busy man for three minutes all told, may, in this fashion, leave another person prostrate after a day of doubt, anxiety and toil.'

The theory was not simply an exercise in superficial cynicism. Parkinson backed it up with statistics. He pointed out, for example, that the number of admiralty officials in the British Navy increased by 78 percent between 1914 and 1928 while the number of ships fell by 67 percent and the number of officers and men by 31 percent. Parkinson concluded that the expansion of administrators tends to take on a life of its own – 'The Officials would have multiplied at the same rate had there been no actual seamen at all'.

While Parkinson aimed his jibes at bureaucracy, the next comic master targeted the absurdities of the corporation and management hierarchies. **Laurence J. Peter** (1919–90) was a Canadian academic. Being a man of the world in possession of sight and the normal faculties, he observed incompetence everywhere he looked. The result was the Peter Principle which said that managers in an organization rise to their level of incompetence, through being promoted until they failed to do well in their current job. 'For each individual, for you, for me, the final promotion is from a level of competence to a level of incompetence', wrote Peter, going on to advise that the final promotion should not be taken as inevitable – 'If at first you don't succeed, you may be at your level of incompetence'.

The greatness of Peter lay in the fact that his humor is grounded very solidly in corporate reality. Anyone who has ever worked for an organization can identify with his observations – 'There are two kinds of failures: those who thought and never did, and those who did and never thought'; 'Fortune knocks once, but misfortune has much more patience'; 'There are two sorts of losers – the good loser, and the other one who can't act'; or 'If you don't know where you are going, you will probably end up somewhere else'.

Peter's work was an antidote to the many hundreds of books which celebrate corporate success stories. We all know that farce and failure dog our lives. Peter simply reminded us of this. Around his basic joke, Peter wove a mass of aphorisms and *bon mots*. These included: 'An economist is an expert who will know tomorrow why the things he predicted yesterday didn't happen'; and 'Originality is the fine art of remembering what you hear but forgetting where you heard it'.

Peter's book, *The Peter Principle* (co-authored with Raymond Hull) also features an essential glossary which includes 'tabulatory giantism: obsession with large size desks' and 'free-floating apex: a supervisor with no subordinates'. Under 'exceptions' the entry is forthright: 'There are no exceptions to the Peter Principle'.

The final comic perspective comes from Scott Adams (born 1957) and his Dilbert cartoon. This is now the biggest selling business book of all time. Adams takes the Peter Principle a stage further. 'Now, apparently, the incompetent workers are promoted directly to management without ever passing through the temporary competence stage', reflects Adams. 'When I entered the workforce in 1979, the Peter Principle described management pretty well. Now I think we'd all like to return to those Golden Years when you had a boss who was once good at something.'[1]

Adams' themes are much the same as Peter's and Parkinson's: failure, incompetence and fear of being caught failing or being incompetent. 'In the old days it was important to be able to run down an antelope and kill it with a single blow to the forehead. But that skill is becoming less important every year,' says Adams. 'Now all that matters is if you can install your own Ethernet card without having to call tech support and confess your inadequacies to a stranger whose best career option is to work in tech support.'

Notes

1   Adams, Scott, 'The Dilbert principle', *Wall Street Journal*, 22 May 1995.

Bibliography

The Peter Principle (with Raymond Hull), William Morrow & Co., New York, 1969.
The Peter Plan, Bantam Books, 1981.
Why Things Go Wrong or the Peter Principle Revisited, William Morrow & Co., New York, 1984.
Peter's Quotations: Ideas For Our Time, Quill, 1993.

Tom Peters

'You can't think your way out of a box, you've got to act.'

Tom Peters

American consultant, speaker and author
Born 1942

Breakthrough ideas

Excellence
Customer service

Key books

In Search of Excellence
Liberation Management

I n 1982 Thomas J. Peters and Robert H. Waterman's *In Search of Excellence* was published. It marked a watershed in business book publishing. Since 1982, the business book market has exploded into a multi-million pound global extravaganza. And, in parallel, the management guru industry has burgeoned.

Tom Peters (born 1942) was born and brought up near Baltimore. He studied engineering at Cornell University and served in Vietnam. He also worked for the drug enforcement agency in Washington. Peters has an MBA and PhD from Stanford where he encountered a number of influential figures including Gene Webb and Harold Leavitt. After Stanford he joined the consultancy firm, McKinsey & Company. He left the firm (prior to the publication of *In Search of Excellence*) to work independently. He continues to travel the world giving seminars.

Tom Peters was both a beneficiary and the instigator of the boom in business books and the rise of the guru business. He was, in effect, the first management guru. While his predecessors were doughty, low-profile academics, Peters was high-profile and media friendly. After *In Search of Excellence* stormed unexpectedly up the bestseller lists, he traveled the world with bewildering speed, delivering seminar after seminar, quote after quote. The McKinsey consultant in his regulation dull suit, Thomas J. Peters, became a celebrity, charging celebrity rates (around $90,000 a day outside of the US). A business sprung up around him. First there were the books, then the videos, the consultancy and the conferences. The medium threatened to engulf the message.

Peters' critics suggest that while he may have raised awareness, he has done so in a superficial way. He has pandered to the masses. Though his messages are often hard hitting they are overly adorned with empty phrase making – 'yesterday's behemoths are out of step with tomorrow's madcap marketplace'- and with insufficient attention to the details of implementation.

And, over the years, the message has been radically overhauled. Tom Peters' ideas have been refined, popularized and, in many cases, entirely changed. While academics shift directions slowly and quietly in the obscurity of academic journals, Peters does so in front of audiences of hundreds. The standard, and often voiced, criticism of Peters is that there is little consistency in his thinking. What he celebrates today is liable to be dismissed in his next book – 'I decide to write a new book when I feel disgusted and embarrassed by my previous one,' he says.[1] His critics suggest that Tom Peters vacillates as readily as he pontificates.

A look at Peters' books proves that this is undoubtedly true. *In Search of Excellence* celebrated big companies. Its selection of 43 'excellent' organizations featured such names as IBM, General Electric, Proctor & Gamble, Johnson & Johnson and Exxon. The choices were hardly original or surprising – though none of the reviews of the book disputed the selection. At the time, Peters and Waterman were McKinsey consultants and their selection reflected a natural bias towards the corporate giants which were McKinsey's customers. (The only risky choice, as Peters recalls, was Wal-Mart, which then proceeded to out-perform virtually all the others.) 'The book's chief failure, in retrospect, was that Waterman and I – both from conventional roots – mainly examined conventional firms', says Peters.

The choices were large, and largely uncontroversial and unsurprising – including the likes of IBM, Hewlett-Packard, Wal-Mart and General Electric. (While the book celebrated the successful techniques employed by large companies many of the techniques are more easily and successfully employed by smaller companies. This also explains the book's perennial appeal.) '*Search* was an out-and-out attack on the excesses of the *rational model* and the *business strategy paradigm* that had come to dominate Western management thinking. What it counseled instead was a return to first principles: attention to customers ('close to the customer'), an abiding concern for people ('productivity through people'), and the celebration of trial and error ('a bias for action'),' wrote Peters later. 'But whether or not Bob Waterman and I were on management's case or on its side, there are more important fish to fry. To wit, an enormous error that resided between the lines: While *Search* condemned the excesses of dispassionate *modern management practice*, it nonetheless celebrated big manufacturing businesses. With the exaltation of IBM and more than one nod to GM, we implicitly endorsed the humongous American technocratic enterprise in general – the institutions that economist John Kenneth Galbraith and business historian Alfred Chandler had not so long before declared almost perfect instruments for achieving America's economic manifest destiny. Make no mistake,

Bob Waterman and I, who came of age in the '50s and '60s, were Galbraith's and Chandler's offspring!'[2]

In Search of Excellence presented, on the surface at least, the bright side of an American crisis. The Japanese were seemingly taking over the industrial world, unemployment was rising, depression was a reality and the prospects for the future looked bleak. Managerial prescriptions were bleak – Robert Hayes and William Abernathy's *Harvard Business Review* article, 'Managing our way to economic decline', summed up the air of despondency. The management world was ready for good news and Peters and Waterman provided it.

Peters views it a little differently: *'In Search of Excellence* was the first book written about things that work. It was purposeful. Hayes and Abernathy trashed American management and wrote it in the Harvard manual. Admittedly, the logic of the book was that American management was screwed up. It was a brutal, upfront attack on American management and McKinsey thinking. Okay it was 75 percent about islands of hope but that was what they were: exceptional. I consider *In Search of Excellence* a bad news book.'[3]

For such a trailblazing book, *In Search of Excellence* is, in retrospect at least, surprisingly uncontroversial. Peters and Waterman admitted that what they had to say was not particularly original. But, they also had the insight to observe that the ideas they were espousing had been generally left behind, ignored or overlooked by management theorists.

Peters and Waterman's conclusions were distilled down into eight crucial characteristics. These have largely stood the test of time:

- a bias for action
- close to the customer
- autonomy and entrepreneurship
- productivity through people
- hands-on values driven
- stick to the knitting
- simple form, lean staff
- simultaneous loose–tight properties.

Two years after *In Search of Excellence* was published, an American business magazine covered its front page with a single headline: 'Oops!'

It then went on to reveal that the companies featured in *In Search of Excellence* were anything but excellent. The article claimed that about a quarter of the 'excellent' companies were struggling.

The single and undeniable fact that the excellent companies of 1982 were no longer all excellent two years later has continued to haunt Peters. 'We started to get beaten up. When the magazine ran the *Oops* story it was a bad week,' says Peters. 'I was certain the phone would stop ringing. I wouldn't disagree that I had been on the road too much and in that respect it was a great wake up call.'

The phone didn't stop ringing and Peters' next two books carried on in much the same vein. *A Passion for Excellence* emphasized the need for leadership. Co-written with Nancy Austin, it was hugely successful but added little in the way of ideas. '*A Passion for Excellence* is probably my sixth favorite of my six books', Peters admits. 'It was a collection of stories collected on the road. It is hopelessly disorganized, a haphazard collection of anecdotes awkwardly shoved into a framework. It came from me talking to zillions of people and seminars, so it wasn't the best written book and the published version is a nightmare, but people still come up to me about the vignettes. People read it for the soundbites.'

But Peters' audience were increasingly restless. They believed what he said. They agreed that customer service was critical and that layer upon layer of bureaucracy was pointless. His next book, *Thriving on Chaos,* was an answer to the big question: how could you become excellent?

Thriving on Chaos opened with the bravado proclamation: 'There are no excellent companies.' This is probably the most quoted single line from Peters' work – either used as proof of his inconsistency, as evidence that he learned from his mistakes or as a damning indictment of his propensity to write in slogans. *Thriving on Chaos* was a lengthy riposte to all those critics who suggested that Peters' theories could not be turned into reality. Each chapter ended with a short list of suggested action points. '*Thriving on Chaos* was the final, engineering-like, tidying up', says Peters. 'It was organized in a hyper-organized engineering fashion.'

The major change in Peters' thinking occurred at the beginning of the 1990s. In effect, Peters dismissed the past and heralded in a brave new world of small units, freewheeling project-based structures, hierarchy-free teams in constant communication. Big was no longer beautiful and corporate structure, previously ignored by Peters, was predominant. After speaking on customer service for the previous decade, Peters noted 'If you've done all the close-to-the-customer things that I begged you to do in my first three books … I'm not sure you'll be any *closer* five years from now than you are today'.

Peters contended that his previous work was marred by paying too little attention to the perennially vexed question of organizational structure. Peters did not mean structure in the traditional hierarchical and functional sense. Indeed, his exemplars of the new organizational structure were notable for their apparent lack of structure. And herein lay Peters' point. Companies such as CNN, ABB and Body Shop thrived through having highly flexible structures able to change to meet the business needs of the moment. Free-flowing, impossible to pin down, unchartable, simple yet complex, these were the paradoxical structures of the future. 'Tomorrow's effective organization will be conjured up anew each day', Peters pronounced.

Key to the new corporate structures envisaged by Peters were networks with customers, with suppliers and, indeed, anyone else who could help the business deliver. 'Old ideas about size must be scuttled. "New big", which can be very big indeed, is "network big". That is, size measured by market power, say, is a function of the firm's extended family of fleeting and semi-permanent cohorts, not so much a matter of what it owns and directly controls,' he wrote.

New organizations demanded new management skills. Peters bade farewell to command and control, ushered in a new era characterized by 'curiosity, initiative, and the exercise of imagination'.

Examining his output, Peters is engagingly candid. 'My books could be by different authors. I have no patience with consistency so regard it as a good thing. I consider inconsistency as a compliment,' he says. 'When I'm writing I think whether people who've influenced me would throw tomatoes at it or not. To some extent I am a translator who is good at finding interesting examples which make it relevant to people.'

To Peters the moment is all important. If what he sees and what he thinks runs totally counter to what he has previously argued, it is simply proof that circumstances have changed. (Not for nothing did

Peters name his boat 'The Cromwell' inspired by Cromwell's comment 'No one rises so high as he who knows not whither he is going.')

Indeed, what distinguishes Peters – and partly explains his success – is that he is not shackled to a particular perspective. While Michael Porter covers competitiveness and Rosabeth Moss Kanter human resources, Peters stalks restlessly from one issue to another. His seminars roam widely, and at times indiscriminately, from customer service to free trade, from politics to health and fitness.

Peters has also proved remarkably adept at picking up ideas at exactly the right time. *In Search of Excellence* was successful because it brought good news at a time of widespread depression; *Thriving on Chaos* was published on the day Wall Street crashed and promised a way through the uncertainty; the sprawling *Liberation Management* anticipated much of the later work on teams and project-led organizations, and its case studies (such as ABB and CNN) have been relentlessly explored. Peters has moved with the flow of ideas – but has always managed to be ahead of the tide.

Tom Peters believes that his fundamental thinking remains largely unchanged. If there is a consistent strand through his work, Peters believes it is 'a bias for action'. Forget the theorizing, get on with the job. This is a message which leads academics to shake their heads at its simplicity. With managers, however, it appears to strike a chord – Peters can claim a long list of adherents including ABB's Percy Barnevik and Northwestern's Herb Kelleher. 'Ideas and strategies are important, of course, but execution is the real challenge', says Barnevik.

While making things happen is a consistent refrain in Peters' books, the shift in emphasis has undoubtedly been dramatic. Over 15 years he has moved from a corporate world view to one centered on individuals. Corporate aid has metamorphosed into self-help, the world of gurus like Kenneth Blanchard and Stephen Covey. 'In the Covey–Blanchard world there is something. It does boil down to personal transformation,' Peters observes.

His recent work has a more personal emphasis. For example, in typically breathless style, he ushers in a new era in the world of brands. 'Regardless of age, regardless of position, regardless of the business we happen to be in, all of us need to understand the importance of branding', says Peters. 'We are CEOs of our own companies: Me Inc. To be in business today, our most important job is to be head marketer for the brand called You.'

Peters argues that Marlboro Friday in 1993 (when Philip Morris slashed the prices of its premium cigarette brand) marked the end of a generation of big brands. The new world of brands is radically different. The big names still exist but they no longer have a monopoly over the art of branding. Peters points to the rise of the Internet as evidence of a new, more personal brand generation. After all, you return to the Web site you trust and gain the most value from. Increasingly we need to promote our own personal brands through such things as developing our contacts or updating our résumés. Self-creation is the order of the day.

'If you're really smart, you figure out what it takes to create a distinctive role for yourself – you create a message and a strategy to promote the brand called You,' says Peters. What is interesting – and paradoxical – is that amid this branding frenzy, Peters' idea of what constitutes a brand remains somewhat traditional. 'The brand is a promise of the value you'll receive', he says, a definition as applicable to a pack of corn flakes as an interesting résumé.[4] Peters has traveled a long way to conclude that, in the end, there is the individual.

The Tom Peters of the late 1990s is a million miles away from the Tom Peters of 1982. His most recent book, *The Circle of Innovation*, takes the style and exuberance that has built up over his recent work a stage further. Boisterous and belligerent, it is a million miles away from the buttoned-down world of McKinsey and the 'straight' *In Search of Excellence*. Peters has moved on. To where he probably doesn't know, but in moving on at all he has taken more risks than most.

Notes

1   Interview with the author.
2   Peters, Tom, *Liberation Management*, Alfred P Knopf, New York, 1992.
3   Interview with the author.
4   Peters, Tom, 'The brand called you', *Fast Company*, August/September 1997.

Bibliography

In Search of Excellence (with Robert Waterman), Harper & Row, New York & London, 1982.
A Passion for Excellence (with Nancy Austin), Collins, London, 1985.
Thriving on Chaos, Macmillan, London, 1988.
Liberation Management, Alfred Knopf, New York, 1992.
The Tom Peters Seminar, Vintage Books, New York, 1994.
The Pursuit of Wow!, Vintage Books, New York, 1994.
The Circle of Innovation, Hodder & Stoughton, London, 1997.

Michael Porter

"Strategic thinking rarely occurs spontaneously.**"**

Michael Porter

American academic and consultant
Born 1947

Breakthrough ideas

Strategy
Competitiveness
The Five Forces Framework

Key books

Competitive Advantage
Competitive Strategy
The Competitive Advantage of Nations

I f Peter Drucker is the intellectual giant of management thinking and Tom Peters its most charismatic populist, **Michael Porter** is perhaps the thinker with the greatest influence. Porter plays golf with the President. This is not simply to keep the President company. He runs workshops at Harvard for newly appointed CEOs – of billion-dollar corporations. He has also acted as a consultant to countries as diverse as Portugal and India. What is astonishing about Porter's allure is that his area of expertise is business strategy. Las Vegas it isn't.

But then again, Porter is precociously talented and intellectually persuasive. Born in Ann Arbor, Michigan in 1947, Porter's father was an army officer and he spent his youth moving around the world. (He later served in the US Army Reserve reaching the rank of Captain.) Porter went to Princeton University where he obtained a degree in aerospace and mechanical engineering. He was also an all-state high school football and baseball player. At Princeton he played intercollegiate golf and was named in the 1968 NCAA Golf All-American team.

Rather than pursuing a career as a professional golfer, Porter took a Harvard MBA (1971) and followed this with a doctorate in business economics (1973). While completing his PhD Porter came under the influence of Richard Caves, the economist, who became his mentor. He joined the Harvard faculty at the age of 26 – one of the youngest tenured professors in the school's august history. 'If anyone is capable of turning management theory into a respectable scholarly discipline, it is Michael Porter', noted *The Economist*.[1]

Porter has served as a counselor on competitive strategy to many leading US and international companies and plays an active role in economic policy with the US Congress, business groups and as an adviser to foreign governments. He serves on the executive committee of the Council on Competitiveness, a private sector group of business, labor and academic leaders formed in 1986.

Porter has also exerted huge local influence on the state of Massachusetts. He wrote *The Competitive Advantage of Massachusetts* (1991) and chaired the state's Council on Economic Growth and Technology in Massachusetts. These initiatives led to new laws and a variety of initiatives.

Porter's genius has lain in producing brilliantly researched and cogent models of competitiveness at a corporate, industry-wide and national level. For example, Porter took an industrial economics framework – the structure–conduct performance paradigm (SCP) – and translated it into the context of business strategy. From this emerged his best known model: the five forces framework, which states that 'in any industry, whether it is domestic or international or produces a product or a service, the rules of competition are embodied in five competitive forces'. These five competitive forces are:

- The entry of new competitors. New competitors necessitate some competitive response, which will inevitably use some of your resources, thus reducing profits.
- The threat of substitutes. If there are viable alternatives to your product or service in the marketplace, the prices you can charge will be limited.
- The bargaining power of buyers. If customers have bargaining power they will use it. This will reduce profit margins and, as a result, affect profitability.
- The bargaining power of suppliers. Given power over you, suppliers will increase their prices and adversely affect your profitability.
- The rivalry among the existing competitors. Competition leads to the need to invest in marketing, R&D or price reductions, which will reduce your profits.

'The collective strength of these five competitive forces determines the ability of firms in an industry to earn, on average, rates of return on investment in excess of the cost of capital. The strength of the five forces varies from industry to industry, and can change as an industry evolves,' Porter observed.

The five forces (outlined in Porter's bestselling *Competitive Strategy*) were a means by which a company could begin to understand its particular industry. Initially, they were passively interpreted as valid statements of the facts of competitive life. Now, however, they are more regularly interpreted as the rules of the game, which have to be changed and challenged if an organization is to achieve any impact in a particular market. 'Porter's translation did not resolve, and could not resolve, the fundamental weakness of the SCP approach. Why did some companies manage the five forces better than others?' notes John Kay of Oxford's Said Business School.[2] The five forces framework was once seen as providing all the answers. Now, the suggestion is that it actually is better used as a means of provoking questions.

Having mapped out the facts of competitive life, Porter nearly left the obvious next question – what can we do about it? – unanswered. A late addition to his book was the concept of generic strategies. Porter argued that there were three 'generic strategies', 'viable approaches to dealing with ... competitive forces'. Strategy, in Porter's eyes, was a matter of *how* to compete.

The first of Porter's generic strategies was differentiation, competing on the basis of value added to customers (quality, service, differentiation) so that customers will pay a premium to cover higher costs. The second was cost-based leadership, offering products or services at the lowest cost. Quality and service are not unimportant, but cost reduction provides focus to the organization. Focus was the third generic strategy identified by Porter. Companies with a clear strategy outperform those whose strategy is unclear or those that attempt to achieve both differentiation and cost leadership. 'Sometimes the firm can successfully pursue more than one approach as its primary target, though this is rarely possible', he said. 'Effectively implementing any of these generic strategies usually requires total commitment, and organizational arrangements are diluted if there's more than one primary target.'

If a company failed to focus on any of the three generic strategies it was liable to encounter problems. 'The firm failing to develop its strategy in at least one of the three directions – a firm that is *stuck in the middle* – is in an extremely poor strategic situation', Porter wrote. 'The firm lacks the market share, capital investment, and resolve to play the low-cost game, the industry-wide differentiation necessary to obviate the need for a low-cost position, or the focus to create differentiation or low cost in a more limited sphere. The firm stuck in the middle is almost guaranteed low profitability. It either loses the high-volume customers who demand low prices or must bid away its profits to get this business away from low-cost firms. Yet it also loses high-margin businesses – the cream – to the firms who are focused on high-margin targets or have achieved differentiation overall. The firm stuck in the middle also probably suffers from a blurred corporate culture and a conflicting set of organizational arrangements and motivation system.'

When *Competitive Strategy* was published in 1980, Porter's generic strategies offered a rational and straightforward method of companies extricating themselves from strategic confusion. The reassurance proved short-lived. Less than a decade later, companies were having to compete on all fronts. They had to be differentiated, through improved service or speedier development, and be cost leaders, cheaper than their competitors.

Porter has moved on to expand the range of his research. It now encompasses countries as well as companies. Indeed, Porter's 1990 book, *The Competitive Advantage of Nations,* must be ranked as one of the most ambitious books of our times. At its heart was a radical new perspective of the role and *raison d'être* of nations. Porter charted their transformation from being military powerhouses to economic units whose competitiveness is the key to power.

The book emerged from Porter's work on Ronald Reagan's Commission on Industrial Competitiveness. 'The book that projected Mr Porter into the stratosphere, read by aspiring intellectuals and despairing politicians everywhere, was *The Competitive Advantage of Nations*', said *The Economist*. 'This work can be read on three levels: as a general inquiry into what makes national economies successful, as a detailed study of eight of the world's main modern economies, and as a series of prescriptions about what governments should do to improve their country's competitiveness.'[3]

Porter's research, in fact, encompassed ten countries: the UK, Denmark, Italy, Japan, Korea, Singapore, Sweden, Switzerland, the US and Germany (then West Germany). Porter has since extended his study to include Japan, India, Canada, New Zealand, Portugal and the state of Massachusetts.

Porter sought to build on the ideas of his previous books to examine what makes a nation's firms and industries competitive in global markets and what propels a whole nation's economy to advance. 'Why are firms based in a particular nation able to create and sustain competitive advantage against the world's best competitors in a particular field? And why is one nation often the home for so many of an industry's world leaders?' he asked. 'Why is tiny Switzerland the home base for international leaders in pharmaceuticals, chocolate and trading? Why are leaders in heavy trucks and mining equipment based in Sweden?'

Porter returned to first principles, an ambitious move in itself given the nature of the nationalistic minefield he ventured into. 'The principal economic goal of a nation is to produce a high and rising standard of living for its citizens. The ability to do so depends not on the amorphous notion of "competitiveness" but on the productivity with which a nation's resources (labor and capital) are employed,' he wrote. 'Productivity is the prime determinant in the long run of a nation's standard of living.'

Unlike Kenichi Ohmae who champions the 'end of the nation state', Porter's research led to different conclusions. He identified a central paradox. Companies and industries have become globalized and more international in their scope and aspirations than ever before. This, on the surface at least, would appear to suggest that the nation has lost its role in the international success of its firms. 'Companies, at first glance, seem to have transcended countries. Yet what I have learned in this study contradicts this conclusion,' said Porter. 'While globalization of competition might appear to make the nation less important, instead it seems to make it more so. With fewer impediments to trade to shelter uncompetitive domestic firms and industries, the home nation takes on growing significance because it is the source of the skills and technology that underpin competitive advantage.'

Porter also laid down a challenge, perhaps to himself, to solve another perennial mystery: 'Much is known about what competitive advantage is and how particular actions create or destroy it. Much else is known about why a company makes good choices instead of bad choices in seeking bases for competitive advantage, and why some firms are more aggressive in pursuing them.' Porter's conclusion was that it is the intensity of domestic competition that often fuels success on a global stage.

To make sense of the dynamics behind national or regional

strength in a particular industry, Porter developed the national 'diamond'. This is made up of four forces:

- Factor conditions – these once would have include natural resources and plentiful supplies of labor; now they embrace data communications, university research and the availability of scientists, engineers or experts in a particular field.
- Demand conditions – if there is strong national demand for a product or service this can give the industry a headstart in global competition. The US, for example, is ahead in health services due to heavy national demand.
- Related and supporting industries – industries that are strong in a particular countries are often surrounded by successful related industries.
- Firm strategy, structure and rivalry – domestic competition fuels growth and competitive strength.

Such frameworks are a typical Porter technique. He has the ability to distil vast amounts of complex data and material into relatively robust frameworks. To some this cheapens his research, but it has attracted a mass audience to his work.

Most recently, Porter has once again returned to first principles to consider the very nature of strategy. He laments that the profusion of management tools has taken the place of strategy. 'Management prefers to lurch from one tool to another rather than formulating a coherent strategy. This may enhance operational effectiveness but the essence of strategy lies in selecting a unique and valuable position rooted in systems of activities that are much more difficult to match.'[4]

Notes

1   'Professor Porter PhD', *The Economist*, 8 October 1994.
2   Kay, John, 'Why gurus should cross the bridge into business', *Financial Times*, 17 November 1997.
3   'Professor Porter PhD', *The Economist*, 8 October 1994.
4   Porter, Michael, 'What is strategy?', *Harvard Business Review*, November/December 1996.

Bibliography

Competitive Strategy, Free Press, New York, 1980.
Competitive Advantage, Free Press, New York, 1985.
The Competitive Advantage of Nations, Free Press, New York, 1990.

Edgar H. Schein

"The company is an economic vehicle invented by society. It has no rights to survive. But value systems and philosophies survive. People take it with them."

Edgar H. Schein

Social psychologist
Born 1928

Breakthrough ideas

Corporate culture
Career anchors

Key books

Organizational Culture and Leadership
Organizational Psychology

S ocial psychologist **Ed Schein** (born 1928) has eschewed a high media profile during a lengthy academic career. Yet his work has exerted a steadily growing influence on management theory, particularly over the last 20 years. His thinking on corporate cultures and careers has proved highly important. Schein is one of the originators of the field of organizational psychology and worked closely with the human resources school of the late 1950s and 1960s.

Ed Schein graduated from Chicago in 1946 and then studied at Stanford. He completed a PhD in social psychology at Harvard and, after graduating in 1952, carried out research into leadership as part of the Army Program. This came to a halt with the end of the Korean War, when Schein and every available psychologist was mobilized to deal with the repatriation of POWs. 'We were shipped to Korea to spend time with repatriated POWs on their 16-day voyage way back. It was a smart move by the government,' Schein recalls. 'I was stuck in Inchon in Korea three extra weeks and started the whole process of interviewing people.'[1]

Returning home, Schein received a letter from Douglas McGregor who knew of Schein's work through Gordon Allport at Harvard and because Schein had taken a couple of seminars at MIT where McGregor was based. 'McGregor asked me to work with him at MIT. He said come here and figure out what you want to do. It was a fated decision. I left traditional social psychology for a business school. In retrospect, it turned out to be a good decision as psychology in business schools became far more interesting.' Schein joined MIT in 1956 and initially worked under the influence of Douglas McGregor. He has remained there ever since. 'I never regretted joining MIT. It is an open, creative place,' he says.

At MIT Schein soon noted the similarities between the brainwashing of POWs and the corporate indoctrination carried out by the likes of GE at its Crotonville training base and IBM at Sands Point. This was the era of corporate man – a grey-suited, obedient character brilliantly exposed in William Whyte's classic *Organization Man*. Schein's first paper was entitled 'Management development as a process of influence', which applied the brainwashing model from prison camps to the corporate world. 'There were enormous similarities between the brainwashing of the POWs and the executives I encountered at MIT', says Schein. 'I didn't see brainwashing as bad. What was bad were the values of the Communists. If we don't like the values, we don't approve of brainwashing.' From this work came Schein's book, *Coercive Persuasion*.

The ability of strong values to influence groups of people is a strand which has continued throughout Schein's work. As he points out, recent trends, such as the learning organization (championed by his MIT colleague Peter Senge), are derivatives of brainwashing – 'Organizational learning is a new version of coercive persuasion,' he says.

Douglas McGregor also recruited Warren Bennis, who joined the MIT team in 1957. In the same year, Schein was directed to learn more about sensitivity group training and met Chris Argyris at the National Training Laboratories at Bethel. The work at Bethel provided long-lasting inspiration for Schein. He continued to visit Bethel every summer for the next 10–15 years. 'I realized I was a group expert who knew nothing about groups. More important than my academic training was my experience and practice working with groups. I learned that you never have pure individualism or pure groupism. There is always a balance.'

The dynamics of groups and Schein's knowledge of brainwashing led to a developing interest in corporate culture, a term which Schein is widely credited with inventing.

His research into the area included work with Ken Olsen and Digital Equipment Corporation (anonymously cited by Schein as Action Co.). 'Ken Olsen at DEC really empowered people. What he did fitted the market of the time but, when the market matured, the approach became dysfunctional. DEC had too many projects and creative people. Olsen couldn't control it. Creativity is functional at certain times and can become dysfunctional.' Interesting to Schein was the fact that though the Digital culture imploded, its executives often took the culture with them when they left to set up their own businesses or to manage elsewhere. 'The Digital culture is dead, but not in individuals. The economic unit has no right to survive, but the culture does,' says Schein. He makes a comparison between the fate of Digital and that of its corporate contemporary Hewlett-Packard. 'HP emerged at the same time as DEC but was better at transforming itself. It diversified, devolving into creative units. Organizational diversity may be more important than individual diversity. Diversity talks about people rather than sub-cultures. One reason for the success of the US is maybe that it has never throttled sub-cultures.'

Schein's work on corporate culture culminated in the 1985 book *Organizational Culture and Leadership*. Schein describes culture as 'a pattern of basic assumptions – invented, discovered, or developed by a given group as it learns to cope with its problems of external adaptation and internal integration – that has worked well enough to be considered valid and therefore to be taught to new members as the correct way to perceive, think, and feel in relation to those problems'.

Instead of regarding everything an organization does as part of its culture, Schein took a more psychological view. Schein's 'basic assumptions' are rephrased and reinterpreted elsewhere in a variety of ways – perhaps the nearest is Chris Argyris' term 'theories-in-use'.

These basic assumptions, says Schein, can be categorized into five dimensions:

- **Humanity's relationship to nature** – while some companies regard themselves as masters of their own destiny, others are submissive, willing to accept the domination of their external environment.
- **The nature of reality and truth** – organizations and managers adopt a wide variety of methods to reach what becomes accepted as the organizational 'truth' – through debate, dictatorship, or through simple acceptance that if something achieves the objective it is right.
- **The nature of human nature** – organizations differ in their views of human nature. Some follow McGregor's Theory X and work on the principle that people will not do the job if they can avoid it. Others regard people in more positive light and attempt to enable them to fulfill their potential for the benefit of both sides.
- **The nature of human activity** – the West has traditionally emphasized tasks and their completion rather than the more philosophical side of work. Achievement is all. Schein suggests an alternative approach – 'being-in-becoming' – emphasizing self-fulfillment and development.

- **The nature of human relationships** – organizations make a variety of assumptions about how people interact with each other. Some facilitate social interaction, while others regard it as an unnecessary distraction.

These five categories are not mutually exclusive, but are in a constant state of development and flux. Culture does not stand still.

Key to the creation and development of corporate culture are the values embraced by the organization. Schein acknowledges that a single person can shape these values and, as a result, an entire corporate culture. (This spawned a wave of interest in the heroic creators of corporate cultures from Henry Ford to IBM's Thomas Watson.) Schein identifies three stages in the development of a corporate culture – 'birth and early growth'; 'organizational mid-life'; and 'organizational maturity'.

Organizational Culture and Leadership clarified the entire area of corporate culture in a way no-one previously had achieved. It spawned a host of research projects and books on the subject.

More recently, Schein's work on culture has identified three cultures of management which he labels 'the key to organizational learning in the 21st century'. The three cultures are the operator culture ('an internal culture based on operational success'); the engineering culture (created by 'the designers and technocrats who drive the core technologies of the organization') and the executive culture formed by executive management, the CEO and immediate subordinates. 'The three cultures of management suddenly came to me. I hadn't thought of it like that before and think that I'm one of the few to realize that we've always taken the point of view of the operators and have overlooked the other two cultures,' says Schein.

He observes that the three cultures rarely co-exist happily – 'We have in most organizations three different major occupational cultures that do not really understand each other very well and that often work at cross-purposes with each other.' The operational culture generally dominates, though recent years have seen the excesses of the executive culture in downsizing and of the engineering culture in re-engineering.

Within Schein's three cultures lies a more controversial sub-text. 'CEOs worry about the financial side rather than whether they are paying enough attention to people and I am beginning to think that it is commonsense that CEOs are like that. Their job is often not to be humane, to see people as impersonal resources. By the time people become CEOs they are preoccupied with survival and money. They respond to capital markets, stockholders, etc. Even if they try or want to be people-oriented, a financial crisis will always get their attention,' he says. 'Engineers also have to engineer people out the equation. Maybe we should ask engineers to be better engineers rather than more humane. We have never got into the mentality of CEOs or engineers in a helpful way. We should be seeking to understand how we can help them to do it better.' This, as Schein sees it, is a simple statement of the facts of corporate life rather than a cynical prescription.

Success is related to how well the three cultures are aligned. It is a precarious balance, easily disturbed. For example, when executives move from one industry to another, cultures are often pushed out of alignment. Schein suggests that John Sculley's move from Pepsi to Apple was doomed from the outset as he was a non-engineer moving to an engineering culture. In contrast, Lou Gerstner's move to IBM offered more potential as IBM was a sales rather than an engineering culture. (Schein goes on to suggest that IBM's downturn could be attributed to forgetting that sales and marketing were the core of the business.)

To resolve the gulf between the three cultures, Schein advocates taking the entire concept of culture more seriously; acknowledging that our old assumptions often no longer work; and learning how to create cross cultural dialogues. Companies need to pay much more attention to understanding the cultures of engineers and CEOs. Schein provides an example: 'At Shell in the US, the CEO set about creating what I would call a learning organization. To do so he had to deal with the hard and then the soft issues. He wanted value to be added all the way down the organization so he taught managers how to add value in the economic sense. Once they understand the economics, he started working on the soft stuff.'

Schein's point is that, in a capitalist system, economic viability is more important than how human resources are managed. 'It is the ends while the better organization of people is the means.' Balance is all. 'The great companies take all their stakeholders seriously. They value customers, employees and stockholders. Saying the customer is king is as stupid as saying the stockholder is king. The great executives understand it is a complex game.'

Another focus of Schein's attentions in recent years has been the subject of careers. He originated key phrases such as the psychological contract – the unspoken bond between employee and employer – and careers anchors. Schein proposed that once mature we have a single 'career anchor', which is the underlying career value that we could not surrender. 'Over the last 25 years, because of dual careers and social changes the emphasis of careers has shifted', he says. 'The career is no longer over arching. It is probably healthy because it makes people more independent. Lifestyle has become the increasingly important career anchor.' This applies to Schein's own career. He identifies his family life as his career anchor. 'I have never had a single mission. Someone once said that my ideas had evolved. I thought that was a great compliment,' he says. 'What I have always enjoyed is my own learning process, finding new things to think about and revisiting old things in new ways. I learn most from what people do and watching them.'

Schein's work and the issues he covers slip in and out of fashion. He shrugs his shoulders. 'When I look at a lot of the fads they come back to the same underlying theories, but we have to keep examining the essentials. In a way it is flattering that issues I have thought and written about keep resurfacing. The puzzle is why we have to keep reinventing.'

Notes

1   Interview with the author, June 1997.

Bibliography

Personal and Organization Change Through Group Methods: The Laboratory Approach (with Warren Bennis), John Wiley, New York, 1965.
Career Dynamics: Matching Individual and Organizational Needs, Addison Wesley, Wokingham, 1978.

Organizational Psychology, Prentice Hall, Englewood Cliffs, NJ, 1980.

Organization Culture and Leadership, Jossey-Bass, 1985 (2nd edn, 1992).

Process Consultation Vol. 1 (revised), Addison-Wesley, Reading, MA, 1988.

The Art of Managing HR, Oxford University Press, Oxford, 1987.

Career Anchors: Discovering Your Real Values, Pfeiffer, San Diego, CA, 1990.

Career Survival: Strategic Job and Roles Planning, Pfeiffer, San Diego, CA, 1994.

Strategic Pragmatism: The Culture of Singapore's Economic Development Board, MIT Press, Cambridge, MA.

Process Consultation, Addison-Wesley, Reading, MA, 1969.

Organizational Psychology (3rd edition), Prentcie Hall, Engelwood Cliffs, NJ, 1980.

Organizational Culture and Leadership, Jossey-Bass, San Francsico, CA, 1985.

Peter Senge

"Real commitment is rare in today's organizations. It is our experience that 90 percent of the time what passes for commitment is compliance."

Peter Senge

American academic
Born 1947

Breakthrough ideas

The learning organization

Key book

The Fifth Discipline

P **eter Senge** (born 1947) is director of the Center for Organizational Learning at the Massachusetts Institute of Technology. He is founding partner of the training and consulting company, Innovation Associates, now part of Arthur D. Little. Senge graduated in engineering from Stanford before doing a PhD on social systems modeling at MIT.

Senge studies how firms and other organizations can develop adaptive capabilities in a world of increasing complexity and rapid change. He argues that vision, purpose, alignment and systems thinking are essential for organizations. In his book *The Fifth Discipline*, Senge gave managers tools and conceptual archetypes to help them understand the structures and dynamics underlying their organizations' problems.

'As the world becomes more interconnected and business becomes more complex and dynamic, work must become more *learningful*,' wrote Senge. 'It is no longer sufficient to have one person learning for the organization, a Ford or a Sloan or a Watson. It's just not possible any longer to "figure it out" from the top, and have everybody else following the orders of the "grand strategist". The organizations that will truly excel in the future will be the organizations that discover how to tap people's commitment and capacity to learn at all levels in an organization.'

These organizations are what have now been labeled 'learning organizations' and it is for this term that Senge is best known. While the phrase is used with great abandon by other theorists as well as executives, it is rarely fully understood – and it is even rarer to actually find a 'learning organization'. 'In the simplest sense, a learning organization is a group of people who are continually enhancing their capability to create their future', explains Senge. 'The traditional meaning of the word *learning* is much deeper than just *taking information in*. It is about changing individuals so that they produce results they care about, accomplish things that are important to them.'[1]

The learning organization emerged from extensive research carried out by Senge and his team at the Center for Organizational Learning. 'For the past 15 years or longer, many of us have been struggling to understand what "learning organizations" are all about, and how to make progress in moving organizations along this path. Out of these efforts, I believe some insights are emerging,' says Senge.

He suggests there are five components to a learning organization:

- **Systems thinking** – Senge champions systems thinking, recognizing that things are interconnected. He regards corporations as complex systems. Picking up on the work of some of MIT colleagues, such as Jay Forrester, Senge introduced the idea of systems archetypes In practical terms this can help managers spot repetitive patterns, such as the way certain kinds of problems persist, or the way systems have their own in-built limits to growth. This has pushed managerial thinking towards contemplating complexity theory, which has spawned numerous books, though few go beyond the basic metaphor.
- **Personal mastery** – Senge grounds this idea in the familiar competencies and skills associated with management, but also includes spiritual growth – opening oneself up to a progressively deeper reality – and living life from a creative rather than a reactive viewpoint. This discipline involves two underlying movements: continually learning how to see current reality more clearly; and the ensuing gap between vision and reality produces the creative tension from which learning arises.
- **Mental models** – this essentially deals with the organization's driving and fundamental values and principles. Senge alerts managers to the power of patterns of thinking at the organizational level and the importance of nondefensive inquiry into the nature of these patterns.
- **Shared vision** – here Senge stresses the importance of co-creation and argues that shared vision can only be built on personal vision. He claims that shared vision is present when the task that follows from the vision is no longer seen by the team members as separate from the self.
- **Team learning** – the discipline of team learning involves two practices: dialogue and discussion. The former is characterized by its exploratory nature, the latter by the opposite process of narrowing down the field to the best alternative for the decisions that need to be made. The two are mutually complimentary, but the benefits of combining them only come from having previously separated them. Most teams lack the ability to

distinguish between the two and to move consciously between them.

For the traditional organization, the learning organization poses huge challenges. In the learning organization managers are researchers and designers rather than controllers and overseers. Senge argues that managers should encourage employees to be open to new ideas, communicate frankly with each other, understand thoroughly how their companies operate, form a collective vision and work together to achieve their goal.

In practice, when working with companies Senge says that he seeks to enable individuals and teams to recognize, articulate and align the goals most critical to them; to understand the complexity of organizations and the 'interconnectedness' within them; and to 'conduct conversations with each other around difficult and volatile issues in a way that creates deep understanding, empathy, innovation, and co-operation rather than ducking and blaming'.

The trouble is that the learning organization is regarded as an instant solution, yet another fad which can be implemented. Earnest attempts to turn it into reality have floundered. 'I know people who've lost their jobs supporting these theories', Senge has admitted. 'Yet they go on. One man told me that by adopting the learning organization model, he'd made what he called "job limiting choices". What he meant was that he could have climbed the corporate ladder faster by rejecting my theories and toeing the company line. But what would that have brought him? A higher pension fund and more stock, maybe. That's not what matters.'[2]

Senge argues that the interest in the concept of the learning organization is proof that institutions and people are ready for major change. 'The learning organization has become one of the prominent management fads of the first half of the 1990s – at least if you judge by the coverage in the business press, by the number of conferences organized and by recognition from prestigious institutions', says Senge. 'Being in the middle of all this had made me acutely aware of the larger forces within which this one little book has been swept along. I have come to believe that there is an opening today for a new movement of meaning and change. Our traditional ways of managing and governing are breaking down. The demise of General Motors and IBM has one thing in common with the crisis in America's schools and "gridlock" in Washington – a wake-up call that the world we live in presents unprecedented challenges for which our institutions are ill prepared.'[3]

Change is not viewed by Senge as an organizational phenomena but as something which must also affect us as individuals. If we do not change; our organizations will not change. This is perhaps where the problem of implementation lies. Organizations regard learning as a route to competitive advantage; individuals regard it as a route to personal advantage. The two extremes have not been bridged. 'The learning organization concept came laden with huge promise which has worryingly disappeared from view', says Phil Hodgson of Ashridge Management College. 'Part of the trouble is that if you give something a label people expect a product. The learning organization is not a product but a process and processes are a lot harder to talk about in board meetings. On the positive side, companies which have incorporated Senge's ideas have often been very successful – once again, however, the fact that the learning organization is a process means that accrediting improvements to it is sometimes difficult.'

Notes

1   Quoted in Napuk, K, 'Live and learn', *Scottish Business Insider*, January 1994.
2   Quoted in Griffith, V., 'Corporate fashion victim', *Financial Times*, 12 April 1995.
3   Senge, Peter, 'A growing wave of interest and openness', Applewood Internet site, 1997.

Bibliography

The Fifth Discipline: The Art and Practice of the Learning Organization, Doubleday, New York, 1990.
The Fifth Discipline Fieldbook: Strategies and Tools for Building a Learning Organization (with Roberts, C., Ross, R., Smith, B., and Kleiner, A.), Nicholas Brealey, London, 1994.

Alfred P. Sloan

"In practically all our activities we seem to suffer from the inertia resulting from our great size. There are so many people involved and it requires such a tremendous effort to put something new into effect that a new idea is likely to be considered insignificant in comparison with the effort that it take to put it across ... Sometimes I am almost forced to the conclusion that General Motors is so large and its inertia so great that it is impossible for us to be leaders."

Alfred P. Sloan

Car industry executive
1875–1966

Breakthrough ideas

The divisionalized organization

Key book

My Years with General Motors

I n 1908, William Crapo Durant (1861–1947) founded the General Motors Company of New Jersey. Less than half a century later, in the early 1950s, the company's Charles E. Wilson, told the US Senate Armed Forces Committee: 'What is good for the country is good for General Motors and what's good for General Motors is good for the country'. At the time, there were few dissenters with such sentiments. For much of this century, GM has stood as a symbol of the might of corporate America.

That it has done so can, to a significant degree, be attributed to **Alfred P. Sloan** (1875–1966) who was the company's legendary chief during its formative years. Researching her case study of GM for *The Change Masters,* Rosabeth Moss Kanter was told by then GM chairman Roger Smith that his aim was to 'return this company to the way Sloan intended it to be managed' – and that was over 30 years after Sloan's death.

As well as being the architect of GM, Sloan was also one of the first managers to write an important theoretical book. The relative dullness of the book, *My Years With General Motors* (1963), should not cloud the size of Sloan's contribution to theory and practice.

Sloan was general manager of the Hyatt Roller Bearing Company at the age of 24 and became president when it merged with United Motors which, in turn, became part of General Motors in 1917. Initially a director and vice-president, Sloan became GM's chief executive in 1946 and honorary chairman from 1956 until his death.

When Sloan took over General Motors the fledgling automobile market was dominated by Ford. Under Henry Ford the company had become a pioneer of mass production techniques (see pp. 65–8). In 1920 Ford was making a car a minute and the famously black Model T accounted for 60 percent of the market. General Motors managed to scrimp and scrap its way to around 12 percent.

With Ford cornering the mass market, the accepted wisdom was that the only alternative for competitors lay in the negligibly sized luxury market. Sloan thought otherwise and concentrated GM's attentions on the, as yet non-existent, middle market. His aim was a car for 'every purse and every purpose'.

At the time, GM was an unwieldy combination of companies with eight models that basically competed against each other as well as against Ford. Sloan cut the eight models down to five and decided that rather than competing with each other, each model would be targeted at a particular segment of the market. 'Back then, if you said the word Pontiac, any consumer in the country could tell you what kind of person drove it,' said *Business Week*.[1] The five GM ranges – the Chevrolet, Oldsmobile, Pontiac, Buick and Cadillac – were to be updated and changed regularly and came in more than one color. Ford continued to offer functional, reliable cars; GM offered choice.

While all this made commercial sense, Sloan inherited an organization that was ill-suited to deliver his aspirations. Ford had been able to achieve standardization and mass production by producing as narrow a product range as possible. Sloan wanted to produce a far greater range from a rag bag of companies – GM had been built up through the regular and apparently random acquisition of small companies. His conclusion was that through better running of the organization of the company, as opposed to the production line, this could be achieved.

The challenge Sloan faced was that any thought of providing some sort of overall corporate culture, structure or direction had apparently been overlooked in GM – though this was principally because it had never been done before. Sloan set about creating a coherent organization from his motley collection. Central to this was his 'organization study' which, said one observer, appeared to 'have sprung entirely from his own head in 1919 and 1920'. This was an examination of the way the organization worked and was a new and novel idea. (Sloan had a modest habit of suggesting that ideas just came to his mind. It should be noted that in virtually all cases, they didn't come to anyone else's mind. Explaining the company's move into advertising, he said: 'I had some consumer studies made in 1922, and we found that people throughout the US, except at the corner of Wall and Broad Streets, didn't know anything about GM. So I thought we should publicize the parent company.')

As a result of his organization study, in the early 1920s Sloan organized the company into eight divisions – five car divisions and three component divisions. In the jargon (invented 50 years later) they were strategic business units.

Each of the units was made responsible for all their commercial operations with their own engineering, production and sales departments, but was supervised by a central staff responsible for overall policy and finance. The operating units were semi-autonomous, charged with maintaining market share and sustaining profitability in their particular area. In a particularly innovative move, the components divisions not only sold products to other GM companies, but also to external companies.

This policy, which Sloan labeled 'federal decentralization', marked the invention of the decentralized, divisionalized organization. (While this was its first sustained practical usage, Sloan's ideas can be traced back to Henri Fayol's functional approach – though there is no evidence that Sloan was an adherent of Fayol's.) 'Alfred Sloan did for the upper layers of management what Henry Ford did for the shopfloor: he turned it into a reliable, efficient, machine-like process', recently observed *The Economist*.[2] It should not be forgotten that Sloan was an engineer.

The multi-divisional form enabled Sloan to utilize the company's size without making it cumbersome. 'The multi-divisional organization was perhaps the single most important administrative innovation that helped companies grow in size and diversity far beyond the limits of the functional organization it replaced', say contemporary thinkers Sumantra Ghoshal and Christopher Bartlett.

Executives had more time to concentrate on strategic issues and operational decisions were made by people in the front line rather than at a distant headquarters. It required a continuous balancing act. By 1925, with its new organization and commitment to annual changes in its models, GM had overtaken Ford, which continued to persist with its faithful old Model T. Sloan's segmentation of the market changed the structure of the car industry – and provided a model for how firms could do the same in other industries.

From a managerial point of view, Sloan and Henry Ford had entirely different approaches. Ford ignored management. Sloan sought to make management highly efficient. His system aimed to eliminate, as far as was possible, the deficiencies and eccentricities of managerial behavior. Sloan, Peter Drucker observed, was entirely focused on 'managing a business so that it can produce effectively, provide jobs, create markets and sales, and generate profits'.[3]

And yet, Sloan was committed to what at the time would have been regarded as progressive human resource management. In 1947 Sloan established GM's employee-research section to look at employee attitudes and he invested a large amount of his own time in selecting the right people for the job – Sloan personally selected every GM executive from managers to master mechanics and, though he was prepared to miss policy meetings, he always attended personnel meetings.

After being lauded as a managerial hero by Alfred Chandler and Peter Drucker, the deficiencies of Sloan's model gradually became apparent. The decentralized structure built up by Sloan revolved around a reporting and committee infrastructure, which eventually became unwieldy. As time went by, more and more committees were set up. Stringent targets and narrow measures of success stultified initiative. By the end of the 1960s the delicate balance, which Sloan had brilliantly maintained between centralization and decentralization, was lost – finance emerged as the dominant function – and GM became paralyzed by what had once made it great.

The merits or otherwise of Sloan's approach have long been debated. The most thoughtful and comprehensive commentary comes from Sumantra Ghoshal and Christopher Bartlett who have pointed to the inward-looking nature of Sloan's approach as one of its major drawbacks. 'Sloan's organization was designed to overcome the limitations of the functional structure in managing large, established businesses. While it did this quite well, at least for a while, it proved incapable of creating and developing new businesses internally. This inability to manage organic expansion into new areas was caused by many factors. With primarily operating responsibilities and guided by a measurement system that focused on profit and market share performance in served markets, the front-line business unit managers in the divisionalized corporation were neither expected to nor could scout for new opportunities breaking around the boxes in the organization chart that defined their product or geographic scope. Besides, small new ventures, as organic developments tended to be at the start of their lives, could not absorb the large central overheads and yet return the profits needed to justify the financial and human investments.'

The multi-divisional form, say Bartlett and Ghoshal, was handicapped by having 'no process through which institutionalized wisdoms can be challenged, existing knowledge bases can be overturned, and the sources of the data can be reconfigured. In the absence of this challenge, these companies gradually become immobilized by conventional wisdoms that have ossified as sacred cows, and become constrained by outmoded knowledge and expertise that are out of touch with their rapidly changing realities'.

They describe the multi-divisional approach as a 'doctrine – it is more than a mere specification of the organization structure: it also describes the roles and responsibilities of corporate, divisional and business unit level managers; relative status and norms of behavior of staff and line functionaries; mechanisms and processes for allocation of resources; and, in general, "the rules of the game" inside the company. Over the last ten years, a variety of changes in market, technological and competitive contexts has rendered this doctrine obsolete and the problems large corporations are facing stem, at least in part, from sticking to this past success formula well beyond the limit of its usefulness.'

Notes

1   Kerry, Kathleen, 'GM warms up the branding iron', *Business Week*, 23 September 1996.
2   'The changing nature of leadership', *The Economist*, 10 June 1995.
3   Drucker, Peter F., *Concept of the Corporation*, John Day, New York, 1972.

Bibliography

My Years with General Motors, Doubleday, New York, 1963.

Frederick W. Taylor

"Hardly a competent workman can be found who does not devote a considerable amount of time to studying just how slowly he can work and still convince his employer that he is going at a good pace."

Frederick W. Taylor

American engineer and inventor
1856–1917

Breakthrough ideas

Scientific Management

Key book

The Principles of Scientific Management

F | **rederick Taylor** (1856–1917) had a profound effect on the working world of the twentieth century and was a man of amazing versatility and brilliance. And yet, his name is either not known, or regarded in a negative light. Taylor, the inventor of what was known as Scientific Management, was the patron saint of mass production; the champion of measurement and of control; the rich man who believed he knew and understood life on the production line better than anyone.

Frederick Winslow Taylor grew up in Philadelphia. His family were affluent. While a teenager he undertook the classic European tour. It was no whistle stop breeze through the continent – Taylor's tour lasted three years. Aged eighteen, and back at home, Taylor apprenticed himself to a Philadelphia maker of steam pumps, the Enterprise Hydraulic Works. (He didn't go to Harvard because of impaired eyesight, though he passed the entrance examination.) His next career move was to the Midvale Steel Company, where he became chief engineer, and from there to become general manager of the Manufacturing Investment Company's paper mills in Maine. In 1893 he moved to New York and began business as a consulting engineer (the forerunner of the management consultant).

Taylor attended the Stevens Institute of Technology in Hoboken, New Jersey. Stevens was a recently established engineering institute then under its first president, Henry Morton. Morton aimed to upgrade mechanical engineering and emphasized a broad-based curriculum that fitted Taylor's wide range of skills. Taylor graduated in 1883. (Henry Gantt – creator of the Gantt chart – graduated from Stevens a year after Taylor.)

While working and studying, Taylor came up with a seemingly endless series of inventions and innovations. He changed the rules of baseball so that pitchers threw overarm rather than underarm and took out over 100 patents for his many and varied ideas. He was also a tennis champion.

At the core of Taylor's view of the working world was his theory of how working life could be made more productive and efficient. This was painfully simple. Taylor was the first and purest believer in command and control. In his 1911 book, *The Principles of Scientific Management*, Taylor laid out his route to improved performance:

'1 Find, say, 10 or 15 different men (preferably in as many separate establishments and different parts of the country) who are especially skillful in doing the particular work analyzed.

'2 Study the exact series of elementary operations or motions which each of these men uses in doing the work being investigated, as well as the implements each man uses.

'3 Study with a stopwatch the time required to make each of these elementary movements and then select the quickest way of doing each element of the work.

'4 Eliminate all false movements, slow movements and useless movements.

'5 Collect into one series the quickest and best movements as well as the best implements.'

This minute examination of individual tasks became known as Scientific Management. Having identified every single movement and action involved in doing something, Taylor could determine the optimum time required to complete a task. Armed with this information, the manager could determine whether a person was doing the job well. 'In its essence, scientific management involves a complete mental revolution on the part of the working man engaged in any particular establishment or industry – a complete mental revolution on the part of these men as to their duties toward their work, toward their fellow men, and toward their employees,' Taylor wrote.

The humble employee was regarded as a robotic automaton. Motivation came in the form of piece work. 'Brutally speaking, our scheme does not ask any initiative in a man. We do not care for his initiative,' said Taylor with typical frankness. Employees had to be told the optimum way to do a job and then they had to do it. 'Each employee should receive every day clear-cut, definite instructions as to just what he is to do and how he is to do it, and these instructions should be exactly carried out, whether they are right or wrong', Taylor advised. Not surprisingly this did not always go down well – in 1911 the introduction of Taylor's methods caused a strike at a munitions factory run by the army.

The man most associated with the application of Scientific Management was Henry Ford (though this is a simplistic reading of Ford's contribution – see pp. 65–8). In his book, *My Life and Work*, Ford gave a chilling insight into the unforgiving logic of Scientific Management. He calculated that the production of a Model T required 7882 different operations. Of these 949 required 'strong, able-bodied, and practically physical perfect men' and 3338 required 'ordinary physical strength'. The remainder, said Ford, could be undertaken by 'women or older children' and '670 could be filled by legless men, 2,637 by one-legged men, two by armless men, 715 by one-armed men and 10 by blind men'. Debased though it was, this was the logical conclusion of Scientific Management.

Taylor practised what he preached and applied his theories to every aspect of his own life. One book about him noted: 'Taylor's personality emerges with great clarity from his writings. His virtual obsession to control the environment around him was expressed in everything he did; in his home life, his gardening, his golfing; even his afternoon stroll was not a casual affair but something to be carefully planned and rigidly followed. Nothing was left to chance if in any way chance could be avoided. Every personal action was thought through carefully, all contingencies considered, and steps taken to guard against extraneous developments. And when, despite all precautions, something did occur to upset his plans he gave evidence of great internal distress – distress that sometimes expressed itself in blazing anger and sometimes in black brooding … one gets the impression of a rigid, insecure personality, desperately afraid of the unknown and the unforeseen, able to face the world with reasonable equanimity only if everything possible has been done to keep the world in its place and to guard against anything that might upset his careful, painstaking plans.'[1]

And yet, there can be no doubting the impact of Taylor's thinking on a wider audience. Mussolini and Lenin were admirers, but so were many thousands of ordinary business people. Astonishingly, a talk by Taylor in New York in 1914 attracted an audience of 69,000. Scientific management had an effect throughout the world. A Japanese engineer translated *The Principles of Scientific Management* (in Japan it became *Secrets for Eliminating Futile Work and Increasing Production*). In Japan it was a bestseller – a foretaste of the Japanese willingness to embrace the latest Western thinking.

Right or wrong, moral or amoral, Taylor's view of the future of industry was accurate. 'In the past the man was first. In the future the system will be first,' he said, and so it proved. Central to this, however, was the role of managers. Scientific management elevated the role of managers and negated the role of workers. Armed with their scientifically gathered information, managers dictated terms. 'Science, not rule of thumb', said Taylor. The decisions of foremen – based on experience and intuition – were no longer considered to be important. Employees were not allowed to have any ideas or sense of responsibility. Their job was to simply to do their job as delineated by the all-seeing and all-knowing manager.

This may appear to be management by dictatorship; management from another time. And yet Taylor's legacy lives on. 'Despite [the] obsolescence of Taylor's premises, we retain the Taylor system, with all the detriments inherent in use of a system which is based on obsolete premises. The most obvious and serious of these detriments is the underemployment of the intelligence and creative capacity of millions of human beings,' says quality guru, Joseph Juran.[2]

Nowhere is this clearer than in the continuing prevalence of the belief that measurement is the crucial part of a manager's work. Obsessive measurement is a slippery slope. 'The first step is to measure whatever can be easily measured. That is OK as far as it goes,' says Robert McNamara. 'The second step is to disregard that which can't be easily measured or to give it an arbitrary quantitative value. This is artificial and misleading. The third step is to presume that what can't be measured easily really isn't important. This is blindness. The fourth step is to say that what can't be easily measured really doesn't exist. That is suicide.'[3]

A more positive slant on Taylor's work is provided by *Fortune*'s Tom Stewart in his book on *Intellectual Capital* – not a subject one would expect Taylor to feature in. 'Taylorism ... not only worked, but for many decades worked brilliantly', says Stewart. 'The essence of Taylorism isn't just drudgery, constant repetition, and narrow job descriptions. The genius of the man was to urge that management apply knowledge as well as the lash: take complex work, apply brainpower to it, and find ways to do it simpler, faster, better. It is fashionable to dump on Taylor, but important to remember that Scientific Management was a great leap forward, not just in terms of productivity but also in terms of the dignity of labor.'[4]

While it is difficult to accept that Taylor enhanced the 'dignity of labor', Stewart's point that Taylor was a creature of his times is worth remembering. His contribution was significant as it encouraged thinkers to consider the nature of work and how best to manage people and resources. For the first time, thinkers began to give serious consideration to work. While Taylor's concepts are now usually regarded in a negative light, the originality of his insights and their importance are in little doubt. While acknowledging Scientific Management as 'one of the great liberating, pioneering insights' Peter Drucker identified its weak points in *The Practice of Management*: 'Scientific Management, despite all its worldly success, has not succeeded in solving the problem of managing worker and work. As so often happens in the history of ideas, its insight is only half an insight. It has two blind spots, one engineering and one philosophical.' Drucker argued that the engineering defect is that 'to take apart and to put together are different things. To confuse the two is grossly unscientific.' The other blemish, said Drucker, was to fail to recognize that 'planning and doing are separate parts of the same job; they are not separate jobs'.[5]

That Taylorism lives on is undoubted. After the death of his heirs, the Stevens Institute of Technology in Hoboken, New Jersey, received around $10 million from Taylor's sizeable estate. In keeping with his principles, Taylor had stipulated how the Institute was to invest the money. Indeed, Taylor specified how much of the income from share dividends could be reinvested. His plan covers the next 180 years and could potentially amount to an $8.6 billion endowment.

Notes

1   J.C. Worthy, *Big Business and Free Men*, Harper & Row, New York, 1959, pp. 74–5.
2   Juran, Joseph, 'The Taylor system and quality control'.
3   Quoted in Crainer, Stuart, *The Ultimate Book of Business Quotations*, Capstone, Oxford, 1997.
4   Stewart, Thomas, *Intellectual Capital*, Nicholas Brealey, London, 1997.

5   Drucker, Peter F., *The Practice of Management*, Harper & Row, New York, 1954.

Bibliography

Shop Management, Harper & Row, New York, 1903.
The Principles of Scientific Management, Harper & Row, New York, 1913.

Alvin Toffler

"If you have the right knowledge, you can substitute it for all the other facts of production. You reduce the amount of labor, capital, energy, raw materials, and space you need in the warehouse. So knowledge is not only a factor of production, it's the factor of production, and none of the powers that be in Washington and in the industrial centers of our country seem yet to fully comprehend it. It scares them. It's threatening."

Alvin Toffler

American futurist
Born 1928

Breakthrough ideas

Adhocracy
Post-industrialization

Key books

Future Shock
The Third Wave
Powershift

A lvin Toffler (born 1928) may not have invented the future; but he all but invented the business of futurology. Toffler, along with John Naisbitt, remains the world's best known purveyor of trends, scenarios and predictions. His work has often been prophetic and is always interesting.

Toffler – who works alongside his wife, Heidi – studied English at New York University. 'I was your typical liberal arts student. Math and science were absolutely the subjects that gave me the most difficulty. But for some reason, I knew at a very young age that technology was important and science was important, and so I took a course in the history of technology and then read, read and read.'[1]

When not discovering the world of science, Toffler wrote poetry, outlined prospective novels, and worked in factories. Toffler's journalistic career evolved slowly, helped along by a commission from IBM to write a report on the long-term social and organizational implications of the computer. He then became a Washington correspondent for a Pennsylvania newspaper and an associate editor of *Fortune* before spending time as a Visiting Professor at Cornell University, a Visiting Scholar at the Russell Sage Foundation and teaching at the New School for Social Research.

Toffler's first high impact work was the 1970 book, *Future Shock* (1970). '*Future Shock* suggested that businesses were going to re-structure themselves repeatedly', says Toffler. 'That they would have to reduce hierarchy and [adopt] what we termed ad-hocracy. This sounded sensational to many readers'.[2] It also sounded laughable to many others. After decades of assembling carefully constructed hierarchies and ornate bureaucracies, companies saw no reason to dismantle them.

The book's origins lay in Toffler's time in Washington where he came to the conclusion that the political systems were hopelessly outdated. (Virtually every other Washington correspondent comes to the same conclusion. Most do not go on to consider how things should be changed.) Some of the ideas were signposted in a 1965 article, 'The future as a way of life', which suggested that accelerating change and uncertainty were going to be characteristics of the future. Toffler regarded the term future shock 'as an analogy to the concept of culture shock. With future shock you stay in one place but your own culture changes so rapidly that it has the same disorienting effect as going to another culture'.[3]

Toffler's theorizing came as a rude awakening to many readers. In 1970 corporate American was at the height of its powers. The oil crisis of the 1970s was yet to happen; corporate giants appeared to have achieved immortality; economists mapped what would happen decades into the future with apparent confidence. At a time of security and arrogance, Toffler preached insecurity and humility. No utopian idealist, Toffler's future was grounded in reality rather than flights of fancy.

In this, Toffler's vision of the future was greatly different from those of other crystal-ball gazers. The mainstream futurists of the early 1970s predicted a leisure age. We would work less and play more. After the decades of wealth creation and rising standards of living, this seemed the inevitable result. How wrong they were. The leisure age failed to materialize. We now work harder in more insecure jobs. Toffler correctly anticipated that technology would enable us to work differently rather than doing away with work altogether – 'Machine synchronization shackled the human to the machine's capabilities and imprisoned all of social life in a common frame. It did so in capitalist and socialist countries alike. Now, as machine synchronization grows more precise, humans, instead of being imprisoned, are progressively freed.'

Toffler differed from mainstream thought in a number of other ways. First, he was not taken in by the burgeoning overconfidence of the time. His starting point was that things needed to change dramatically. The second crucial area of difference was that Toffler had a keen awareness of the technological potential. The future he envisaged was driven by technology and knowledge. These two themes are constant throughout his work. 'The image of the office of the future is too neat, too smooth, too disembodied to be real. Reality is always messy. But it is clear that we are rapidly on our way, and even a partial shift towards the electronic office will be enough to trigger an eruption of social, psychological, and economic consequences. The coming word-quake means more than just new machines. It promises to restructure all the human relationships and roles in the office as well,' he later wrote in *The Third Wave*.

Toffler's subsequent work has simply added emphasis to his early arguments. His books appear every ten years and map out the technological leaps necessary for survival in the next ten years – *The Third Wave* appeared in 1980 and *Powershift* in 1990. Toffler's latest work is (the premature) *War and Anti-War* (1993) which argues that 'as new civilizations emerge they bring with them new forms of warfare and as new forms of warfare emerge, new forms of peacefare are required'.

Toffler's argument of the 1980s was encapsulated in *The Third Wave*. While others looked at the impact of technology or the impact of increased amounts of information, Toffler sought out a panoramic view. 'Humanity faces a quantum leap forward. It faces the deepest social upheaval and creative restructuring of all time. Without clearly recognizing it, we are engaged in building a remarkable new civilization from the ground up. This is the meaning of the Third Wave,' he wrote. Toffler ushered in the new technological era and bade farewell to the Second Wave of industrialization. 'Old ways of thinking, old formulas, dogmas, and ideologies, no matter how cherished or how useful in the past, no longer fit the facts', Toffler wrote. 'The world that is fast emerging from the clash of new values and technologies, new geopolitical relationships, new lifestyles and modes of communication, demands wholly new ideas and analogies, classifications and concepts.'

'The death of industrialism and the rise of a new civilization' meant mass customization rather than mass production. 'The essence of Second Wave manufacture was the long "run" of millions of identical standardized products. By contrast, the essence of Third Wave manufacture is the short run of partially or completely customized products,' wrote Toffler. This notion of mass customization has since been picked up by a wide variety of thinkers and, in some areas, is already in existence.

From a technological perspective, Toffler has been amazingly accurate in his predictions. Such has been the pace of change that Toffler can appear to have under-stated the likely technological leaps. In 1980, for example, Toffler had to explain what a word processor is – and mentioned its alternative labels, 'the smart typewriter' or 'text editor'. He envisaged the office of the future: 'The ultimate beauty of the electronic office lies not merely in the steps saved by a secretary in typing and correcting letters. The automated office can file them in the form of electronic bits on tape or disc. It can (or soon will) pass them through an electronic dictionary that will automatically correct their spelling errors. With the machines hooked up to one another and to the phone lines, the secretary can instantly transmit the letter to its recipient's printer or screen.'

In 1980, to the vast majority of Toffler's readers, this read like science fiction. Just a few years later it was reality for many in the industrialized world (or de-industrialized world, according to Toffler's perspective). In a 1996 interview, he reflected: 'The single, most important educational gain in America in the last 15 or 20 years has been the fact that 20, 30 or 40 million Americans have learned to use a PC ... What happened was, through an informal process of people-to-people learning, an enormous bank of skills was distributed through our society. No school. Schools didn't matter in that process. Virtually none. That says to me, if we understood people-to-people learning, and distributed intelligence, we could transform and accelerate the learning processes in fabulous ways that have nothing to do with schoolrooms and seats.'[4]

Toffler has also gone on to explore the wider implications of such changes, within organizations and within countries and regions. The company of the future, he predicts, will be a 'multipurpose institution', driven to redefine itself through five forces:

- **Changes in the physical environment** – companies are having to undertake greater responsibility for the effect of their operations on the environment.
- **Changes in the 'line-up of social forces'** – the actions of companies now have greater impact with those of other organizations such as schools, universities, civil groups and political lobbies.
- **Changes in the role of information** – 'As information becomes central to production, as "information managers" proliferate in industry, the corporation, by necessity, impacts on the informational environment exactly as it impacts on the physical and social environment', writes Toffler.
- **Changes in government organization** – the profusion of government bodies means that the business and political worlds interact to a far greater degree than ever before.

- **Changes in morality** – the ethics and values of organizations are becoming more closely linked to those of society. 'Behavior once accepted as normal is suddenly reinterpreted as corrupt, immoral or scandalous', says Toffler. 'The corporation is increasingly seen as a producer of moral effects.'

The organization of the future, Toffler envisages, will be concerned with ecological, moral, political, racial, sexual and social problems, as well as traditional commercial ones.

Toffler's perspective became even broader with the 1990 book, *Powershift*. In this he accurately predicted the growth of regionalism and the profusion of local media. This, in one of his ungainly phrases, is the 'de-massifying' of our culture. In many ways, Toffler has come full circle. The limitations of the institutions that ignited his interest in the 1960s largely remain. The ticking bomb underneath the Western world continues to tick. 'All the social institutions designed for the second wave – for a mass production, mass media, mass society – are in crisis. The health system, the family system, the education system, the transportation system, various ecological systems – along with our value and epistemological systems. All of them,' he says. 'And the emerging third-wave civilization is going to collide head-on with the old first and second civilizations. One of the things we ought to learn from history is that when waves of change collide they create countercurrents. When the first and the second wave collided we had civil wars, upheavals, political revolutions, forced migrations. The master conflict of the 21st century will not be between cultures but between the three supercivilizations – between agrarianism, industrialism and post-industrialism.'[5]

Notes

1 'Alvin Toffler: still shocking after all these years', *New Scientist*, 19 March 1994.

2 Gibson, Rowan (editor), *Rethinking the Future*, Nicholas Brealey, London, 1997.

3 'Alvin Toffler: still shocking after all these years', *New Scientist*, 19 March 1994.

4 Interview with Alvin Toffler, *Star Tribune*, March 1886.
5 Schwartz, Peter, 'Shock wave (anti) warrior', *Wired*, 1993.

Bibliography

Future Shock, Bodley Head, London, 1970.
The Third Wave, Bantam, New York, 1980.

Robert Townsend

"Big companies are small companies that succeeded."

Robert Townsend

American executive
Born 1920

Breakthrough ideas

Debunking corporate life

Key book

Up the Organization

B orn in 1920, **Robert Townsend** did all the right things to become corporate man. He was highly educated – at Princeton and Columbia – and held a number of important executive positions. He was partner in charge of research at Hass & Company and spent 13 years as director of American Express. Townsend joined Avis Rent-a-Car in 1962 and was the company's President until it was absorbed into the ITT empire.

This experience equipped him wonderfully for a career change. The straight exec, Robert Townsend transformed himself into a witty commentator on the excesses of corporate life. The new model Townsend first appeared with the bestseller *Up the Organization* (1970), sub-titled 'How to stop the corporation from stifling people and strangling profits'. The British management writer Robert Heller called the book 'the first pop bestseller on business management' which 'owed much of its success to Townsend's derisive title'. There was also a hilariously funny book behind the title page. Its sequel was *Further Up the Organization* (1984); and, most recently, Townsend has written *The B2 Chronicles* (1997) which recounts the story of a company called QuoVadoTron and includes characters such as Crunch, Dooley and Archibald.

Townsend has not returned to corporate life and now 'divides his time between books, boats and family' and undertakes a little consultancy work. There is a degree of irony in Townsend pursuing a consultancy sideline as his quip on consultants – 'They are the people who borrow your watch to tell you what time it is and then walk off with it' – remains one of the most quoted put-downs of an entire industry.

Townsend's genius lies in debunking the modern organization for its excess, stupidity and absurdity. He is also acutely aware of the boredom of the corporation. 'In the average company the boys in the mailroom, the president, the vice-presidents, and the girls in the steno pool have three things in common: they are docile, they are bored, and they are dull', observes Townsend. 'Trapped in the pigeonholes of organization charts, they've been made slaves to the rules of private and public hierarchies that run mindlessly on and on because nobody can change them.'

Townsend is the ultimate skeptic. Those with power, or who think they have power, are dangerous beings. 'The sin of hubris is inevitably and inexorably followed by Nemesis,' warns Townsend. He is, by turn, playful, indignant, critical and practical. 'A personnel man with his arm around an employee is like a treasurer with his hand in the till', he notes. Commonsensical aphorisms speckle his prose.

There is a serious side to Townsend. 'There's nothing fundamentally wrong with our country except that the leaders of all our major organizations are operating on the wrong assumptions', he writes. 'We're in this mess because for the last two hundred years we've been using the Catholic Church and Caesar's legions as our patterns for creating organizations, And until the last forty or fifty years it made sense. The average churchgoer, soldier, and factory worker was uneducated and dependent on orders from above. And authority carried considerable weight because disobedience brought the death penalty or its equivalent.'

His greatest vehemence is reserved for Harvard Business School – 'Don't hire Harvard Business School graduates', he advises. 'This elite, in my opinion, is missing some pretty fundamental requirements for success: humility; respect for people on the firing line; deep understanding of the nature of the business and the kind of people who can enjoy themselves making it prosper; respect from way down the line; a demonstrated record of guts, industry, loyalty down, judgment, fairness, and honesty under pressure.'

More useful, if still obtuse, is Townsend's observation that 'top management (the board of directors) is supposed to be a tree full of owls – hooting when management heads into the wrong part of the forest. I'm still unpersuaded they even know where the forest is.'

Townsend has no time for the adornments of executive office and his list of 'no-nos' includes: reserved parking spaces; special-quality stationery for the boss and his elite; muzak; bells and buzzers; company shrinks; outside directorships and trusteeships for the chief executive ('Give up all those non-jobs. You can't even run your own company, dummy'); and the company plane. He is, in fact, preaching a brand of empowerment and participation that was 20 years ahead of its time. Humorous it may be but, as with all great humor, there is a serious undercurrent.

Bibliography

Up the Organization, Michael Joseph, London, 1970.

Further Up the Organization, Random House, New York, 1984.

The B2 Chronicles: Uncommon Wisdom for Un-corporate America, Berkley Publishing Group, 1995.

Reinventing Leadership (with Warren Bennis), William Morrow & Co., New York, 1997.

Fons Trompenaars

"The international manager needs to go beyond awareness of cultural differences. He or she needs to respect these differences and take advantage of diversity through reconciling cross-cultural dilemmas. The international manager reconciles cultural dilemmas."

Fons Trompenaars

Dutch consultant and researcher
Born 1952

Breakthrough ideas

Managing globalization
Cultural issues

Key book

Riding the Waves of Culture

W hile other management thinkers rant and rave about the intricacies of strategic management and marketing, Dutch consultant and author, **Fons Trompenaars** (born 1952) paints on a larger canvas. Not for Trompenaars the world of miniatures. His subject is the universal one of cultural diversity. How do we think? How do we behave in certain situations? How does that affect the way we manage businesses? And what are the skills essential to managing globally?

'Basic to understanding other cultures is the awareness that culture is a series of rules and methods that a society has evolved to deal with the recurring problems it faces', says Trompenaars. 'They have become so basic that, like breathing, we no longer think about how we approach or resolve them. Every country and every organization faces dilemmas in relationships with people; dilemmas in relationship to time; and dilemmas in relations between people and the natural environment. Culture is the way in which people resolve dilemmas emerging from universal problems.'

The roots of his interest in the perils, practice and potential of cross-cultural life go back to Trompenaars' childhood. Brought up by a Dutch father and a French mother, he later studied at top American business school Wharton, which played a part in convincing him that the American management model was neither perfect nor universally applicable.

Prior to arriving at Wharton in 1979, Trompenaars received a Dutch masters in business economics, a more academic form of the MBA. 'While MBAs give brilliant answers to the wrong questions, we specialized in brilliant questions with no answers', he explains with characteristics gusto.[1] Trompenaars' studies at Wharton were funded by a one-year scholarship from the EEC which involved negotiating a heavyweight interviewing panel of the late Gunnar Hedlund, Andre Laurent and Geert Hofstede.

'I became interested in management and culture. At the time there was nothing in the field. The first articles by Hofstede were beginning to appear. People wandered what it was,' he recalls. 'Wharton had a fantastic program on social systems. I am still excited by that period. I met people like Russ Ackoff.' Among the other luminaries Trompenaars encountered at Wharton were Eric Trist, Fred Emery and Stafford Beer who was a guest lecturer. 'It was the foundation of my thinking. I got sucked into the program,' says Trompenaars.

The idea was that after a year he would return to Holland as an academic, but he secured sponsorship from Shell for a further three years. Shell gave Trompenaars complete freedom and, in 1982, he received his PhD and joined the oil giant. 'I was enormously arrogant, I had been to Wharton, but Shell treated me like any other graduate. They didn't care less about Wharton,' says Trompenaars.

He spent three years with Shell, finishing up working on a culture change project. He then worked part-time for the company before founding the Center for International Business Studies. Trompenaars is now developing his research and ideas further through the Trompenaars–Hampden-Turner Group.

Trompenaars' book, *Riding the Waves of Culture*, was published in 1993. It is one of those slow-burning bestsellers. Indeed, its sales have increased each quarter ever since publication. 'When I wrote the book I wrote it for myself', says Trompenaars.

Now in his mid-forties, Trompenaars continues to have a troubled relationship with the American business world, which tends to regard his work as concerned with diversity, racial and sexual, rather than to do with different cultures. Even so, he has his American fans – Tom Peters was an enthusiastic reviewer of *Riding the Waves of Culture*. Calling it a masterpiece, Peters noted: 'What's not okay is cultural arrogance. If you come to another's turf with sensitivity and open ears – what the Zen teachers call beginner's mind – you're halfway home. I think Trompenaars is correct when he says we'll never master anybody else's culture. That means keeping a beginner's mind in perpetuity is a must for successful – and less stressful – dealings throughout the emergent global village.' Others remain suspicious and leap to defend the American approach. Gary Hamel has acerbically issued a challenge: 'Funny how American companies are out-competing their European competitors in Asia and Latin America. Name any region of the world that looks to Europe for its managerial inspiration.'

Undeterred by such hype and hyperbole, Trompenaars remains more cosmopolitan man than corporate man. He is still dismissive of the American (or any other) managerial model – 'It is my belief that you can never understand other cultures. I started wondering if any of the American management techniques I was brainwashed with in eight years of the best business education money could buy would apply in the Netherlands, where I came from, or indeed in the rest of the world.' The answer he provides is simply that they do not. (Trompenaars points out that Americans are adept at reconciling cultural differences – teamworking, for example, is highly important in American companies.)

To the ethereal world of culture, Trompenaars has brought enthusiastic vigor. His books are based around exhaustive and meticulous research. Typically, *Riding the Waves of Culture* drew from over 900 seminars, presented in 18 countries. The Trompenaars database is a large and impressive beast – his latest book emerged from a 58-item questionnaire among 34,000 middle and senior managers from some 58 countries. This produced two million responses. 'I love research but wouldn't survive if that was all I did,' says Trompenaars. 'The essence of what I do is the transformation of fairly complex models into an appealing, practical setting. There is now a tendency to be too theoretical so it is the transformation into what managers can use that is important.'

The complexity of the research simply, in Trompenaars' eyes, matches the complexity of the subject. 'Management is beyond simple rationalization', he says. (The corollary of this is that anyone who simplifies or rationalizes the world of business is an impostor.)

For all the nationalistic nerves it touches, at the heart of Trompenaars' research is a relatively simple proposition: the only positive route forward for individuals, organizations, communities and societies is through reconciliation. 'Our hypothesis is that those societies that can reconcile better are better at creating wealth. More successful companies are those which reconcile more effectively,' says Trompenaars. The rich don't get even; they get on with each other.

As a result, how international managers reconcile differences is the very essence of their job. Of course, it is easy to make such statements while managing in the global environment – even for Trompenaars' most fervent of disciples – remains wrought with difficulty. 'Globalization is just starting and people are realizing its implications', he says.

As a key to the complexity, in his earlier work Trompenaars presented a number of fundamentally different cultural perspectives while acknowledging that within a country attachment to any given cultural trait varies widely. The first of these intriguing pairings is the conflict between what Trompenaars labels the 'universalist' and the 'particularist'. Universalists (including Americans, Canadians, Australians and the Swiss) advocate 'one best way', a set of rules that applies in any setting. Particularists (South Koreans, Chinese and Malaysians) focus on the peculiar nature of any given situation.

Trompenaars examined the extremes by way of archetypal situations. In the universalist–particularist conflict, he presented the following dilemma: You are in a car with a close friend who has an accident in which a third party is injured. You are the only witness, and he asks you to testify falsely about his driving speed. In such a situation, universalists won't lie for their friend while particularists will. The difference becomes even more pronounced if the injury is severe. The universalist becomes even more adherent to the rules while the particularist's sense of obligation grows. (In this example, 74 percent of South Koreans would assist their friend and lie, compared to just five percent of Americans.)

Such results allow Trompenaars to provide advice on how business dealings between the two parties might work. Universalists doing business with particularists should, for example, 'be prepared for meandering or irrelevancies that do not seem to be going anywhere'; moreover, we should not 'take get to know you chatter as small talk'. It is important to particularists. Particularists doing business with universalists should 'be prepared for rational and professional arguments and presentations'.

The cultural imponderables and wide range of basic differences in how different cultures perceive the world provides a daunting picture of the world riddled with potential pitfalls. 'We need a certain amount of humility and a sense of humor to discover cultures other than our own; a readiness to enter a room in the dark and stumble over unfamiliar furniture until the pain in our shins reminds us of where things are', says Trompenaars. Most managers, it seems, are more intent on protecting their shins than blundering through darkened rooms.

Honing in on the great imponderables is Trompenaars' latest book, *Mastering the Infinite Game*, written with long-term collaborator, Charles Hampden-Turner of Cambridge's Judge Institute of

Management Studies. Hampden-Turner was also co-author of the 1994 book *The Seven Cultures of Capitalism* and is now credited as co-author of *Riding the Waves of Culture.*

The duo argue that the massive and dramatic success of the East Asian 'tiger economies' can be attributed to 'seven major integrations'. Central to these are cultural differences which mean that the lost managerial souls of the West find themselves 'playing Finite Games in which individuals win or lose by specific criteria in universal contests'. In contrast, the East Asians are playing an Infinite Game 'with rules which are adapted by the exceptions they encounter, with contests from which all players learn co-operatively'.

Not surprisingly, Trompenaars and Hampden-Turner identify fundamental differences in Western and Eastern values. The West believes in rule by laws (universalism) while the East believes in unique and exceptional circumstances (particularist); winning is opposed by negotiating consensus; success is good opposes the belief that the good should succeed. The differences between West and East have been much debated and there is little to disagree about in Trompenaars and Hampden-Turner's list. But that is not their argument. Instead, their argument remains the same: reconciling different values is key to success – and it is something that Eastern cultures have proved marvelously adept at achieving. While the East settles the difference, the West remains obsessed with splitting the difference. It is a cultural imponderable that is enough to make even Fons Trompenaars despair.

Notes

1 Interview with the author, November 1997 (as are all other quotes unless otherwise stated).

Bibliography

Riding the Waves of Culture (with Charles Hampden-Turner), Nicholas Brealey, London, 1993.

The Seven Cultures of Capitalism (with Charles Hampden-Turner), Piatkus, London, 1994.

Mastering the Infinite Game (with Charles Hampden-Turner), Capstone, Oxford, 1997.

Sun-Tzu

"Opportunities multiply as they are seized."

Sun-Tzu

Chinese soldier philosopher
c. 500 BC

Breakthrough ideas

Strategy and competitive tactics

Key book

The Art of War

M anagerial metaphors are sadly uninspired but have usually proved long lasting. Two metaphors spring to mind as archetypes of the industrial age. First, the organization as machine (see the sections on Frederick Taylor and Max Weber for its inspiration). The second regards competition as war. This remains a powerful image. At a sales conference somewhere in the world, a CEO is talking about outflanking the competition, obliterating the competition. Business is war. Books as diverse as Carl Von Clausewitz's *On War* (1908), BH Liddell-Hart's *Strategy* (1967) and Miyamoto Mushashi's *A Book of Five Rings* (1974) have explored the link. Military role models – whether they are Napoleon, Montgomery, MacArthur, Colin Powell or Norman Schwarzkopf – are keenly seized upon by executives. The military, with its elements of strategy and leadership, is alluring and the link between the military and business worlds has existed since time immemorial. Its starting point, as far as it is possible to discern, is **Sun-Tzu's** *The Art of War* written 2500 years ago.

The authorship of *The Art of War* remains, perhaps understandably, clouded in mystery. It may have been written by Sun Wu, a military general who was alive around 500 BC. His book is reputed to have led to a meeting between Sun Wu and King Ho-lü of Wu. Sun Wu, not having a flip chart available, argued his case for military discipline by decapitating two of the King's concubines. This proved his point admirably. The book's actual title is *Sun Tzu Ping Fa* which can be literally translated as 'The military method of venerable Mr Sun'.

The book returned to grace bookshelves in the 1980s. Its return to popularity can be attributed to a number of reasons. First, Western industry felt itself under siege. Japanese companies appeared to be staging a relentless onslaught. Warfare seemed a more appropriate metaphor than ever before. Second, there was a rise in interest in Eastern managerial models and thinking. Kenichi Ohmae charted the Japanese take-on strategy, while Pascale and Athos examined the Japanese art of management. The East was fashionable. The third impetus to Sun-Tzu's comeback was Michael Porter's work on competitive advantage. Strategy and competitive advantage also became fashionable. Reading Sun-Tzu was a great deal easier on the mind than coming to terms with Michael Porter. Kill or be killed appealed to executive machismo in a way the five forces framework failed to do.

And this was how Sun-Tzu was (and continues to be) generally regarded. In the same way as Machiavelli is pigeonholed under helpful hints on amoral leadership, Sun-Tzu is filed under means of destroying competition and sending them to oblivion. Simple really. The attraction of the military analogy is that it is clear who your enemy is. When your enemy is clear, the world appears clearer if you are a military general or a managing director. Sun-Tzu is an aggressive counterpoint to the confusion of mere theory. After all, among his advice was the following: 'Deploy forces to defend the strategic points; exercise vigilance in preparation, do not be indolent. Deeply investigate the true situation, secretly await their laxity. Wait until they leave their strongholds, then seize what they love.'

Managers lapped up such brazen brutality. Yet *The Art of War* is more sophisticated than that. Why destroy when you can win by stealth and cunning? 'If you are near the enemy, make him believe you are far from him. If you are far from the enemy, make him believe you are near,' wrote the master. Michael Porter never made it that simple. 'A sovereign should not start a war out of anger, nor should a general give battle out of rage. For while anger can revert to happiness and rage to delight, a nation that has been destroyed cannot be restored, nor can the dead be brought back to life,' wrote Sun-Tzu. 'To subdue the enemy's forces without fighting is the summit of skill. The best approach is to attack the other side's strategy; next best is to attack his alliances; next best is to attack his soldiers; the worst is to attack cities.'

Sun-Tzu also offered sound advice on knowing your markets. 'Advance knowledge cannot be gained from ghosts and spirits ... but must be obtained from people who know the enemy situation.'

The final attraction of Sun-Tzu was that managers were drawn to Zen-like aphorisms. Confucian analogies appear to be anathema to hard headed modern executives. Often, however, they appear to find them reassuring. 'For the shape of an army is like that of water', said Sun Tzu. 'The shape of water is to avoid heights and flow towards low places; the shape of the army is to avoid strength and to strike at weakness. Water flows in accordance with the ground; an army achieves victory in accordance with the enemy.' Quite how this might help you manage a ball bearing maker in Illinois more effectively is difficult to imagine.

While the imagery of warfare continues to exert influence over managers, it appears to be on the wane. Contemporary business metaphors are as likely to emerge from biology and the environment as from the traditional sources of engineering and warfare. For example, American consultant James Moore argues that 'in guiding their companies from one era to the next, managers need to understand how their ecosystem works'. If they fail to do so, they risk extinction. Moore says that the creation of business 'ecosystems' is a matter of evolution rather than revolution – 'Life arrives only through spectacular stamina, patience and luck'. What is important in his metaphor is that ecosystems rely on rich, complex and constantly changing systems of mutual reliance and benefit. To view the business world in this way is daunting, but provides an opportunity. Companies must anticipate the next stage in the development of their ecosystem. Moore suggests that products that fail because they are too late or too early for the marketplace have probably done so because they are not 'sensitive to the current state of capability building within an ecosystem'.

The message is that innovation must be attuned to the ecosystem if it is to succeed. It is only by being constantly aware of the nuances of their environment that companies can survive. Otherwise they will quickly become corporate dodos.

This all sounds very modern and profound. But is it a million miles away from much of the wisdom of Sun-Tzu? I doubt it.

Bibliography

The Art of War (transl. Griffith), Oxford University Press, Oxford, 1963.

Thomas Watson Jr

"I believe that the real difference between success and failure in a corporation can very often be traced to the question of how well the organization brings out the great energies and talents of its people. What does it do to help these people find common cause with each other? And how can it sustain this common cause and sense of direction through the many changes which take place from one generation to another?"

Thomas Watson Jr

American executive and diplomat
1914–94

Breakthrough ideas

Corporate culture and values

Key book

A Business and Its Beliefs

C ommentators tend to have mixed feelings about **Thomas Watson Jr** (1914–93). To some he was the son who inherited control of a corporate juggernaut and did little to put his own stamp on its destination. To others he was the man who brought IBM into the technological era and who mapped out how values and culture could shape an entire organization. In 1987 Watson was hailed by *Fortune* as 'the most successful capitalist in history'.

Whichever interpretation is correct, Watson had a significant role in the shaping of the modern IBM – a company whose trials and tribulations continue to fill the media.

Watson's father, the redoutable Thomas Watson Sr (1874–1956), built the industrial colossus IBM from what had previously been the nondescript Computing, Tabulating, Recording Company. Watson Jr attended Brown University and served in the Air Corps during World War II. He joined IBM in 1946 and worked as a salesman. (At that time the company had just launched its Selective Sequence Electronic Calculator and had revenues of $119 million.) Watson Jr became chief executive in 1956 and retired in 1970. He was then US ambassador in Moscow until 1980.

Watson Jr was always in the shadow of his father – 'The secret I learned early on from my father was to run scared and never think I had made it', he said – but under him IBM was propelled to the forefront of the technological and corporate revolution of the 1960s and 1970s. Most notably, Watson invested heavily in the development of System/360 which formed the basis of the company's success in the 1970s and 1980s.

Watson's real claim to managerial fame does not, however, lie in the company's technological achievements. Indeed, these were something he himself sometimes questioned. In 1965, Watson despaired at IBM's weak response to Seymour Cray's development of the CDC 6600. 'Contrasting this modest effort of 34 people including the janitor with our vast development activities, I fail to understand why we have lost our industry leadership position by letting someone else offer the world's most powerful computer', said Watson. How could a minnow out-innovate a giant? Cray had a quick riposte: 'It seems Mr Watson has answered his own question.'

In terms of management thinking, what IBM stood for was more important than what it made. Under Watson, the corporate culture and the company's values became all-important. They were the glue that kept a sprawling international operation under control.

The three basic beliefs on which IBM was built were: give full consideration to the individual employee; spend a lot of time making customers happy; and go the last mile to do things right. These had been established under Watson Sr, a man who knew all about customer service long before it was taken up by the gurus. But, while Watson Sr was content to drum the message home, his son took it a step further.

Watson Jr codified and clarified what IBM stood for – most notably in his book, *A Business and Its Beliefs* (1963). Central to this were the company's central beliefs (or what would now be called core values). Watson said that a culture could only be sustained by 'a sound set of beliefs, on which it premises all its policies and actions. Next, I believe that the most important single factor in corporate success is faithful adherence to those beliefs ... beliefs must always come before policies, practices, and goals. The latter must always be altered if they are seen to violate fundamental beliefs.'

Beliefs, said Watson, never change. Change everything else, but never the basic truths on which the company is based – 'If an organization is to meet the challenges of a changing world, it must be prepared to change everything about itself except beliefs as it moves through corporate life ... The only sacred cow in an organization should be its basic philosophy of doing business.'

Whether IBM collapsed because it failed to change or adapt its beliefs to new times is difficult to determine. Watson saw it coming. 'I'm worried that IBM could become a big, inflexible organization which won't be able to change when the computer business goes through its next shift', Watson told Chris Argyris of Harvard in the 1950s when Argyris did some work for the company. Watson saw the future but couldn't mobilize the corporate culture he did so much to clarify, in structures or practices that enabled IBM to pick up the baton.

'For 20 years IBM was in charge of the transformation agenda in the computer industry. Then the industry became driven by the vision and strategy of other companies. IBM's problems are not about implementation but foresight,' says Gary Hamel.

Bibliography

A Business and its Beliefs, McGraw Hill, New York, 1963.

Max Weber

"The organization of offices follows the principle of hierarchy; that is each lower office is under the control and supervision of a higher one.**"**

Max Weber

German sociologist
1864–1920

Breakthrough ideas

Bureaucratic model of organization

Key book

The Theory of Social and Economic Organization

I n his 1992 book, *Liberation Management,* Tom Peters championed a new form of business organization. 'We're all in Milan's *haute couture* business and Hollywood's movie business ... everyone must be an expert in a fast-paced fashionized world', he announced with typical bravado. The new organizational reality, according to Peters, was anarchic, exciting, freewheeling. Order and the dull regime of corporate life were dead. Long live chaos, innovation and experimentation.

Meanwhile, many organizations continued to be highly successful by completely ignoring Peters' advice. They succeeded because they were very well organized, because they refused to experiment recklessly, because their systems and processes were geared to efficiency and nothing else. They may not have had Harold Geneen as CEO or been founded by Henry Ford, but Geneen and Ford would have been able to identify them as their kind of organization.

The original champion of the latter approach, a rigidly constrained corporate culture and structure, was the German sociologist, **Max Weber** (1864–1920).

Weber has had a bad press – in the business world at least. His depiction of corporations run by an overbearing bureaucratic machine struck a chord with corporate life in the early part of the century. But, just because Weber described bureaucracy does not mean that he approved of it.

Weber was multi-talented and spent his life seeking out some understanding of the relationships between science, the law, politics, knowledge and action. After studying legal and economic history, Weber was a law Professor at the University of Freiburg and later at the University of Heidelberg. He studied the sociology of religion and in this area he produced his best known work, *The Protestant Work Ethic and the Spirit of Capitalism.* In political sociology he examined the relationship between social and economic organizations. Towards the end of his life, Weber developed his political interests and was on the committee that drafted the constitution of the Weimer Republic in 1918.

In terms of management theorizing Max Weber has become something of a *bête noir*, the sociological twin of Frederick Taylor, the king of scientific rationality. Weber 'pooh-poohed charismatic leadership and doted on bureaucracy; its rule-driven, impersonal form, he said, was the only way to assure long-term survival' observed Peters and Waterman in *In Search of Excellence*.[1]

Weber did not dote on bureaucracy. he was not the doting type. Instead, he simply observed what he saw emerging in the fledgling industrial world. Weber argued that the most efficient form of organization resembled a machine. It was characterized by strict rules, controls and hierarchies and driven by bureaucracy. This, Weber termed the 'rational–legal model'. At the opposite extreme were the 'charismatic' model and the 'traditional' model. In the charismatic model, a single dominant figure ran the organization. Weber dismissed this as a long-term solution – once again Weber was the first to discuss this phenomena and examine its ramifications. No matter what Peters and Waterman say, history bears Weber out – an organization built around a single charismatic figure is unsustainable in the long term.

The final organizational form Weber identified was the traditional model where things were done as they always have been done – such as in family firms in which power is passed down from one generation to the next.

If it was pure efficiency you required there was, said Weber, only one choice: 'Experience tends universally to show that the purely bureaucratic type of administrative organization – that is, the monocratic variety of bureaucracy – is, from a purely technical point of view, capable of attaining the highest degree of efficiency and is in this sense formally the most rational known means of carrying our imperative control over human beings', Weber wrote. 'It is superior to any other form in precision, in stability, in the stringency of its discipline, and in its reliability. It thus makes possible a particularly high degree of calculability of results for the heads of the organization and for those acting in relation to it. It is finally superior both in intensive efficiency and in the scope of its operations and is formally capable of application to all kinds of administrative tasks.'

In *The Theory of Social and Economic Organization* Weber outlined the 'structure of authority' around seven points:

1 A continuous organization of official functions bound by rules.
2 A specified sphere of competence.

3   The organization of offices follows the principle of hierarchy.
4   The rules that regulate the conduct of an office may be technical rules or norms. In both cases, if their application is to be fully traditional, specialized training is necessary.
5   In the rational type it is a matter of principle that the members of the administrative staff should be completely separated from the ownership of the means of production or administration.
6   In the rational type case, there is also a complete absence of appropriation of his official position by the incumbent.
7   Administrative acts, decisions and rules are formulated and recorded in writing, even in cases where oral discussion is the rule or is even mandatory.

Modern commentators usually cannot resist the urge to scoff at Weber's insights. The bureaucratic business world he described was denuded of life and inspiration. And yet it largely came to pass.

Look at William Whyte's 1956 classic, *The Organization Man*, and its descriptions of corporate life. 'The fundamental premise of the new model executive ... is, simply, that the goals of the individual and the goals of the organization will work out to be one and the same. The young men have no cynicism about the "system", and very little skepticism – they don't see it as something to be bucked, but as something to be co-operated with ... they have an implicit faith that the organization will be as interested in making use of their best qualities as they are themselves, and this, with equanimity, they can entrust the resolution of their destiny to the organization ... the average young man cherishes the idea that his relationship with the organization is to be for keeps.' Whyte described a world where the organization choked inspiration in the name of efficiency. The individual was subsumed under the bureaucratic machine.

And, if you wish for further proof, look at the success of Scott Adams' Dilbert, based on the mundanity and regularity of corporate life.

So, the bureaucratic model as outlined by Weber to a large extent became reality. It was an undoubtedly narrow way of doing things and one which seems out of step with our times. Yet, in the early part of the twentieth century, it was a plausible and effective means of doing business. Like all great insights, it worked, for a while at least.

Notes

1   Peters, Tom, and Waterman, Robert, *In Search of Excellence*, Harper & Row, New York, 1982.

Bibliography

The Theory of Social and Economic Organization, Free Press, New York, 1947.
The Protestant Ethic and the Spirit of Capitalism, Scribner's, New York, 1958.
Economy and Society, University of California Press, 1978.

Appendix

No such compendium of thinkers could ever claim to be 100 percent foolproof. There is always room for dissension and discussion. Many others could have been among the 50 thinkers I have featured. Perhaps some *should* have been included. By way of recompense, here is a further collection of thinkers with strong cases for inclusion. Once again the thinkers are organized alphabetically.

Russ Ackoff

Russ Ackoff (born 1919) is chairman of INTERACT and Professor Emeritus at Wharton School. He is the author or co-author of 19 books, including *Creating the Corporate Future, Management in Small Doses, Ackoff's Fables* and *The Democratic Corporation*. Ackoff graduated from the University of Pennsylvania in 1941 in architecture. His doctorate at the same university was in science. He argues that interaction between different functions and individuals should be the driving force of organizations rather than functional separation. Fons Trompenaars met Ackoff while at Wharton and recalls that 'He was a guru in the real sense. Now everyone is a guru.'

John Adair

John Adair (born 1934) is a British leadership expert who has had a colorful career working on Arctic trawlers among other things. He emphasized the distinction between managing and leading. He developed the idea of Action Centred Leadership and estimated that half of the performance in teams could be attributed to the individual and the other half to the quality of leadership.

David Arnold

The British academic, David Arnold (born 1956) is an assistant professor at Harvard Business School. He has a degree in English Literature and a Masters in modern drama and worked in publishing, becoming marketing manager of the UK's Ashridge Management College. Finding himself fascinated, Arnold took an MBA and joined the Ashridge faculty – one of the few examples of a gamekeeper turning poacher. He later did a doctorate at Harvard and now teaches the core marketing course on the school's first-year MBA programme and an international marketing course. He is also taking over responsibility for the International Marketing Management element of the MBA programme.

Arnold's research centres on international marketing issues and he is also the author of *The Handbook of Brand Management*. Among his current research projects is one on emerging markets. Another focuses on customer management and he has also looked at the evolution of international distribution channels.

Charles Babbage

Charles Babbage (1792–1871) was born in London and became a Professor of Mathematics at Cambridge University (1828–39). He produced perhaps the first business bestseller in his study of British factories, *On the Economy of Machines and Manufactures* (1832). His work and observations were only a step away from Frederick Taylor's at the end of the nineteenth century (though there is no evidence that Taylor read Babbage). 'It is of great importance to know the precise expenses of every process as well as of the wear and tear of machinery which is due to it', wrote Babbage. Taylor went on to utilize the same enthusiasm for measurement to human performance. Babbage is best known for his attempts at building two calculating machines – 'the difference engine' and the 'analytical engine'. 'Errors using inadequate data are much less those using no data at all', he shrewdly noted. These are regarded as the precursors of today's computers.

Christopher Bartlett

Australian-born, Christopher Bartlett is MBA Class of 1966 Professor of Business Administration at Harvard Business School. Bartlett (born 1943) has an economics degree from the University of Queensland and masters and doctorate degrees from Harvard. He previously worked as a McKinsey consultant and as a manager. He joined the Harvard faculty in 1979. Bartlett is best known for his work with Sumantra Ghoshal (see p. 73). Their books include *Managing Across Borders* (1989) and *The Individualized Corporation* (1997). Bartlett's research focuses on corporate transformation and managing companies in a global environment.

Stafford Beer

Stafford Beer (born 1926) studied philosophy at London University. He served in the British Army during World War II where he became involved in operations research. He later worked in the steel industry as a production controller and an operations research manager. He founded and directed the department of operations research and cybernetics at United Steel. (Cybernetics is simply regarded by Beer as the science of effective organization.)

As part of his work on cybernetics, Beer developed the Viable System Model, a model of effective organizations. This identified five functions which all systems need to be viable. Within the model, the management of system behavior centers on defining and controlling essential variables, on developing corporate strategies and planning, and on integrating and co-ordinating different organizational parts. Elsewhere, Beer has argued that the functions of management are policy making, decision making and control. His books include *Brain of the Firm* (second edition 1985); *The Heart of Enterprise* (1994); and *Decision and Control* (1994).

Meredith Belbin

The British psychologist, consultant and academic Meredith Belbin (born 1926) is the doyen of the theory of teamworking. He read Classics and Psychology at Cambridge University before becoming a researcher at the Cranfield College of Aeronautics. He worked in Paris for the Organization for Economic Co-operation and Development; with the Industrial Training Research Unit at University College, London; in a number of manufacturing companies; and at Henley Management College.

Belbin's books include *Management Teams* (1984), *Team Roles at Work* (1993) and *The Coming Shape of Organization* (1996).

Eric Berne

Eric Berne (1910–70) was a Canadian psychiatrist who worked in California. He identified three ego states that dictated behavior – child, parent and adult – and applied these to group dynamics.

Julian Birkinshaw

Julian Birkinshaw (born 1964) is an assitant professor at Stockholm School of Economics' Institute of International Business. His initial research was carried out at the University of Western Ontario where he gained an MBA and a PhD in business administration. This was the basis for his continuing work on international organizations and how their subsidiaries can sometimes be innovative and entrepreneurial leaders rather than timid corporate followers. Birkinshaw is also researching how network organizations identify and leverage their core competencies. His research suggests that top performing units are good at giving knowledge away as well as bringing it in. Low performers tend to be good at neither.

Robert Blake

Robert Blake (born 1918) is Professor of Social Psychology at the University of Texas at Austin. He was involved in research at the National Training Laboratories in the 1950s and worked at the Tavistock Clinic in London. He is best known for his work with Jane Mouton (see p. 281). In 1961 they co-founded the company, Scientific Methods, 'to provide theory and practice in effective problem-solving teamwork'.

Their most famous innovation was the 'managerial grid' (see the 1964 book, *The Managerial Grid*). The managerial grid designated various styles of leadership. It showed how a leader could simultaneously maximize both production and people-oriented methods of management. It identified four extremes of management style and measured them on two dimensions: concern for production and concern for people.

Blake has also developed a new approach to learning which he calls 'Synergogy'.

Kenneth Blanchard

Cornell educated, Kenneth Blanchard launched an entirely new business book genre with his 1982 book, *The One Minute Manager* (co-authored with Spencer Johnson). It was much ridiculed by academics but bought in huge numbers – it has now sold over seven million copies, been translated into more than 25 languages and been imitated by a host of others. Blanchard has gone on to write a succession of similar books including *Raving Fans*, on customer service, and *Everyone's A Coach* with football coach, Don Shula. Blanchard's message is the sugary, but popular, one that we can all be, and inspire, winners and that a high achieving, healthy, balanced and happy life is achievable by all of us.

Edward de Bono

Edward Francis Charles Publius de Bono was born in Malta in 1933 and studied medicine at the Royal University of Malta. He was a Rhodes scholar to Oxford where he read psychology, physiology and medicine. Between 1976 and 1983 he lectured in medicine at Cambridge University. Since 1971 he has been director of the Cognitive Research Trust and Secretary General, since 1983, of the Supranational Independent Thinking Organization.

De Bono is best known as the inventor and apostle of lateral thinking, an idea which has spawned 50 books and secured worldwide fame (as well as no little fortune – de Bono organizes projects from his private island of Tessera in Venice). Lateral thinking is not sequential, vertical or necessarily rational. Instead it seeks out original perspectives by turning ideas on their head. It also makes use of analogy and random word association to break free from more conventional thinking. 'Concepts are the currency of creativity. Creativity is the way ahead,' says de Bono.

His books include *The Use of Lateral Thinking* (1967); *Teaching Thinking* (1976); and *I am Right;You are Wrong* (1990). In *Who's Who*, de Bono lists his interests as travel, toys and thinking.

Richard Boyatzis

The study behind Boyatzis' book *The Competent Manager: a model for effective performance* (1982) involved over 2000 managers who held 41 different jobs in 12 different public and private organizations. The result was a generic model of managerial competencies applicable in different contexts and organization types. The model comprises 12 competencies in six clusters. In the 1990s competencies have been an increasing part of the managerial agenda.

James MacGregor Burns

James MacGregor Burns is a political scientist. Not simply a theorist, he has stood, unsuccessfully, for Congress as a Democrat and worked in John F. Kennedy's presidential campaign.

His books include *Congress on Trial* (1949); *Government by the People* (with Jack Peltason, 1950); *Roosevelt: The Lion and the Fox* (1956); *John Kennedy: A Political Profile* (1960); *The Deadlock of Democracy* (1963); *Presidential Government: The Crucible of Leadership* (1965); *Roosevelt: The Soldier of Freedom* (1970); *Uncommon Sense* (1972) and *Edward Kennedy and the Camelot Legacy* (1976).

In the business sphere, Burns is known for a single work, *Leadership*. Burns suggested that 'leadership as a concept has dissolved into small and discrete meanings. A superabundance of facts about leaders far outruns theories of leadership.' He provided a useful definition of the subject: 'Leadership over human beings is exercised when persons with certain motives and purposes mobilize, in competition or conflict with others, institutional, political, psychological and other resources so as to arouse, engage and satisfy the motives of followers'. Aside from this thoughtful definition, Burns identified two vital strands of leadership – transformational and transactional leadership.

Tom Burns

Warren Bennis has described the 1961 book, *The Management of Innovation* as a 'major classic'. The book was based on a study of a relatively small number of Scottish companies. In it the sociologist, Burns, and his co-author psychologist, G.M. Stalker, identified the 'organic' organization characterized by networks, shared vision and values, and teamworking, echoing many contemporary theorists. Burns, a professor of sociology at Edinburgh University until his retirement in 1981, contended that such organizations were better equipped to deal with change and insecurity than organizations built around bureaucracy and command and control.

Andrew Campbell

Andrew Campbell (born 1950) is a director of the Ashridge Strategic Management Centre, London, and was previously a consultant with McKinsey & Company. He is the author (with Michael Goold) of the highly influential *Strategies and Styles* (1987); *Strategic Synergy* (with Kathleen Luchs, 1992); and *Break Up!* (with Richard Koch, 1996).

Campbell (along with his various colleagues) has examined the role of corporate centers in diversified companies. He has argued the case for and the place of strategic planning and concluded there are three dominant styles: strategic planning, strategic control and financial control. The best style for a particular company depends on the nature of the business and its long-term strategic objectives.

Campbell's most significant work is *Corporate-Level Strategy* (with Goold and Marcus Alexander, 1994) which argued that most large companies are now multibusiness organizations. Such multibusiness companies through their very size offer economies of scale and synergies between the various businesses which can be exploited to the overall good. Goold, Campbell and Alexander calculated that in over half multibusiness companies the whole is worth less than the sum of its parts. Instead of adding and nurturing value, the corporation actually negates value. It is costly and its influence, though pervasive, is often counter-productive. If corporate level strategy is to add value there needs to be a tight fit between the parent organization and its businesses. Successful corporate parents focus on a narrow range of tasks and create value in those areas, and align the structures, processes and central functions of the parent accordingly.

Peter Cohan

Peter Cohan (born 1957) runs his own consulting company in Marlborough, Massachusetts. He worked for the consulting firm, Index Systems, and after studying for an MBA at Wharton, joined Monitor, the consulting firm of Harvard's Michael Porter. Cohan's work and thinking is a distillation of some of the ideas championed in reengineering and by Porter. To these, Cohan has added his own experience from working on strategic planning with the Bank of Boston, as director of reengineering at Liberty Mutual and as a consultant to high-tech companies in Silicon Valley and Asia. To the reengineering concept he has added humanity. He is the author of *The Tech-*

nology Leaders. In it, Cohan provides a marriage of reengineering with Porter through his concept of the value triangle.

Stephen Covey

Stephen Covey (born 1932) is founder, chairman and president of the Covey Leadership center at Provo, Utah. He has an MBA from Harvard Business School and spent the bulk of his career at Brigham Young University where he was first an administrator and then professor of Organizational Behavior. His doctoral research looked at 'success literature'. In 1984 he founded his Leadership Center aiming to 'serve the worldwide community by empowering people and organizations to significantly increase their performance capability in order to achieve worthwhile purposes through understanding and living principle-centered leadership'.

Covey reached a huge global audience with the success of *The Seven Habits of Highly Effective People* (1989) which has sold over six million copies. Along the way, the devout Mormon transformed himself into an end-of-the-century Dale Carnegie. 'He has sold himself with a brashness that makes the over-excited Tom Peters look like a shrinking violet,' noted *The Economist*. Another commentator observed that 'Mr Covey has a knack of dressing up spiritual principles in pinstripes'. In fact, Covey's 'principles' are a mixture of the commonsensical and the hackneyed – 'be proactive; begin with the end in mind; put first things first; think win/win; seek first to understand then to be understood; synergize; sharpen the saw'. Yet, it is their very simplicity and accessibility which partly explains Covey's astonishing success. The Covey Leadership Center now employs over 700 people and has an annual turnover of $70 million.

Philip Crosby

Philip Crosby began his working life on an assembly line, rising to become quality manager for Martin-Marietta. At the company he came up with the concept of 'zero defects'. Crosby then spent 14 years as corporate vice president for ITT.

He set up his own company in 1979 to promote his quality theories. At the height of the quality bandwagon, Philip Crosby Associates advised 200 of the *Fortune 500*. At one time the company had 300 employees and revenues of $80 million. Crosby was called to give evidence at the Congressional Committee investigating the Challenger disaster. In 1985 Philip Crosby Associates was floated for $30 million.

In 1989, Crosby sold his company to the UK consultancy Proudfoot for $67 million. Crosby stayed on as creative director for a salary of £500,000. In 1997 he bought the company back for less than $1 million.

Crosby's books include *Quality Is Free* (1979), *Quality Without Tears* (1984) and various others on the same theme.

Richard Cyert

Richard Cyert (born 1921) is based at Philadelphia's Carnegie-Mellon University. Educated at the University of Minnesota and Columbia University, Cyert's research has covered economics, behavioral science and management. His most influential book was *A Behavioral Theory of the Firm* (originally published in 1963 but revised in 1992) which he co-authored with James March (see p. 281). The book explored the rationality, or otherwise, of management decision making. Cyert and March concluded that decisions were not always rational and advocated a more creative approach, a 'technology of foolishness', with greater experimentation.

Terence Deal

Terence Deal, a Professor at Peabody College, Vanderbilt University, is best known for his work with Allan Kennedy of McKinsey & Co. Their 1982 book, *Corporate Cultures: The rites and rituals of corporate life* argued that strong cultures lead to strong businesses and that cultures are driven by values, heroes, roles and rituals.

Fred Emery

Fred Emery worked at the Tavistock Clinic in London and collaborated with Einar Thorsrud in the development of theories of industrial democracy. They co-authored *Form and Content in Industrial Democracy*.

Jay Forrester

Jay Forrester (born 1918) is an engineer and creator of system dynamics, which has applications to the modeling of industrial development, cities and the world. MIT-based, Forrester believes that systems are all embracing and has developed a system to map any business situation. His work had considerable influence on systems theory and the ideas explored by Peter Senge in his examination of learning organizations.

Henry Gantt

Gantt graduated a year after Frederick Taylor from the same engineering college in New Jersey. He went on to develop the Gantt chart, a means of representing progress in a project.

Arie de Geus

Arie de Geus joined the Royal Dutch/Shell Group in 1951 and spent over 35 years with the company, eventually becoming group planning coordinator. His retirement has seen de Geus take on a variety of academic positions, including one at London Business School. He is also a board member of the Organizational Learning Center at MIT's Sloan School and on the board of the Nijenrode Learning Centre in the Netherlands.

De Geus has emerged as one of the most thoughtful commentators on corporate life expectancy.

De Geus began by disabusing managers of notions of corporate immortality. His research charted the regular and widespread demise of companies that were, at one time, thought immortal. His interests have now developed logically to consider what allows some companies to reach a ripe old age – such as the 700 year-old Swedish company, Stora – and what is it that sentences others to an early death.

The survivors are labeled by de Geus as 'living companies'. They are characterized by an awareness that they are made up of a community of human beings. They are more than mere producers or providers. They are thoroughly human and humane.

The living companies are, says de Geus, dedicated to long-term development. Managers regard themselves as 'stewards' rather than as temporary functionaries. Here, somewhat in Peter Sellers vein, de Geus brings in the homespun image of managers as careful gardeners, encouraging growth and renewal, but willing to scythe away when necessary. The image is something of a cliché, but that does not mean that its message can be ignored or that it is easily achieved. The living company, says de Geus, survives because it learns, adapts and evolves. It is a combination which is likely to continue to prove beyond the reach of virtually all organizations.

Andrew S. Grove

'Business is about communications, sharing data and instantaneous decision making. If you have on your desk a device that enables you to communicate and share data with your colleagues around the world, you will have a strategic advantage,' says Andy Grove (born 1936), the Hungarian-born co-founder of Intel. Grove is increasingly regarded as a management thinker as well as highly successful practitioner. He is the author of *Only the Paranoid Survive*.

Frank and Lilian Gilbreth

Frank Gilbreth (1868–1924) and his wife Lilian (1878–1972) were innovative and entrepreneurial exponents of Scientific Management.

They took Frederick Taylor's ideas forward through more intensive study of what workers actually did, labeling their approach 'motion study'. 'Eliminating unnecessary distances that workers' hands and arms must travel will eliminate miles of motions per man in a working day as compared with usual practice', they argued. Frank was a builder who became an inventor and consultant. He combined some of his talents to built a scaffold that helped make him the fastest bricklayer on a building project.

Lilian Gilbreth continued preaching her husband's efficiency message after his early death. She even used motion study to ensure the smooth running of domestic life. As she brought up 12 children this example of theory being turned into practice should not be sniffed at.

Luther Gulick

Luther Gulick was part of a President Roosevelt's committee on administrative management in the 1930s. 'Real efficiency must be built into the structure of a government just as it is built into a piece of machinery', he said. His greatest contribution to management thinking was the acronym PODSCORB, which summarized the managerial roles as Planning, Organizing, Directing, Staffing, Co-ordinating, Reporting and Budgeting.

Michael Hammer

Michael Hammer (born 1948) is an electrical engineer, former computer science professor at MIT and President of Hammer and Company, a management education and consulting firm. He is, along with James Champy (see p. 31), one of the founding fathers of re-engineering, the managerial fashion of the early 1990s. The roots of the idea lay in the research carried out by MIT from 1984 to 1989 on 'Management in the 1990s'.

Hammer and Champy co-wrote the bestselling, *Reengineering the Corporation* and Hammer wrote a sequel, *The Reengineering Revolution* (with Steven Stanton, 1995). Amid the media attention,

Hammer proved himself highly quotable, proclaiming that he was intent on reversing the industrial revolution – 'I think this is the work of angels. In a world where so many people are so deprived, it's a sin to be inefficient.' Unfortunately, many reengineered companies found themselves to be sinners.

Robert Hayes

Robert Hayes (born 1936) is best known for the 1981 *Harvard Business Review* article he co-authored with his Harvard Business School colleague, William Abernathy, 'Managing our way to economic decline'. This sounded the death knell for post-war industrial expansionism and unveiled the deficiencies at the heart of American management. 'We believe that during the past two decades American managers have increasingly relied on principles which price analytical detachment and methodological elegance over insight', concluded Hayes and Abernathy. A spell of breastbeating and eulogies to Japanese management followed.

Later Hayes moved on to provide a more positive manifesto for the future with the 1984 book, *Restoring Our Competitive Edge* (co-written with Stephen Wheelwright). Hayes argued that well-run factories throughout the world have similarities. It tackled the mythology of Japanese production techniques and argued the case for a competitive and practically implemented manufacturing strategy.

Thomas Hout

Co-author and co-protagonist with George Stalk of the fad of time-based competition, another brilliantly conceived Boston Consulting Group matrix. Their 1900 book, *Competing Against Time*, led to a flurry of interest in the subject and to growing interest in 'lean' production methods.

Allen Kennedy

McKinsey consultant and co-author, with Terence Deal (see p. 274) of *Corporate Cultures*. Kennedy was also influential in the development of the research and concepts behind Peters and Waterman's *In Search of Excellence*.

Charles Kepner

Charles Kepner and Benjamin Tregoe's *The Rational Manager* (1965) offered 'a systematic approach to problem solving and decision making'. 'The capacity to reason systematically is unquestionably a basic necessity for any manager', argued Kepner and Tregoe. The techniques detailed in *The Rational Manager* laid the basis for the duo's consultancy firm's enduring success and were updated in *The New Rational Manager*.

John Kotter

John Kotter (born 1947) is Konosuke Matsushita professor of Leadership at Harvard Business School. He is a graduate of MIT and Harvard, and joined the Harvard faculty in 1972. In 1980, aged 33, Kotter was given tenure and full professorship – one of the youngest full professors in the history of Harvard.

Kotter has proved himself amazingly prolific and wide ranging in his subject matter. His books include *The General Managers* (1982); *Power and Influence* (1985); *A Force for Change* (1990); *Corporate Culture and Performance* (with J.L. Heskett, 1992); *The New Rulers* (1996); *Matsushita Leadership* (1996); and *Leading Change* (1996).

Harold Leavitt

The American psychologist Harold Leavitt is author of *Managerial Psychology* (1978) among other books. He invented a typology that separated 'corporate pathfinders' into three types:

- **Type One** – Visionaries who are bold, charismatic, original, often eccentric, brilliant and imposing. (These include Jesus Christ, Gandhi, Martin Luther King and John F. Kennedy.)
- **Type Two** – Analysts who deal with numbers and facts rather than opinions. They are characterized by being rational, calculating and controlling. (Examples include Harold Geneen and Jimmy Carter.)
- **Type Three** –Doers who emphasize fixing and implementing. (These include Lyndon Johnson, Eisenhower and Napoleon.)

More recently Leavitt has championed the role of what he calls 'hot groups'. These are lively, high-achieving, small teams dedicated to the completion of a particular task.

Rensis Likert

The American psychologist Rensis Likert (1903–81) developed four types – Systems 1 to 4 – of management style. The first is exploitative and authoritarian; the second, 'benevolent autocracy'; the third, 'consultative' and the fourth 'participative'. The latter was seen by Likert as the best option – both in a business and a personal sense. He also proposed System 5, in which there was no formal authority. His key book is *New Patterns of Management* (1961).

Jay Lorsch

Jay Lorsch graduated from Antioch College in 1955 and also studied at Columbia University and Harvard Business School. He was a Lieutenant in the US Army Finance Corp from 1956 until 1959 and is now Director of Research and Professor of Human Relations at Harvard Business School.

In a development from Douglas McGregor's original argument, Lorsch and fellow academic John Morse argued that 'the appropriate pattern of organization is contingent on the nature of the work to be done and the particular needs of the people involved'. They labeled their approach 'contingency theory', a pragmatic juxtaposition of Theories X and Y.

More recently, Lorsch's research has concentrated on the roles and responsibilities of boards of directors, corporate governance, CEO succession and the problems encountered by top management in knowledge-intensive companies.

James March

James March (born 1918) is based at Carnegie-Mellon University. He is co-author of *A Behavioral Theory of the Firm* with Richard Cyert (see p. 274).

Chris Meyer

Chris Meyer (born 1949) is a director of the Ernst & Young Centre for Business Innovation, Boston, Massachusetts. He is a sometime economist and Harvard MBA who has transformed himself into a high-tech consultant and author. While at Mercer Management Consulting, Meyer founded the company's practice in IT industries and has been seeking to understand more about the emerging information economy ever since. He joined Ernst & Young in 1995 and heads the firm's Center for Business Innovation – an 'R&D shop' that aims to identify the issues that will be challenging business in the future and defining responses to them.

Meyer also established the Bios Group, Ernst & Young's initiative to develop complexity-based solutions for management. The entire challenge of making complexity theory understood and practical lies at the heart of Meyer's current work. In the information economy the small things are connected in a myriad of ways to create a 'complex adaptive system'. Meyer is the author of *Blur*, co-authored with the futurist, Stan Davis.

Jane Mouton

Jane Mouton (1930–87) is known for her work alongside Robert Blake (see p. 269). She was a mathematician and an ex-student of Blake's at the University of Texas. She led T-groups at the National Training

Laboratories and, in the 1960s, achieved prominence with the development of the managerial grid.

William Ouchi

William Ouchi is Professor of Management at the Anderson Graduate School of Management at UCLA, where he has been based since 1979. He formerly taught at the Universities of Stanford and Chicago. Ouchi is the author of the 1981 bestseller, *Theory Z*. Ouchi's book was a major contributor to the fascination in the 1980s, and later, with Japanese management. Ouchi sub-titled the book 'The Japanese challenge', and took as his starting point Douglas McGregor's unfinished contemplation of the theory beyond Theories X and Y. In the Japanese practices of lifetime employment and company values, Ouchi found a rich source of material echoing many of the ideas initially contemplated by McGregor. Ouchi is also author of *The M Form Society* (1984).

C. Northcote Parkinson

Charles Northcote Parkinson (1909–93) studied history at Cambridge and then undertook a PhD at King's College London. He subsequently held a variety of academic posts in the UK and the US, and later in his career was Raffles Professor of History at the University of Malaya. His theories on the machinations of administrative life were developed during five years of army service during World War II.

He is famous for Parkinson's Law that work expands to fill the time available. Parkinson's sequel to *Parkinson's Law* was *The Law and the Profits* (1960) which introduced Parkinson's Second Law: expenditure rises to meet income.

C.K. Prahalad

Indian-born, C.K. Prahalad is Harvey C Fruehauf Professor of Business Administration at the University of Michigan's Graduate School of Business Administration. He is best known for his work with Gary Hamel (see p. 79) including a series of influential *Harvard Business Review* articles and the bestselling *Competing for the Future* (1994). Prahalad studied at Harvard, the Indian Institute of Management and the University of Madras.

Reg Revans

In the 1920s Reg Revans (born 1907) worked at Cambridge's Cavendish Laboratories alongside five Nobel Prize winners. An Olympic athlete, he later became the first director of education and training at the National Coal Board. He concluded that colliery managers and miners themselves needed to acknowledge the problems they faced and then attempt to solve them. Revans spent two years underground to examine the real problems facing miners. This reinforced his idea that learning comes when problems are aired and shared in small groups of 'comrades in adversity'. The pits that tried Revans' methods recorded a 30 percent increase in productivity.

His theory, christened action learning, is deceptively simple. It is concerned with learning to learn by doing, a process for which Revans created a simple equation – $L = P + Q$ – learning occurs through a combination of programmed knowledge (P) and the ability to ask insightful questions (Q).

In the 1960s, Revans was apparently set on an academic career. The UK's first professor of industrial administration at Manchester University, he was involved in the debate about the nature of the city's soon-to-be-established business school. Again, action learning ruffled establishment feathers and Revans departed for Belgium to lead an experiment launched by the Foundation Industrie-Université with the support of the country's leading business people and five universities.

Here he found more fertile ground. The Belgians responded to the idea of action learning with enthusiasm. With minimal attention from the rest of the world, the Belgian economy enjoyed a spectacular renaissance – during the 1970s Belgian industrial productivity rose by 102 percent, compared with 28 percent in the UK. Revans continues to preach his message and numbers among his adherents the African National Congress.

Donald Schön

Donald Schön (1930–97) was educated at Yale, the Sorbonne and Harvard University. After teaching philosophy at UCLA and the University of Kansas, he joined consultants Arthur D. Little in 1957 and later worked for the US Department of Commerce. He was then President of the Organization for Social and Technical Innovation at MIT where he also became Ford Professor of Urban Studies and Education. Working with Harvard Business School's Chris Argyris (see p. 5), Schön pioneered the concept of 'action science', an investigative and intimate approach to dealing with problems and errors. Schön gave the 1970 Reith Lectures for the BBC from which was born the book, *Beyond the Stable State* (1978). Argyris and Schön co-authored *Organizational Learning* (1978) and *Theory in Practice: Increasing Professional Efficiency* (1974).

Fritz Roethlisberger

Fritz Roethlisberger (1898–1974) was based at Harvard Business School throughout his career. His most significant work was his contribution to the Hawthorne experiments. He was the author of *Management and the Worker* (with W.J. Dickson, 1939) and *Man-In-Organization* (1968).

Richard J. Schonberger

Richard Schonberger (born 1937) was trained as an industrial engineer. He was one of the first to bring Japanese management and production techniques to Western audiences. He is the author of *Japanese Manufacturing Techniques* (1982); *World Class Manufacturing* (1986); and *Building a Chain of Customers* (1990). More recently, Schonberger has argued that quality has merely dented the castle walls and organizations have yet to scale the ramparts. He believes that in many organizations, perhaps the majority, long-established functional divides remain in place. If these are to be overcome collaboration is the way forward. Companies should be 'collaboratively linking the entire production system to the customer-service/distribution sub-system'.

Once all-conquering, Schonberger laments that TQM has proved too limited a weapon. Internal collaborations are preferable to internal warfare but often they produce results too slowly or invisibly. There is a need for 'multi-echelon' agreements linking one company to another and which are 'sweeping in scope' – 'The object is service to customers not functional glory'.

E.F. Schumacher

The German economist, E.F. Schumacher (1911–77) is famous for the phrase 'Small is beautiful' though it was actually thought up by his publishers. His 1973 book of that title was an antidote to the all powerful conglomerates which held corporate sway at the time. Its organic, people-centered approach to life and business won many admirers (including Jimmy Carter). Schumacher's ideas emerged from time he spent working with the UK's National Coal Board. Here he worked with Reg Revans who counters that 'Small is dutiful' would be a more appropriate manifesto.

Peter Schwartz

Peter Schwartz (born 1946) is President of Global Business Network, a futurist think tank based in California.

Ricardo Semler

In 1990 and again in 1992, Ricardo Semler (born 1957) – majority owner of a Sao Paulo manufacturing company, Semco S/A, which specializes in marine and food-service equipment – was elected business leader of the year by a poll of 52,000 Brazilian executives. His book *Maverick!* was an international bestseller. In Brazil it was on the bestseller list for 200 weeks. The book told Semler's remarkable story of empowering the company's workforce. 'Democracy has yet to penetrate the workplace', said Semler. 'Dictators and despots are alive and well in offices and factories all over the world.'

Semler has studied at Harvard Business School and has written articles for the *Harvard Business Review*. He was Vice-President of the Federation of Industries of Brazil and is a member of the board of SOS Atlantic Forest, Brazil's foremost environmental organization.

Herbert Simon

Herbert Simon (born 1916) is a cognitive scientist and economist who won the Nobel prize for economics in 1978. In a management context, he is known particularly for his work on problem solving and decision making. 'The secret of problem solving is that there is no secret. It is accomplished through complex structures of familiar simple elements,' he says. 'Intuition is not a process that operates independently of analysis. It is a fallacy to contrast "analytic" and "intuitive" styles of management. Intuition and judgment – at least good judgment – are simply analyses frozen into habit and into the capacity for rapid response through recognition.' While it is difficult to see intuition and judgment as 'analysis frozen into habit' Simon's point that problem-solving methods co-exist is accurate. His books include *Administrative Behavior* (fourth edition, 1997), *Human Problem Solving* (with A. Newell, 1972) and *The New Science of Management Decision* (1977). Simon is based at Carnegie-Mellon University where he is Professor of Computer Science and Psychology.

Wickham Skinner

Wickham Skinner (born 1924) did much during the 1970s and 1980s to alert Western companies to the progress being made by the Japanese in manufacturing methods. Based at Harvard Business School, Skinner's *Manufacturing in Corporate Strategy* (1977) and *Manufacturing: The formidable competitive weapon* (1985) provided blueprints of what could be done. Few listened.

Adrian Slywotsky

Adrian Slywotsky (born 1951) trained as a lawyer and has an MBA from Harvard. He was founding partner of Corporate Decisions, a consulting company based in Boston, now part of Mercer Management Consulting. His approach to strategy focuses on customer needs. He is the author of *Value Migration*.

George Stalk

George Stalk, along with Thomas Hout, of the Boston Consulting Group launched the fashion for 'time-based competition' with their 1990 book *Competing Against Time*. 'As time is compressed, share increases,' is the basic and simple message.

Paul Strassmann

Paul Strassmann (born 1929) is a long-time student of the information age. 'The capital-based industrial economy has been superseded by the management-dominant information economy', he argues. He is the author of *The Business Value of Computers*.

Don Sull

Don Sull (born 1963) has a degree, an MBA and a doctorate from Harvard. He has worked with McKinsey & Company as a consultant and was involved in the $1 billion leveraged buy-out of tyre maker, Uniroyal Goodrich. He is now an assistant professor at London Business School.

Sull's research currently centers on something he calls 'active inertia'. This is a term to describe the corporate tendency to carry on doing what they have always done when they are faced with a crisis. Rather than freezing rabbit-like in the glare of change, managers and organizations carry on in much the same way as before.

Benjamin Tregoe

Partner in the consulting firm Kepner-Tregoe and co-author of *The Rational Manager*. (See Charles Kepner, p. 279).

Eric Trist

Eric Trist was one of the founders of the Tavistock Institute in London. 'Our approach was closely akin to action research as conceived by Kurt Lewin, except that it had a socio-clinical basis. It depended on a collaborative relationship being established between ourselves and the organization with which we worked on problems of change needed and, when understood, desired by them.'

Lyndall Urwick

Lyndall Urwick (1891–1983) was the British champion of management thinking and education in the first half of the twentieth century. He was an eager proponent of Frederick Taylor's Scientific Management (he read Taylor's book in the World War I trenches) and did much to publicize the theories of both Taylor and Henri Fayol. In

Scientific Principles of Organization he developed and expanded on the ideas of both of his inspirations.

Urwick had a degree in modern history from Oxford and briefly worked in his family's glove making business. In 1921 he joined the Rowntree confectionery business. He was an early champion of management training. He was director of the International Management Institute in Geneva and was instrumental in the establishment of Henley Administrative Staff College (now Henley Management College). Urwick was one of the founders of the UK's Institute of Management and set up his own consulting firm Urwick, Orr in 1934.

Robert Waterman

Robert Waterman (born 1936) joined the consulting firm McKinsey & Company in 1963. During the late 1960s and early 1970s he worked extensively with companies that were restructuring and decentralizing. He then worked at McKinsey's Australian office. He spent a year teaching at IMEDE in Lausanne, Switzerland before returning to work at McKinsey's San Francisco office. There he met Tom Peters (see p. 187) who became Waterman's co-author of *In Search of Excellence*. Waterman left McKinsey in 1984 and has kept a fairly low profile ever since. He continues to work as a consultant and has produced two books, *The Frontiers of Excellence* (1994) and *The Renewal Factor* (1987) which thoughtfully develop many of the customer-oriented and humanistic themes developed in *In Search of Excellence*.

William Whyte

If Arthur Miller's *Death of a Salesman* is the classic 1950s drama portraying the sorrows of selling, William H. Whyte Jr's *The Organization Man* (1956) is a less dramatic accompanying volume describing the mind-numbing mundanity of life shackled to the desk constrained by rigid corporate rules and hierarchy.

Times have changed, says Sumantra Ghoshal: '*Organization Man* was written when capital was a scarce commodity. Now, knowledge, initiative and creativity are the key resources.'

Norbert Wiener

Norbert Wiener (1894–1964) was a mathematician and founder of cybernetics. Wiener was a child prodigy who went to university aged 11. He studied at Harvard, Cornell, Cambridge and Göttingen Universities. He was a Professor of Mathematics at MIT from 1932 until 1960. During World War II he worked on guided missiles. His major book was *Cybernetics* (1948), concerned with 'control and communication in the animal and the machine'.

Master Bibliography

Igor Ansoff

Corporate Strategy, McGraw Hill, New York, 1965.
Strategic Management, Macmillan, London, 1979.
Implanting Strategic Management, Prentice Hall, London, 1984.

Chris Argyris

Personality and Organization, Harper, New York, 1957.
Understanding Organizational Behavior, Dorsey Press, Homewood, IL, 1960.
Organizational Learning (with Donald Schön), Addison Wesley, Reading, MA, 1978.
On Organizational Learning, Blackwell, Cambridge, MA, 1992.

Chester Barnard

The Functions of the Executive, Harvard University Press, Cambridge, MA, 1938.
Organization and Management, Harvard University Press, Cambridge, MA, 1948.

Warren Bennis

The Planning of Change (with Benne K.D. & Chin, R., 2nd edn), Holt, Rinehart & Winston, 1970.
Leaders: The Strategies for Taking Charge (with Burt Nanus), Harper & Row, New York, 1985.

On Becoming a Leader, Addison-Wesley, Reading, MA, 1989.
Why Leaders Can't Lead, Jossey-Bass, San Francisco, CA, 1989.
An Invented Life: Reflections on Leadership and Change, Addison-Wesley, Reading, MA, 1993.
Organizing Genius (with Patricia Ward Biederman), Addison Wesley, Reading, MA, 1997.

Marvin Bower

The Will to Manage: Corporate success through programmed management, McGraw Hill, New York, 1966.
The Will to Lead: Running a business with a network of leaders, Harvard Business School Press, Cambridge, MA, 1997.

Dale Carnegie

How to Stop Worrying and Start Living, Pocket Books, 1985.
How to Enjoy Your Life and Your Job, Pocket Books, 1986.
How to Win Friends and Influence People, Pocket Books, 1994.
How to Develop Self-Confidence and Influence People by Public Speaking, Pocket Books, 1995.

James Champy

Reengineering the Corporation (with Michael Hammer), HarperBusiness, New York, 1993.
Reengineering Management, HarperBusiness, New York, 1995.

Alfred Chandler

Strategy and Structure, MIT Press, Boston, MA, 1962.
The Visible Hand: The Managerial Revolution in American Business, Harvard University Press, Cambridge, MA, 1977.
Managerial Hierarchies (with Deams, H., eds), Harvard University

Press, Cambridge, MA, 1980.
Scale and Scope: The Dynamics of Industrial Capitalism, Harvard University Press, Cambridge, MA, 1990.

W. Edwards Deming

Quality, Productivity and Competitive Position, MIT Centre for Advanced Engineering Study, MIT, Cambridge, MA, 1982.
Out of the Crisis, Cambridge University Press, Cambridge, MA, 1988.

Peter Drucker

Concept of the Corporation, John Day, New York, 1946.
The New Society, Heinemann, London, 1951.
The Practice of Management, Harper & Row, New York, 1954.
Managing for Results, Heinemann, London, 1964.
The Effective Executive, Harper & Row, New York, 1967.
The Age of Discontinuity, Heinemann, London, 1969.
Management: Tasks, Responsibilities, Practices, Harper & Row, New York, 1973.
Managing in Turbulent Times, Harper & Row, New York, 1980.
Innovation and Entrepreneurship, Heinemann, London, 1985.
The New Realities, Heinemann, London, 1989.
Managing the Nonprofit Organization, HarperCollins, 1990.
Managing for the Future, Dutton, 1992.
Post-Capitalist Society, Harper, New York, 1993.
Managing in Times of Great Change, Butterworth Heinemann, Oxford, 1995.
Adventures of a Bystander, John Wiley, New York, 1998 (originally published in 1978).

Henri Fayol

General and Industrial Management, Pitman, London, 1949.

Mary Parker Follett

The New State: Group Organization – The Solution of Popular Government, Longman, London, 1918.
Creative Experience, Longman, London, 1924.
Dynamic Administration, Harper & Brothers, New York, 1941.
Freedom and Coordination, Pitman, London, 1949.

Henry Ford

My Life and Work, Doubleday, Page & Co, New York, 1923.

Harold Geneen

Managing (with Alvin Moscow), Doubleday, 1984.
The Synergy Myth, St Martin's Press, 1997.

Sumantra Ghoshal

Managing Across Borders (with Christopher Bartlett), Harvard Business School Press, Boston, MA, 1989.
The Individualized Corporation (with Christopher Bartlett), Harvard Business School Press, Boston, MA, 1997.

Gary Hamel

Competing for the Future (with CK Prahalad), Harvard University Press, Cambridge, MA, 1994.
Competence-Based Competition (editors Hamel and Aimé Heene), John Wiley, New York, 1995.

Charles Handy

Understanding Organizations, Penguin Books, London, 1976.
The Future of Work, Basil Blackwell, Oxford, 1984.
Gods of Management, Business Books, London, 1986.
The Making of Managers (with John Constable), Longman, London, 1988.
The Age of Unreason, Business Books, London, 1989.
Inside Organizations: 21 Ideas for Managers, BBC Books, London 1990.
Waiting for the Mountain to Move and other reflections on life, Arrow, London, 1991.
The Empty Raincoat, Hutchinson, London, 1994.
Beyond Certainty: The changing world of organizations, Century, London, 1995.
The Hungry Spirit, Hutchinson, London, 1997.

Frederick Herzberg

The Motivation to Work (with Mausner, B., and Snyderman, B.), Wiley, New York, 1959.

Geert Hofstede

Uncommon Sense About Organizations: Cases, studies and field observations, Sage Publications, 1997.
Cultures and Organizations: Software of the mind, McGraw Hill, New York, 1995.
Culture's Consequences: International differences in work-related values, Sage Publications, 1984.
Game of Budget Control, Garland Publishing, 1984.
European Contributions to Organizational Theory (with M. Sami Kassem), Longwood Press, 1976.

Elliott Jaques

The Changing Culture of a Factory, Tavistock, London, 1951.
A General Theory of Bureaucracy, John Wiley, New York, 1976.
Free Enterprise, Fair Employment, Crane Russak & Co., 1982.
Requisite Organization (2nd edn), Cason Hall & Co., 1996.

Joseph M. Juran

Managerial Breakthrough, McGraw Hill, New York, 1964.
Juran on Planning for Quality, Free Press, New York, 1988.

Rosabeth Moss Kanter

Men and Women of the Corporation, Basic Books, New York, 1977.
The Change Masters, Simon & Schuster, New York, 1983.
When Giants Learn to Dance, Simon & Schuster, London, 1989.
The Challenge of Organizational Change (with Stein, B.; & Jick, T.D.),
    Free Press, New York, 1992.
World Class: Thriving locally in the global economy, Simon & Schuster,
    New York, 1995.
Rosabeth Moss Kanter on the Frontiers of Management, Harvard Busi-
    ness School Press, Boston, MA, 1997.

Philip Kotler

Marketing Management: Analysis, Planning and Control, Prentice Hall,
    Englewood Cliffs, NJ, 1967 (9th edn 1997).
Marketing Decision Making: A Model Building Approach, Holt, Rinehart
    & Winston, New York, 1971 (Later revised in 1983 and in 1992,
    re-published by Prentice Hall under the title *Marketing Models*
    with co-authors Garry L. Lilien and K. Sridhar Moorthy).
Readings in Marketing Management, Prentice Hall, Englewood Cliffs,
    NJ, 1972 (re-titled *Marketing Management and Strategy* for 1983
    revised edition).

Simulation in the Social and Administrative Sciences (with Harold Guetzkow and Randall L. Schultz), Prentice Hall, Englewood Cliffs, NJ, 1972.

Creating Social Change (with Gerald Zaltman and Ira Kaufman), Holt, Rinehart and Winston, New York, 1972.

Marketing for Nonprofit Organizations, Prentice Hall, Englewood Cliffs, NJ, 1975 (Re-titled *Strategic Marketing for Nonprofit Organizations* with Alan Andreasen as co-author).

Principles of Marketing, Prentice Hall, Englewood Cliffs, NJ, 1980 (7th edition, 1996).

Cases and Readings for Marketing for Nonprofit Organizations (with OC Ferrell and Charles lamb), Prentice Hall, Englewood Cliffs, NJ, 1983 (later re-named *Strategic Marketing for Nonprofit Organizations: Cases and Readings*).

Marketing Essentials, Prentice Hall, Englewood Cliffs, NJ, 1984.

Marketing – An introduction, Prentice Hall, Englewood Cliffs, NJ, 1987.

Marketing Professional Services (with Paul N. Bloom), Prentice Hall, Englewood Cliffs, NJ, 1984.

Strategic Marketing for Educational Institutions (with Karen Fox), Prentice Hall, Englewood Cliffs, NJ, 1985.

The New Competition: What Theory Z Didn't Talk About – Marketing (with Liam Fahey and Somkid Jatusripitak), Prentice Hall, Englewood Cliffs, NJ, 1985.

Marketing for Health Care Organizations (with Roberta N. Clarke), Prentice Hall, Englewood Cliffs, NJ, 1987.

High Visibility (with Irving Rein and Martin Stoller), Dodd, Mead & Co, New York, 1987.

Social Marketing: Strategies for Changing Public behavior (with Eduardo Roberto), Free Press, New York, 1989.

Marketing for Congregations: Choosing to Serve People More Effectively (with Norman Shawchuck, Bruce Wrenn and Gustave Rath), Abingdon Press, Nashville, TN, 1992.

Marketing Places: Attracting Investment, Industry and Tourism to Cities, States and Nations (with Donald H. Haider and Irving Rein), Free Press, New York, 1993.

Marketing for Hospitality and Tourism (with John Bowen and James makens), Prentice Hall, Englewood Cliffs, NJ, 1996.

Standing Room Only: Strategies for Marketing the Performing Arts (with Joanne Scheff), Harvard Business School Press, Boston, MA, 1997.

The Marketing of Nations: A Strategic Approach to Building National Wealth (with Somkid Jatusripitak and Suvit Maesincee), Free Press, New York, 1997.

Museum Strategies and Marketing: Designing the Mission, Building Audiences, Increasing Financial Resources (with Neil Kotler), Jossey-Bass, San Francisco, CA, 1998.

Ted Levitt

Innovation in Marketing, McGraw Hill, New York, 1962.
The Marketing Mode, McGraw Hill, New York, 1969.
The Marketing Imagination, Free Press, New York, 1983.
Thinking About Management, Free Press, New York, 1991.

Kurt Lewin

A Dynamic Theory of Personality, McGraw Hill, New York, 1935.
Principles of Topological Psychology, McGraw Hill, New York, 1936.
Resolving Social Conflicts: Selected Papers on Group Dynamics (ed. Gertrude Lewin), Harper & Row, New York, 1948.
Field Theory in Social Science: Selected Theoretical papers (ed. D. Cartwright), Harper & Row, New York, 1951.

Douglas McGregor

The Human Side of Enterprise, McGraw Hill, New York, 1960.

Nicolo Machiavelli

The Prince, Penguin, London, 1967.

Abraham Maslow

Motivation and Personality, Harper & Row, New York, 1954 (third edition, Harper & Row, 1987).

Towards a Psychology of Being (second edition), Van Nostrand Reinhold, New York, 1982.

The Journals of Abraham Maslow, Brooks/Cole, Monterey, CA, 1979.

Eupsychian Management, Irwin-Dorsey, Homewood, IL, 1965 (republished as *Maslow on Management*, John Wiley, New York, 1998).

Konosuke Matsushita

Not For Bread Alone, Berkeley Publishing, 1994.

Elton Mayo

Human Problems of an Industrial Civilization, Macmillan, New York, 1933.

Social Problems of an Industrial Civilization, Harvard University Press, Cambridge, MA, 1945.

Henry Mintzberg

The Nature of Managerial Work, Harper & Row, New York, 1973.

The Structuring of Organizations, Prentice-Hall, Englewood Cliffs, NJ, 1979.

Structures In Fives: Designing Effective Organizations, Prentice-Hall, Englewood Cliffs, NJ, 1983 (This is an expurgated version of the above).

Power In and Around Organizations, Prentice Hall, Englewood Cliffs, NJ, 1983.

Mintzberg on Management: Inside Our Strange World of Organizations, Free Press, New York, 1989.

The Strategy Process: Concepts, Contexts, Cases (with J.B. Quinn), 2nd edition, Prentice Hall, Englewood Cliffs, NJ, 1991.

The Rise and Fall of Strategic Planning, Prentice Hall International, Hemel Hempstead, 1994.

Akito Morita

Made in Japan (with Edwin M. Reingold and Mitsuko Shimonura), Dutton, New York, 1986.

John Naisbitt

Megatrends, Warner Books, 1984.
Global Paradox, William Morrow & Co., New York, 1994.

Kenichi Ohmae

The Mind of the Strategist, McGraw Hill, New York, 1982.
Triad Power: The Coming Shape of Global Competition, Free Press, New York, 1985.
The Borderless World, William Collins, London, 1990.
The Evolving Global Economy (editor) Harvard Business School Press, Boston, MA, 1995.
The End of the Nation State, HarperCollins, London, 1995.

David Packard

The HP Way, HarperBusiness, New York, 1995.

Richard Pascale

The Art of Japanese Management (with Anthony Athos), Penguin, London, 1981.
Managing on the Edge, Viking, London, 1990.

Laurence J. Peter

The Peter Principle (with Raymond Hull), William Morrow & Co., New York, 1969.
The Peter Plan, Bantam Books, 1981.
Why Things Go Wrong or the Peter Principle Revisited, William Morrow & Co., New York, 1984.
Peter's Quotations: Ideas For Our Time, Quill, 1993.

Tom Peters

In Search of Excellence (with Robert Waterman), Harper & Row, New York & London, 1982.
A Passion for Excellence (with Nancy Austin), Collins, London, 1985.
Thriving on Chaos, Macmillan, London, 1988.
Liberation Management, Alfred Knopf, New York, 1992.
The Tom Peters Seminar, Vintage Books, New York, 1994.
The Pursuit of Wow!, Vintage Books, New York, 1994.
The Circle of Innovation, Hodder & Stoughton, London, 1997.

Michael Porter

Competitive Strategy, Free Press, New York, 1980.
Competitive Advantage, Free Press, New York, 1985.
The Competitive Advantage of Nations, Free Press, New York, 1990.

Edgar H. Schein

Personal and Organization Change Through Group Methods: The Laboratory Approach (with Warren Bennis), John Wiley, New York, 1965.
Career Dynamics: Matching Individual and Organizational Needs, Addison Wesley, Wokingham, 1978.
Organizational Psychology, Prentice Hall, Englewood Cliffs, NJ, 1980.
Organization Culture and Leadership, Jossey-Bass, 1985 (2nd edn, 1992).

Process Consultation Vol. 1 (revised), Addison-Wesley, Reading, MA, 1988.

The Art of Managing HR, Oxford University Press, Oxford, 1987.

Career Anchors: Discovering Your Real Values, Pfeiffer, San Diego, CA, 1990.

Career Survival: Strategic Job and Roles Planning, Pfeiffer, San Diego, CA, 1994.

Strategic Pragmatism: The Culture of Singapore's Economic Development Board, MIT Press, Cambridge, MA.

Process Consultation, Addison-Wesley, Reading, MA, 1969.

Organizational Psychology (3rd edition), Prentcie Hall, Engelwood Cliffs, NJ, 1980.

Organizational Culture and Leadership, Jossey-Bass, San Francsico, CA, 1985.

Peter Senge

The Fifth Discipline: The Art and Practice of the Learning Organization, Doubleday, New York, 1990.

The Fifth Discipline Fieldbook: Strategies and Tools for Building a Learning Organization (with Roberts, C., Ross, R., Smith, B., and Kleiner, A.), Nicholas Brealey, London, 1994.

Alfred P. Sloan

My Years with General Motors, Doubleday, New York, 1963.

Frederick W. Taylor

Shop Management, Harper & Row, New York, 1903.

The Principles of Scientific Management, Harper & Row, New York, 1913.

Alvin Toffler

Future Shock, Bodley Head, London, 1970.
The Third Wave, Bantam, New York, 1980.

Robert Townsend

Up the Organization, Michael Joseph, London, 1970.
Further Up the Organization, Random House, New York, 1984.
The B2 Chronicles: Uncommon Wisdom for Un-corporate America, Berkley Publishing Group, 1995.
Reinventing Leadership (with Warren Bennis), William Morrow & Co., New York, 1997.

Fons Trompenaars

Riding the Waves of Culture, Nicholas Brealey, London, 1993.
The Seven Cultures of Capitalism (with Charles Hampden-Turner), Piatkus, London, 1994.
Mastering the Infinite Game (with Charles Hampden-Turner), Capstone, Oxford, 1997.

Sun-Tzu

The Art of War (transl. Griffith), Oxford University Press, Oxford, 1963.

Thomas Watson Jr

A Business and its Beliefs, McGraw Hill, New York, 1963.

Max Weber

The Theory of Social and Economic Organization, Free Press, New York, 1947.

The Protestant Ethic and the Spirit of Capitalism, Scribner's, New York, 1958.

Economy and Society, University of California Press, 1978.

Index